THE AMERICAN
TELEGRAPHER

CLASS AND CULTURE

A SERIES EDITED BY
MILTON CANTOR AND BRUCE LAURIE

THE AMERICAN
TELEGRAPHER

A SOCIAL HISTORY,
1860–1900

EDWIN GABLER

RUTGERS UNIVERSITY PRESS
NEW BRUNSWICK AND LONDON

TO MY MOTHER AND FATHER

Library of Congress Cataloging-in-Publication Data

Gabler, Edwin, 1949–
  The American telegrapher : a social history. 1860–1900 / Edwin
Gabler.
  p.   cm.—(Class and culture)
  Bibliography: p.
  Includes index.
  ISBN 0-8135-1284-0 ISBN 0-8135-1285-9 (pbk.)
  1. Western Union Telegraph Company Strike. 1883. 2. Trade-
unions-Telegraphers—United States—History—19th century.
3. Telegraphers—United States—History—19th century. I. Title.
II. Series.
HD5325.T252   1883
331.89′2813841′0—dc19   87-19878
                                                              CIP
British Cataloging-in-Publication information available

All illustrations appearing in this publication are used courtesy of
the National Museum of American History, Smithsonian Institution. Permission to quote from the Garrett Family Papers (Ms. no.
979) and the Baltimore & Ohio Railroad Papers (Ms. no. 2003) has
been granted courtesy of the Museum and Library of Maryland
History Division of the Maryland Historical Society. Permission to
quote from the Reading Railroad Company Papers (Ms. no. 1520)
has been granted courtesy of Hagley Museum and Library.

CONTENTS

ACKNOWLEDGMENTS

This book is ultimately a collective effort, and I must thank those who helped me research and write it.

For varied and indispensable help in my library and archival forays, I am grateful to Edla Holm, Ute Bargmann, Marion Grader, and Virginia Garrand, of the library of the University of Massachusetts at Amherst; Michael Nash, Christopher Baer, and Marge McNinch, of the Hagley Museum and Library; Margaret Jasko, of the Western Union Corporation; Warren Wirebach, of the Dauphin County Historical Society; Donna Ellis, of the Maryland Historical Society; and Jane Odom and Robert Harding of the Archives Center, and James Roan of the library, Smithsonian Institution.

I have been privileged to hold a postdoctoral fellowship in the Division of Electricity and Modern Physics, National Museum of American History, Smithsonian Institution, which has allowed me to complete this study and take part in an exciting and diverse scholarly community whose commitment to history is an eminently public one. In particular, thanks are due Bernard S. Finn, division curator, for bearing my electrical illiteracy with patience and helping me better appreciate the technological dimensions of telegraphy. Anastasia Atsiknoudas and Elliott Sivowitch, also of the division, were helpful too. And special thanks are due Carl H. Scheele, curator of the Division of Community Life, who, it turned out, had been a B & O Railroad telegrapher as a young man, and who shared his experiences, adventures, and thoughts about the craft with me.

ACKNOWLEDGMENTS

My gratitude extends to those who offered comments, criticism, suggestions, and other professional courtesies. Greg Field taught me how to conquer price relatives and the pocket calculator. Marlie Wasserman, Marilyn Campbell, and Lois Krieger, of the Rutgers University Press, have provided wise editorial guidance. Walter Licht read a draft of my manuscript with a critical and insightful eye. Richard Edwards put the learning and perspective of an eclectic economist at my disposal. Ronald Story has been a continuing source of imaginative historical thinking. My debts to Robert Griffith—intellectual and personal—are so many and so longstanding as to be embarrassing. I can never hope to adequately repay them, but only acknowledge them, and note that they are the paradoxical kind of debts that make you richer. It was in Bruce Laurie's seminar that I wrote what became the germ of this book, and it is to Bruce Laurie's depth, discipline, and example that this book owes its existence.

THE AMERICAN
TELEGRAPHER

1

A MILD SORT OF REVOLUTION

A little more than a century ago, in 1883, a strike involving thousands of men and women captured the nation's attention. That in itself was not startling. Strikes were no longer novel in postbellum America. Less than a decade before, in 1877, a far more dramatic and singularly bloody eruption of railroad workers had forced Americans to reckon with a growing schism between labor and capital in a country in transition from farm and workshop to city and factory. But contemporaries found the telegraphers' Great Strike of 1883 remarkable. Its very breadth was noteworthy, for it was a nationwide walkout of operators from small branch offices where one or two worked and from large city offices employing hundreds. The strike's adversaries heightened its importance. On one side stood the Western Union Telegraph Company, perhaps the nation's most powerful single firm and a model of the revolutions in business organization, science, and technology that were creating unparalleled dislocation, complexity, wealth, and poverty. Opposing it was a union of telegraphers and linemen, itself part of a larger body, the Knights of Labor, whose values and aspirations in many ways inverted those of the new world that the Western Union represented: an insistence on the dignity and independence of labor rather than its subdivision and degradation for profit, and a belief in the fraternity and sorority of all who produced the nation's wealth. And the telegraphers themselves made the strike unique. Here were laborers who looked very much like capitalists —young men in top hats and young women in tasteful finery—but whose wallets held union cards rather than bond coupons, and whose professions of solidarity went out to others who, like them, were oppressed by the "wages system."

The Great Strike of 1883 was no ordinary labor dispute. Yet the strike itself was part of a larger story whose significance went well beyond a single walkout or union or company. The strike is really a starting place for a broader and deeper inquiry into the changing nature of work and workers, and ultimately of society, in late nineteenth-century America—changes whose consequences remain with us still.

On one level, this is a study of a particular occupation in a particular historical period. I have tried to show what it meant to be a telegrapher in the years of America's industrial puberty: how operators were made, how much they made, what their work was like, and how they themselves shaped that work. I have also asked who the telegraphers were: whether old or young, male or female, and what kinds of families and backgrounds were likely to send someone to the key.

Because so many operators worked directly or indirectly for a pioneer big business, their story necessarily involves an excursion into economic history, and that, too, is part of this study. Corporations beginning to refashion production and distribution were likewise transforming the nature and meaning of employment, and I have used the telegraphers' experience to try to understand why and how this took place.

But as its subtitle indicates, this is also a social history of operators, and while that certainly encompasses the occupational and economic aspects of telegraphy, it must also synthesize them with much else of importance to recreate the complex reality of which the operators and their fellow Americans were part a hundred years ago. Telegraphers were members of a new social class taking form in the period. Like all classes it was dynamic, in constant motion, and difficult to render in any static, schematic way; yet it was far from shapeless. It was a lower middle class of white-collar workers. Even today the term "white-collar workers" seems something of an oxymoron; it was decidedly so in 1883. Their social perch was an anomalous and precarious one that often swayed them in two different, and to a great extent opposite, directions: toward the "old" middle class of bourgeois solidity, polite employment, and gentility; but also toward the growing mass of wage earners, most of them skilled or unskilled manual workers. The wonder is not that telegraphers were pulled both ways, but that they could have so identified themselves as dependent working people as to form trade unions and to join a great reform upsurge—the Knights of Labor—which held all differences among employees less important than their common plight as "producers." The bond between the telegraphers and the Knights was a tense and awkward one, which brought out the worst, as well as the best, in both partners. But that, precisely, is what makes the telegraphers important to understanding the Knights phenomenon and the era in which it occurred.

A brief word about the plan of this study: I begin with a narrative of the Great Strike of 1883 as an apt introduction to the world of the operators and, to borrow a paradigm from classical music, as an exposition of themes to be developed. Chapter 2 sketches the telegraph industry and the rise of the Western Union, fundamental forces shaping the operators' work and lives. Chapter 3 is a social portrait of the craft with particular emphasis on matters of class and culture, and Chapter 4 is a complementary study of women telegraphers, who deserve treatment in their own right. Chapter 5 is about power—formal and informal, political and nonpolitical, in trade unions and outside of them—since power, broadly defined, was what the great upheavals of the Gilded Age were all about. Specifically, the chapter examines the telegraphers' responses to their changing fortunes in the industry, their turn to unionism, to broad social reform and a liaison with the Knights of Labor, and, for some of them, their turn to the state.

On July 16, 1883, after a thirty-five-minute wait, the Executive Committee of the Brotherhood of Telegraphers of the United States and Canada found itself in the boardroom of the Western Union Company's massive brick-and-granite headquarters at 195 Broadway in New York, facing general manager Thomas T. Eckert. Like the building, Eckert cut an imperious figure: a tall, acquiline, thick-necked, mustachioed man who had earned a set of general's stars during the Civil War for his stewardship of the military telegraphs. His character matched his mien. A close associate judged him "stern and at times implacable toward those who have deviated from the path of rectitude" and recalled how the general had once amazed Abraham Lincoln by breaking iron pokers over his forearm to prove how cheaply they were made. Accustomed to command and obedience, Eckert now faced an embryonic mutiny. The men assembled before him represented an operators' union and had come to place a bill of grievances in his hand.[1]

District master workman John Campbell, a bespectacled, slim, schoolmasterish-looking man given to a "quick, decided way of speaking," who had spent twenty of his thirty-five years before a telegraph key and was now the brotherhood's leader, presented his union's demands to Eckert: that compulsory Sunday work be abolished; that day shifts be reduced to eight hours and night shifts to seven; that men and women operators receive equal pay for equal work; that the remuneration and conditions of linemen, railroad telegraphers, and those employed on the automatic Wheatstone system be improved; and that all current salaries be raised by 15 percent. When Campbell had finished, Eckert spoke.

"Have you a list of the aggrieved persons?"

"We have not, sir," answered Campbell.

"I would like a list of those you represent. Can you not supply the information?"

"Our organization is very widespread, and it would take a long time to—"

"Oh," Eckert parried, "you can have all the time you desire."

And so the brief, fruitless ritual went. Eckert claimed (falsely, as the Western Union's president later admitted) that he had no way of knowing whether the committee actually represented his employees and again demanded a list. The committee, predictably, again refused. The legacy of secrecy within the union's parent body, the Knights of Labor, was still strong despite recent steps to discard its furtive forms, but more important, the brotherhood faced the prospect of a struggle with the most powerful corporation in the country, and to furnish the Western Union with a membership roster would be suicidal. For Eckert, recognizing the brotherhood's legitimacy was equally unthinkable—an admission that the prerogatives of capital had limits, and that employees, like employers, might also pursue self-interest through combination. If the Executive Committee had hoped to bargain with Eckert, it left disappointed. "Don't forget the list," the general told the departing delegation. "As I remarked before, you can have all the time you want."[2]

But time, as the brotherhood's leaders viewed things, was in short supply. Acting on a mandate of their constituent local assemblies to petition the Western Union and several lesser companies for a redress of grievances, they were authorized, failing a satisfactory response, to lead the nation's commercial telegraphers in a strike on July 18. As the deadline approached, there were last-minute consultations with national officers of the Knights of Labor in New York, and then an ultimatum from the union: if the telegraph companies would not deal with the brotherhood in some way, the brotherhood would paralyze the companies.

Long-standing antagonism between operators and their employers underlay the dispute. As corporate telegraph consolidation grew in the years following the Civil War, so also did operator discontent, prompting telegraphers to cautiously flirt with labor organization in the 1860s, and to go a step further in 1870 with a brief and disastrous strike against the Western Union. The company prospered nonetheless, growing so robustly that the word *monopoly*, used to describe the Western Union in 1883, was less an epithet than a virtual reality. And all the while operators contrasted the company's financial health with their own lot, decrying a widening gap between their skill and worth and their income and status. Once again they turned to unionism, this time linking their cause in 1881 with that of the Knights of Labor, a promising alliance that sought to unite all "producers" and replace a competitive society with a cooperative one. The Brotherhood of Telegraphers—District Assembly 45 of the Knights—in the best spirit of the order, was an industrial union comprising all who created the telegraph companies' wealth, whether smartly dressed operators who manipulated delicate and temperamental instruments or rough-hewn linemen shod with muck-encrusted climbing boots. It was, in fact, in a dispute over a lineman that the fledgling brotherhood exchanged preliminary blows with telegraph managers in May 1883, the same month that union members approved recourse to a strike should the companies spurn the bill of grievances drafted in March.[3]

By the second week of July, the press began recording signs of trouble in the industry. There were rumors of an operators' strike, the report of a stillborn messenger boys' walkout in Boston, and then, on the eleventh, a surprise announcement from Western Union head-quarters: as of July 1, day-shift operators would put in nine hours' "actual service," night men seven hours, and all work beyond that, including Sunday shifts, would be paid at regular rates based on a seven-hour day. Beset by talk of an operators' revolt, the company was apparently granting a concession. A Boston telegrapher discerned "signs of weakness" in the gesture and thought that his union's goals might be won "without the necessity of determined action on the part of the brotherhood."[4] But few operators saw the move as more than a ploy. "Why it's no concession at all," said one New Yorker. "Concession be hanged!" exploded another. A third dismissed it as a "sop" that would "not have the least effect on the work of the brotherhood." By July 14, the *Boston Globe* was reporting—accurately, as it turned out—that the union would present its demands in two days, giving the Western Union and the smaller companies forty-eight hours in which to respond or bring a strike down upon their heads.[5]

Despite the concession of July 11, the Western Union showed no inclination to dicker with its operators, and after Eckert's rebuff on the sixteenth, the brotherhood girded itself accordingly.[6] In New York, the local assembly's master workman John Mitchell spoke confidently of his colleagues being "well enough 'fixed' to enjoy two weeks' vacation." The men in Baltimore spoke of an even more impressive treasury, which would enable them to hold out for six months. The union was amassing men as well as money, and one dispatch claimed a thousand new recruits for the brotherhood in only three days.[7] Expectation and tension increased at the possibility that the communications network upon which an industrializing America was growing more dependent would be rendered dumb and useless if it came to a strike. Yet rumors of compromise persisted. On Tuesday, July 17, the *Cleveland Plain Dealer* hinted at a settlement afoot that would grant the operators improvements in wages and hours while withholding recognition of their brotherhood. A more authoritative announcement came from the citadel at 195 Broadway the following day. The Western Union's board of directors had appointed a subcommittee to examine employee grievances. Encouraged, the brotherhood extended the strike deadline another twenty-four hours. "Things are looking rather better than they did this morning," an operator in Boston told a reporter Wednesday afternoon, noting that the union's leaders "held out considerable hope that our memorial will receive a favorable decision by the directors' Committee." Such optimism proved chimerical. Before the day had passed, General Eckert, in an open telegram to the general superintendent of the firm's Western Division, Colonel Robert C. Clowry, rejected the brotherhood petition point by point, adding, for good measure, an indictment of the organization for using deceptive recruiting methods and for the alleged wire cutting of its linemen members in New York. The union, in turn, denounced the Western Union directors' subcommittee as "a game of bluff" and gave notice that the strike deadline extension would be final.[8]

Both sides continued digging breastworks. The company assembled lists of potential replacements for rebellious operators from among those currently unemployed or working private wires. The Western Union could also draw on its own large labor pool to break a strike. In Philadelphia, district superintendent John E. Zeublin returned to the city with a complement of fifty telegraphers in tow culled from surrounding rural posts. A company director in New York explained that in the event of a walkout, some one hundred branch offices in the city would close, freeing their operators to act as a reserve force to meet the emergency. At Western Union headquarters, an anonymous wag stuck a calendar in the elevator, circling the original strike date and next to it writing, "the Impending Crisis."[9]

On Thursday morning, July 19, three hours before the strike deadline, John Campbell wired Eckert a final plea to negotiate: "It is with an earnest desire for the harmonious settlement of difficulties and regard for the social and business interests of the people that we send this last appeal for the recognition of the rights and redress of the grievances of your employes." The general's silence was the company's answer. A *New York Tribune* reporter stationed at the main office recorded a "constant passing to and fro of operators, apparently carrying messages and signals," a scene replicated in scores of other offices around the nation. At the small Harrisburg, Pennsylvania, Western Union office, an observer found the operators' "mysterious air and whispered consultation" a sure sign "that something important was about to happen."[10]

At 12:11 P.M. (noon Washington time), Frank R. Phillips, a chubby twenty-five-year-old telegrapher, broke the tension and commenced the revolt at Western Union headquarters with a whistle blast that stopped the business of the great operating room cold. Exuberant but orderly, 300 or more of his colleagues joined Phillips in quitting the building. The largely youthful strikers filed out onto the street, where sympathetic lunchtime throngs cheered and applauded them. Inside, manager William J. Dealy watched the exodus calmly as his boss, district superintendent Walter C. Humstone, rushed to the operating room with a brace of policemen, just in case. They were not necessary. "Commit no unlawful act," John Campbell had cautioned his followers in his official strike order, and they seemed to be scrupulously heeding his advice.[11]

Similar tableaux, on a smaller scale, took place elsewhere that afternoon. Passersby near Western Union offices in Chicago and Philadelphia gave vocal support to the telegraphers emerging from their workplaces. "This is the only way to bring the monopoly to terms," exclaimed one sympathetic Philadelphian to the strikers. The crowds in Chicago seemed especially taken by the young women operators bringing up the rear of the procession "with smiling faces, and swinging their still unopened lunch boxes on their arms." A Boston paper reported that "they were greeted with such remarks as 'Good girls,' 'You're the daisies,' 'The girls are no slouches, after all,' and similar expressons of approval on the part of the spectators." For a labor dispute, the walkout seemed surprisingly free of acrimony. At Cleveland, at Philadelphia, even at the large Chicago office, some departing operators and their managers shook hands, expressed regret at the turn of events, and wished each other well. At other places, the strike simply happened. After his force had quietly left, Atlanta's manager, J. M. Stephens, surveyed the denuded operating room and laconically told a reporter, "It looks like Sunday."[12]

The rebellion had not paralyzed the Western Union, but it did severely shock it, confusing and disrupting service across the continent. The truncated telegram addressed to a hapless Albany resident that read "AUNT'S WILL IS OPEN. YOU ARE LEFT" may not have been typical, but it reflected the chaos of the strike's first hours. One company officer described himself as "flabbergasted" by the blow, and David Homer Bates, then assistant general manager, later confessed that "the business of the company between its principal offices was considerably delayed" during the early phase of the walkout. Customers handing in completed telegram blanks at Western Union receiving counters were greeted by placards informing them that messages would only be accepted "subject to delay and mailing en route if necessary." An account of the stricken New York office peopled the operating room with "young and middle-aged men with a fagged-out appearance" and a host of messengers who sat idly at keys. The situation was so grim that chief operators and even senior managers were supposed to have manned instruments.[13]

Though groggy, the Western Union returned the punch. It closed most branch offices in New York City and summoned their operators to the vital facilities at 195 Broadway. It actively recruited scabs, among them former telegraphers who had abandoned the craft for other pursuits. And it sought to boost the stamina and morale of its nonstriking employees. "Extend to those in your division, both men and women, my best thanks," Eckert wired superintendent Clowry in Chicago, "and leave nothing undone to provide for their wants. Spare no expense in this respect." The general was as good as his word. Cots appeared in company offices to rest relays of operators, rented carriages shuttled loyal "girls" between work and home, and free meals and cigars—the latter ordinarily banned from operating rooms—were provided to telegraphers who remained. This corporate largesse proved considerable. After the strike, Western Union president Norvin Green told a Senate committee that the cost of salary bonuses and other inducements to scabs had set the firm back more than its revenue losses.[14]

But the company got its money's worth. Matt Davin, a telegrapher of twenty-four years' experience who joined the strike after nearly a week of scabbing, recounted his ordeal during the first day at Boston: "I was ordered from my instrument at the Board of Trade at 12.30 on the day of the strike. I sat down at the New York wire, received without interruption until 10.30 P.M., when I rested myself by sending a little. I then began receiving again, and continued taking 'copy' until 5.30 A.M. In all my experience that was the biggest 'roast' I ever had." The next morning, loyal Boston operators resumed their places at their desks "with an air of weariness" born of the previous night's grueling service.[15]

Things were no better for the great monopoly as the walkout passed its second day. In New York, a *Times* man caught up with a bevy of check-girls as the young messengers left work at 195 Broadway. They told of scabs baffled by the important duplex and quadruplex instruments that handled much of the company's first-line business, and who wrote "wretched copy" in pencil rather than the usual pen and ink. "You would kill yourself laughing," said one of the girls, "if you could see some of them work." But the *Times* was in no mood to laugh. Its columns were heavily dependent on the wires, and the paper now complained of bungled dispatches, many of them turned out in a hand "like that of schoolboys."[16]

Thus besieged, Western Union headquarters was rich in rumor and speculation the first week of the strike. On July 21, the *Boston Globe* spoke of dissension and squabbling within the highest circles of the firm. Jay Gould, the Western Union's principal stockholder and its presumed master, the story went, was dismayed by the powerful blow delivered by the operators and was pressing his colleagues to meet the brotherhood's demands. More dramatically, two days later, the *Globe* ran an account of an alleged confrontation between Gould and Eckert in a hallway at 195 Broadway during which the diminutive stock jobber as good as called the burly manager "a fool or a knave." The company denied the whole affair, and an Atlanta daily had Gould declaring that the strike was in fact a good thing for enabling the Western Union to close marginal offices. For all its color, the Gould-Eckert rift was probably apocryphal. What was unquestionably genuine were the troubles their corporation now faced.[17]

The striking operators, conversely, were sanguine. Daily meetings bolstered their solidarity and spirits. The prelude to one such rally in New York, on July 21, involved hundreds of telegraphers and linemen marching in procession behind a small, rebuslike flag that bore the words *Western Union* and the picture of a padlock. There were more accessions to the strikers' ranks as well. About thirty messenger boys entered a New York meeting on the twenty-first to the accompaniment of a standing ovation from the audience. By the twenty-fourth, the union claimed 2,000 new members across the nation, among them the chief operators who reportedly quit at New York, and night chief Billy Lewis, of the Louisville office, who certainly did.[18] Nor was the brotherhood shy about gaining converts. "Skirmishing committees" sent out operators to intercept and "capture" potential scabs. Posted primarily at railway depots and outside telegraph offices, the union men (and sometimes women) met incoming strikebreakers, sought to dissuade them from taking the company's part, and frequently wound up initiating them into the operators' organization. "The boys here are very jubilant," declared the Detroit brotherhood of its skirmishing forays. "Everything that looks like an operator is taken to our spacious parlors, where they are wined, dined, etc." At New York, Augusta, Georgia, Cleveland, Philadelphia, Indianapolis, New Orleans, Boston, and Buffalo the story was the same.[19]

Organizational acuity extended to other brotherhood operations. "Pigeons" remained behind in various offices, ostensibly loyal employees who were in fact union spies using the company's own facilities to send coded messages coordinating the strikers' campaign.[20] And like the Western Union, the Brotherhood of Telegraphers understood the power of the press in molding public attitudes. Local assemblies in large cities formed special press committees to supply journalists with strike bulletins and as flattering a picture of the brotherhood and its crusade as possible.[21]

To paint such a picture, the union laid great emphasis on its members' responsibility and sobriety. "Strike," after all, smacked of conflict, of social instability and violence, of an America engulfed in class war—the paroxysm on the railroads of only six years before had been "strike" writ large. Mindful of those implications, and also reflecting many operators' gentlemanly self-image, the brotherhood aimed to conduct its battle with the Western Union on the highest plane. "Advise the members to be temperate in language," John Campbell wired the Cleveland local assembly on July 21, "and under no circumstances to violate the laws." When stories of alleged wire cutting of Western Union circuits appeared in the first week of the walkout, the brotherhood not only denounced such tactics, but offered a reward in Chicago to help catch any saboteurs.[22]

Temperate behavior also meant a cold water diet for the duration. Operators at New Orleans and Baltimore took the pledge, and at the first strike meeting in New York, John Mitchell presented his assembled fellows with a resolution to swear off drink that passed, the *Tribune* noted, "with an 'aye' that shook the building." When a Saint Louis man tried to have a bottle of whisky brought onto an excusion steamer about to cast off with a load of striking telegraphers, local brotherhood chief Mortimer Shaw intercepted the boy sent to fetch the contraband. "You and that whiskey cannot come on this boat together," he told the youthful courier. "You must either turn that over or stay off the boat." The boy surrendered the bottle, Shaw ceremoniously dropped it into the Mississippi, and the operators left on their abstinent cruise. A visitor to strike headquarters in Baltimore on a Sunday found a reassuring vignette of well-scrubbed and well-mannered young men, "all sprucely dressed. Some of them wore white neckties and had prayer books in their hands, having just returned from church."[23]

These efforts were not in vain; someone was indeed watching and nodding approvingly. "Have the telegraphers inaugurated a new order of strike?" the *Boston Globe* asked. "The universal good order that marks their movement—the refraining from all compulsory and vio-ˡ‿nt measures and the keeping strictly within the legitimate limits of the strike—are so unusual in such manifestations that they excite much comment and gain and keep for the brotherhood the warmest sympathy." And sympathy in the most conservative of places. "One prominent merchant remarked that he did not approve of the strike," the *Globe* reported, "but sympathized with the strikers. Others, while deprecating strikes in general, were hopeful that in this case the strikers would succeed." The august *New York Times* assured its readers that the telegraphers were "not a rabble of workmen misled by demagogues, but a body of intelligent men and women, quite capable of thinking for themselves," a verdict that *Harper's Weekly* echoed when it pronounced them "intelligent and voting labor . . . chiefly American, and of characteristic American intelligence and feeling." Both the Board of Aldermen in New York and Chicago's City Council passed resolutions lauding the operators' cause.[24]

Antimonopolism and hatred of the men behind the Western Union—and Jay Gould in particular—had much to do with the pro-brotherhood sentiment. "If there is any monopoly in this country that ought to be crushed," declared Chicago merchant Julian S. Ramsey, "it is the Western Union Telegraph Company." In late July, a silk manufacturer from New York named John D. Cutter proposed to do just that by forming a new enterprise, the Merchants' and Telegraphers' Association, to break the dependence of his fellow businessmen on the communicatons giant. And greedy corporations were run by greedy men. One daily pointed out that the broad support for the strike was as much due to "the moral character and public disservices of Mr. JAY GOULD" as to the operators' exemplary behavior.[25]

Nor was praise for the brotherhood universal. At times the operators were met with ambivalence, chilly neutrality, or outright hostility. The *New York Sun*, originally sympathetic, executed an about-face and called the strikers "highwaymen and cutthroats," joining Whitelaw Reid's *New York Tribune*, which found the union's bill of grievances "as a whole . . . unreasonable" and "especially objectionable in the way it was presented." From the Pioneer Valley of western Massachusetts the *Hampshire Gazette and Northampton Courier* spoke out against the strike for threatening republican values. "Why should a free-born American citizen 'stop work' or resume work," it wondered, "at the 'order' of anybody on the face of the earth?" The *Atlanta Constitution*, although no friend of the Western Union, was still troubled by the operators' challenge to freedom of contract and the beneficence of laissez-faire—and by the specter of "a parcel of men" whose means were coercion and whose ends included "arbitrary demands." The council of Montreal's Board of Trade likewise condemned what it judged the brotherhood's dictation to the companies, but down at Baltimore the members of the Corn and Flour Exchange chose to remain aloof from the conflict. So did those of the New York Produce Exchange, but not without some internal conflict of their own. No sooner had the exchange members assembled on July 27 to discuss the strike when one of them, W. W. Merrill, "sprang forward with his arms extended and shouted a motion to adjourn." In response, the *Tribune*'s man on the scene reported, "he was promptly hissed down." Speakers went on to vigorously damn the Western Union, vent general antimonopoly sentiments, suggest that the exchange acquire its own wire service, and recommend a negotiated settlement of the strike. But when a Mr. Mackey proposed that the exchange officially endorse the brotherhood, tempers and voices rose.

"I move," declared Mackey, "that this Exchange expresses its unequivocal sympathy with the strikers."

"No! No!" angry cries from the audience protested.

"There's too much of this monopolizing spirit over the country," Mackey went on undeterred, "they have the workingman under their heel—"

"Question! Question!" the hostile shouts interrupted him again. Mackey's motion failed to carry. Less turbulent but equally noncommittal was Massachusetts governor Ben Butler's reaction to the strike. When Boston operators invited him to take part in a support rally, Butler gingerly balanced his corpulent frame astride the middle of the fence and pleaded that the imperatives of office bound him to remain disinterested.[26]

But it was the breadth of sympathy for the brotherhood that was noteworthy, and more than moral support came its way. Boston businessmen reportedly offered strikers amounts ranging from $5 to

$1,000 early in the contest, and dispatches from elsewhere also had bankers, brokers, and merchants chipping in to aid the cause.[27] The owners of excursion steamers in several cities provided brothers and sisters complimentary respite from the July heat. In Boston, operators skated without charge in the Tremont Rink. Combining support for the telegraphers with a passion for the national game, crowds in Philadelphia, Washington, Boston, and New York paid to watch baseball nines swat and field. At Pittsburgh, a company of amateur minstrels entertained some 2,500 people and succeeded in raising $500 for the union, and at Madison Square Garden in New York, the far from the amateur bandmaster Patrick Gilmore lent his services in a benefit concert.[28] Prominent individuals also made donations. Buffalo's Mayor Manning gave $50 to the operators. Congressman J. H. McLean of Saint Louis and Cleveland's ex-Mayor Rose each sent double that amount. And a former telegrapher named Thomas A. Edison fattened the brotherhood strike fund with a gift of $700.[29]

Even more important than the widespread public backing for the walkout was the attitude of working people toward the striking brotherhood. As a branch of the steadily growing Knights of Labor, District Assembly 45 could expect the fraternal support of the order, and the solidarity of the parent body with the operators seemed unbroken. Grand master workman Terence V. Powderly, in Philadelphia on August 3 to help celebrate the birthday of Knights founder Uriah S. Stephens, declared that the brotherhood appeared financially sound, called the operators' actions "proper," and vowed that his organization would "stand by them to the last moment." When a reporter had asked Washington, D.C., operator Robert L. De Akers the previous day whether "the Knights of Labor act as a unit in making this strike a test case," De Akers assured him that they did indeed. Having the hearts and pocketbooks of the Knights on their side was an exhilarating tonic for the telegraphers.[30]

Working-class support was not limited to fellow Knights. Central trade bodies lined up behind the operators, as did individual unions: screwmen and cotton yard men in New Orleans; seamen in Cleveland; tanners and curriers in Boston; journeymen horseshoers, longshoremen, and brownstone cutters in New York; and others provided encouragement and cash.[31] Printers displayed a special alacrity and generosity, and could do much more than talk solidarity. At Elmira, New York, typographers passed a resolution of sympathy with the brotherhood that one of the town's papers, the *Advertiser*, refused to print; that evening, another Elmira journal, the *Gazette*, came out with a pro–Western Union editorial. Indignant printers called retaliatory strikes at both places.[32]

Widespread support meant widespread interest in the strike. The peculiar nature of the walkout caught the public fancy, all the more so because midsummer tended to dullness. With little else to flavor the bland news diet of July and August—President Chester A. Arthur's junket to the West graced more than one front page—the brotherhood's struggle with Gould's monopoly provided conversational spice at the supper tables, waiting rooms, workshops, and bar rails of America. The *New York Morning Journal* acknowledged the strike with the verses of "Tick, Tick, Tick!" one of whose quatrains exclaimed:

> O, woe to the Western U,
> And the holders of its shares!
> O, woe to the sender of news,
> As he madly stamps and swears!

Life, the humor magazine, devoted an installment of its "Popular Science Catechism" to the strike, satirizing the Western Union for using incompetent scab operators. A *Life* competitor, *Puck*, took note too, with a spoof of the exaggerated claims of success of both sides in the conflict. Quick-witted merchants also capitalized on the affair's topicality. Readers of the August 3 *Boston Globe* found this shouting for their attention:

> A GREATER STRIKE
> THAN THE
> TELEGRAPH TROUBLES

> Nearly everyone is interested in the strike of the telegraph operators although, whichever way it may turn out, it will be no pecuniary benefit to them. But the strike in which all Boston has a pecuniary interest is the strike which the Misfit Parlors, 4 Haywood Pl., have made, and which enables them to place fine custom-made clothing on the market.

An Atlanta dry-goods house made similar use of the walkout.[33]

If most people did not themselves use the telegraph, the newspapers that they read did, and the Western Union, like the brotherhood, was determined to keep its version of the contest before the public eye. The company's spokesman at Washington, superintendent Zeublin, eagerly provided newspapermen with the Western Union point of view. A week into the strike, Zeublin, whose flowing patriarchal beard belied his forty years, regaled journalists by describing arrangements to board and feed scabs that wisely limited their fare to soup and vegetables because "meats would make them sleepy at night." Pronouncements even closer to the center of corporate power came from press agent William B. Somerville at 195 Broadway, head of the Western Union news wire department and a kind of embryonic public relations man for the firm whose press conferences became as much a daily fixture of the struggle as brotherhood strike meetings.[34] They earned him a nickname as well. When his increasingly optimistic bulletins reporting various circuits as "O.K." conflicted with reports of continued disruption of Western Union services, skeptics flippantly christened him "O.K. Somerville," and for the remainder of the strike "O.K." became shorthand for the dubious veracity of the telegraph giant.[35] Nor was the company's public standing helped any by its close and dominant relationship with the Associated Press, the nation's major wire service. The brotherhood, naturally enough, claimed that AP dispatches distorted, fabricated, or suppressed news to suit the Western Union cause, but at least two journalists echoed the charges.[36]

Somerville's was not the only voice to speak for the Western Union. One enterprising reporter managed to locate and interview no less than five of the company's directors on the same day. Russell Sage extolled the benefits to the public of monopoly in lowering prices. Cyrus W. Field and an anonymous fellow board member spoke of their duty to the firm's investors ("we have small stockholders, many of them widows and orphans"), and C. P. Huntington reminded his inquisitor that he, too, had once been a "laboring man." Sidney Dillon, chatting with the reporter in pauses amidst his work of signing a stack of railroad bonds (each of which an attending office boy blotted in turn) attacked the union for trying to restrict the secrets of telegraphy to its membership. And all but one of the directors, for some reason, seemed especially indignant that the strike had begun with a whistle blast.[37]

Signals of another kind by late July suggested a marked turn of events in the Great Strike. On July 25, the brotherhood and the American Rapid Telegraph Company announced that they had reached a settlement (the terms of which, however, were not made public for another two weeks—a move that caused some operators to chafe and complain of the secrecy involved). The agreement was heartening news for the strikers, the first victory for their young union in its challenge to corporate power. Yet as telegraphic corporate power went in 1883, the American Rapid was still small game. The operators would have to wring concessions and recognition from more than a third-rate company.[38]

For the time being, a second-rate company would do. As news of the American Rapid accord broke, there were hints that the Baltimore & Ohio, too, would reach an understanding with the strikers. Although nowhere near the size of the Western Union, the B & O, a subsidiary of the famous railroad, was its closest rival, and were it to follow the Rapid's lead, it would strengthen the brotherhood considerably in its contest with the great monopoly. Something was indeed going on between the brotherhood and the B & O. John Campbell later claimed that as early as July 21 the company, like the American Rapid (both bitter foes of the Western Union), had secretly sent emissaries to meet with the strikers. No doubt it had, and a surviving letter suggests that the B & O's liaison was Josiah C. Reiff, a Wall Street adventurer with a fondness for telegraph securities. By the thirtieth, Eugene J. O'Connor, chair of the brotherhood Executive Committee, revealed that delicate negotiations between the two parties were in progress, complicated by B & O acting president Robert Garrett's fears of the ramifications for his rail empire of dealing with a union. Garrett's anxieties eventually overcame his desire for a settlement— according to John Campbell, because some brotherhood members, their tongues lubricated by drink, had prematurely bragged of having won B & O recognition, and so frightened off the skittish Garrett. Whatever the cause, the parley languished and the B & O continued to resist the operators.[39]

Despite the rebuff, the union looked and sounded plucky as July gave way to August. Eugene O'Connor claimed 6,000 to 7,000 accessions to the brotherhood since the start of the strike, and local assemblies prepared to dispense strike allowances to those claiming need—$5 a week for single operators, $7 for those supporting others —on the accustomed August 1 payday.[40] The brotherhood did suffer setbacks. Here and there, strikers defected and returned to work. Six or seven forsook the cause at Boston, where one journalist detected "a general feeling of despondence among the members of the brotherhood." Other reporters were more impressed by the local strikers' continued determination—dramatically manifested at a strike meeting where 200 telegraphers solemnly rededicated themselves to their cause.[41]

Operators stiffened their resolve with the more tangible fillip of strike pay. In New York, around 800 of them drew an allotment, although quite a few, perhaps 400 others, "having saved considerable amounts preparatory to this movement," declined to dip into the brotherhood war chest.[42] The strikers, in any event, seemed well situated. Union officials spoke with pride and assurance of their organization's financial health. And beyond the brotherhood strike fund lay the massed support of fellow Knights of Labor, whose membership assessments, at ten cents a head, could yield the telegraphers $80,000 a week. All this made for a sanguine operator rank and file—despite a few contrary and nagging tocsins: that after strike pay was disbursed in New York some operators were reported to feel "fairly if not generously dealt with"; that the expected assessments from the Knights had been delayed; that the Boston local assembly, while claiming an adequate reserve of cash, announced on July 30 that it had decided, in order "to be well prepared for contingencies," to accept the offers of businessmen and the public of monetary aid and establish a "skirmishing fund." But all this was surely of minor concern in light of frequent and emphatic brotherhood statements that the union was solvent, even affluent.[43] Hadn't grand master workman Powderly himself said that the telegraphers stood on solid pecuniary ground? He had—in public. Privately, he found them sinking. "I fear they must lose the battle," he confided to grand secretary Robert Layton on August 6, "though I talk to the contrary." Two days later, again to Layton, Powderly repeated his gloomy forecast. "Well if the Tel. Ops. fail now it wont be your fault and I am afraid for them, for I dont think they made ample preparation, if they did I know nothing of it."[44]

There was good reason for Powderly's quiet alarm. On August 1, as Eugene O'Connor cheerily announced "an immense improvement in the outlook for our cause," the placards in Western Union offices warning customers that telegrams were only accepted "subject to delay" disappeared.[45] Four days later, in a tacit admission that they had still not brought the Western Union to terms, brotherhood officers directed their railway operator members to present the B & O and Gould-affiliated lines with a bill of grievances and, if spurned, to strike against them. Such a strike had great potential to wreak mischief and inconvenience for the roads. There was heady talk of 7,000 to 10,000 more operators quitting their keys to join those already out, and even indications that other railroad workers—including the conservative engineers—might follow the telegraphers. But a rail operators' strike was also very risky at this point. "The moral [*sic*] effect of a failure," one troubled operator predicted, "will undoubtedly be bad; some of the weak-kneed brothers will regard it as an indication of weakness on the part of the Brotherhood, and it will be a very difficult matter to keep them from going back to work. . . . If on the other hand they [the railroad operators] leave their work, we will feel encouraged and will yet win the fight." As the strike order went out, the *New York Times* found John Campbell and Eugene O'Connor "somewhat anxious" but still talking of victory. The focus of the conflict shifted now to the thousands of telegraphers in the depots and towers that punctuated the railway lines. The brotherhood held its collective breath and awaited their response.[46]

Sputtering feebly, then dying, the new walkout was a miserable failure. By August 13, weary and disheartened union organizers returned to Baltimore after unsuccessful attempts to initiate new members on the B & O system. The results along the other roads were equally frustrating. Nor had the promise of support from the train crews been more than talk. Peter M. Arthur of the Brotherhood of Locomotive Engineers, a paragon of the narrow and selfish trade unionist, studiously distanced himself from the telegraphers' struggle. "We have paddled our own canoe for twenty years," he smugly declared, "and I hope we shall always continue to do so."[47]

The telegraphers' canoe, though, had just lost its paddle. New signs of desperation, heretofore absent or muted, emerged on the brotherhood side. Reports of sabotage, principally wire cutting, became more frequent in early August. On the seventh, district superintendent Thomas Roche announced from Boston that forty-one wires passing under the Connecticut River had been severed, demonstrating "a growing weakness on the part of the strikers," and the next day, his counterpart in New York, Walter Humstone, claimed a further eighty-nine Western Union wires rendered useless. Brotherhood officials denied responsibility and repeated pledges to help prosecute offenders, expel them from the union, and provide repair crews to make good the damage. James Smith, the master workman of New York's striking linemen, added the promise of a "slugging" for the miscreants as well. Probably never more than a small minority of strikers was involved in the guerrilla campaign against the wires, but the carefully cultivated brotherhood image of a gentlemanly contest with the telegraph monopoly suffered.[48]

It suffered even more when people, rather than property, were threatened. In the first two weeks of the strike, while the operators' prospects looked bright, there had been isolated charges of union intimidation, but in the aftermath of the railroad fiasco and amid hints of strained finances, resistance took on a darker hue.[49] On August 6, William ("Buffalo Bill") Steele, a scab lineman expelled by the New York brotherhood the week before for disorderly conduct, taunted a group of striking linemen, provoked a fight, and inflicted a minor stab wound on one of them. Pummeled by the others and then arrested, Steele left a scar on the brotherhood as much as on his victim. When it turned out that some of the union men involved in the incident had violated the temperance pledge, master workman John Mitchell reminded the local assembly that it was "impossible to win this strike and drink whiskey too."[50]

It was not the last violent incident to taint the brotherhood. The day after the knife fracas, general manager Eckert offered a $1,000 reward for the arrest and conviction of the two men who assaulted F. Jesson, a scab operator in New York. Also on August 7, a Pittsburgh strikebreaker named H. E. Safford was the target of a missile reportedly thrown by two union men. Safford ran to a bridge tollhouse, seized the gatekeeper's mace, and turned on his assailants, beating one of them severely. Attempts at coercion did not always end so bloodily. At Bismarck, Dakota Territory, strikers and their allies adopted the novel tactic of mobbing the local Western Union office, forcing the operator to quit, and then ensconcing him in a hotel bed. But the more typical incidents were less whimsical. Early on August 16, an exchange of words in a Cincinnati saloon between strikers and a scab resulted in the latter being "badly beaten and disabled from work," and before the sun rose another Queen City nonstriker, Henry Schwab, suffered a dislocated shoulder at the hands of brotherhood supporters. Friends of the cause sadly shook their heads. "Hitherto," noted the *New Orleans Picayune*, "the strikers have won praise from all by gentlemanly conduct." The noble crusade, faltering, had lurched toward the gutter.[51]

But it never fell into it, and this the operators' many sympathizers seemed to realize. "Your cause is worthy and righteous," Mayor Albert Palmer of Boston wrote the operators, "your demands are just," sentiments that the aging patrician reformer Wendell Phillips shared when he assured them that he sided with their struggle "heart and soul." Allegations of union lawlessness did not stop about 1,500 Bostonians from attending a benefit concert at Tremont Temple on August 16 that enriched the telegraphers' coffers by over $800. In New York, a U.S. Senate committee investigating the plight of working people and the growing gulf between employing and employed classes offered the strikers a fair and often sympathetic hearing. When one senator asked John Campbell to define "strike," the brotherhood chief, choosing his words with exquisite care, called it "a mild sort of revolution."[52]

Public and private encouragement were still not enough to undo the union's reverses. Through the first two weeks of August, reports of strikers wavering, losing followers, exhausting their funds, or seeking to cut their losses and negotiate with the monopoly made for dissonant counterpoint against chipper union statements of the campaign's vigor. When the Western Union's Walter Humstone spoke of an imminent brotherhood collapse on August 10, a trio of strike leaders at New York "all laughed heartily" in response. But their mirth was forced and painful. The day before, Philadelphia master workman C. L. Laverty had frankly called the situation desperate. "We have played our trump card," he said of the railroad walkout, "and lost." Other brotherhood leaders saw things equally grimly by now. *Telegraphers' Advocate* editor John B. Taltavall, who was close to the union's officers, later disclosed that as early as August 5 no senior brotherhood man doubted "that the fight was lost, unless a miracle rescued the order from defeat."[53] And for those reading the daily papers with a cool and discerning eye, there were signs enough of a Western Union triumph in the offing: a story from Boston about a waning of enthusiasm and growing boredom at strike meetings; another from New York that told of rank-and-file misgivings and anxiety about their organization's tactics; from Charleston, South

Carolina, operators "very sore" about "repeated appeals" to the national brotherhood for assistance that went unanswered; a "somewhat gloomy" ambience surrounding strike headquarters at Chicago; and from Philadelphia and Baltimore, dispatches ulcerated with such phrases as "internal fights," "treasury is greatly depleted," "break in the ranks," and "backsliding operators."[54]

By the third week of August the rebellious telegraphers' pockets were empty and their force spent. In what the friendly *New York Times* bluntly referred to as "the dying gasp of the brotherhood," a supposedly independent committee of strikers not representing the telegraphers' union met with Eckert on August 15 to ask on what terms the men and women might return to their desks. The committee was a virtual admission of defeat, and General Eckert seemed to relish the occasion. When the delegation called on him, he did not deign to offer them seats, and so they stood during the entire session, like naughty children called into the principal's office. Nor did he miss the opportunity to pounce on one of the members, Thomas O'Reilly, when the latter answered Eckert's query about whom he represented by blurting out, "I represent the Wheatstone operators upstairs."

"Upstairs?" Eckert challenged him. "Show me your authority."

"I mean," O'Reilly corrected himself, "the striking Wheatstone operators."

The general refused to deal with the committee, saying only that they could follow the routine procedure of applying individually to their superintendents if they wished to "receive consideration" to be rehired. And that was that. Shortly afterward, John Campbell sent an open letter to Eckert in which he characterized the general's treatment of the delegation as "arrogant and decidedly disrespectful," and added, a bit disingenuously, that in sending the committee the telegraphers had "wanted to be convinced and to convince the public that the company did not intend to deal fairly with them independently of the brotherhood," and that they now had "all the proof they wanted." But indignation did little to check the defeatism that Eckert's performance had worsened.[55]

Close to yielding, brotherhood leaders still nursed a frail hope that by reaching an arrangement with the B & O Telegraph Company they might outmaneuver the Western Union. Their contact with the B & O through Josiah Reiff continued at least through August 15, the day of the "independent" committee incident, when Reiff reported to Robert Garrett that the encounter with Eckert had "made them very angry and more determined toward the WU, but their temper is not at all changed toward the B & O. As I assured you, they feel their cause will be strengthened by building up the opposition." Reiff went on to suggest a meeting between Garrett and John Campbell who, he reported, "is sure if he could see you personally the matter could be fixed in a few minutes so your men would get back the next day." He proposed that Campbell travel incognito to Newport for the meeting carrying a visiting card identifying him as "Mr. Morse," and his fertile brain hit on the added scheme of orchestrating an exchange of public letters between Garrett and Thomas Edison to ease a covert settlement with the brotherhood—a ruse that Edison agreed to participate in. But the indecisive Garrett remained more fearful of labor unions than of the Western Union and Reiff's efforts at arbitration proved wasted.[56]

Two days later, on August 17, Campbell formally acknowledged what most of those familiar with the contest already knew and declared the strike at an end. In Boston, Eugene O'Connor had just finished rousing the local assembly with a fighting speech when Campbell's telegram arrived. Voice quavering and on the verge of tears, he handed the message to master workman Charles E. Chute, but Chute, too, fell victim to his emotions and was unable to read the order aloud. Regaining self-control, O'Connor finally took the wire back from Chute, declared, "My heart is absolutely broken," and then informed his comrades that their union had capitulated. The assembled operators, the *Globe* recorded, "were apparently struck dumb with amazement. . . . It was with an air of stupefaction that one of the prominent members arose and requested a second reading of the fatal despatch."[57]

Reaction to the defeat was not so passive everywhere. At Chicago, master workman A. J. Morris told over 400 strikers at Ulich's Hall that they need not heed Campbell's order to give up, and telegrams were read from local assemblies in Cincinnati, Cleveland, and Saint Louis that echoed Morris's call for continued resistance. That afternoon, some 300 operators, along with "several hundred sympathizing trades unionists," defiantly paraded through Chicago's central business district as they sang the well-known antimonopoly ditty about hanging Jay Gould to a sour apple tree. Some tried to preserve a semblance of solidarity and integrity despite their defeat. In Memphis, the operators asked to return in a body, and at New Orleans, they resolved that married ex-strikers have preference in reinstatement, but managers at both offices rejected these scraps of autonomy and declared that hiring practices would remain a company prerogative. From New York, a contented Thomas Eckert issued a bulletin describing the scene at Western Union headquarters. "The first floor is now crowded with strikers," it read. "The end has evidently come."[58]

When the initial shock subsided, the vanquished operators asked themselves why they had lost.

For one thing, some said, the strike had been poorly managed, strategically and tactically sloppy and amateurish. The timing had been all wrong. Midsummer was the telegraph companies' slowest season—something that several observers had pointed out even in the first roseate days of the walkout.[59] The plan of calling out the commercial operators at once without including the vital press and railroad telegraphers at the same time was faulted too.[60] Beyond that, there were charges that the surrender had been premature, and that the Western Union, far weaker than was generally imagined, could yet have been beaten had the brotherhood only persevered. One of the returning men at Boston, "upon finding the business of the company in so mixed a condition, cried because the strikers did not hold out still longer."[61]

Some saw the men leading their union as the villains of the piece. Disgusted strikers in Toledo excoriated John Campbell—whose nickname before the debacle had been "Honest John"—as "the Judas Iscariot of the Brotherhood." In Chicago, Boston, and New York, there was bitter and suspicious talk about the collapse having been a sellout, a "put-up job" by duplicitous union officers.[62]

But the greatest anger, frustration, and sense of betrayal was directed at the Knights of Labor. On the eve of the capitulation, a leader of the New York brotherhood, admitting defeat, called the Knights "the most gigantic of frauds," and one of his associates condemned the order as a "politico-Communistic organization, profuse in promises and criminal in their non-fulfillment of such promises." Van Cullen Jones, an eleven-year veteran of the key and a prominent Boston operator, ascribed his union's "unfortunate termination of the struggle" to the Knights' failure "as an organized body" to make good on pledges of financial aid to the brotherhood. From Baltimore, Pittsburgh, and Saint Louis, similar indictments were broadcast.[63] Not even the humor column of the *Telegraphers' Advocate* escaped the sour aftertaste of the affair, offering: "There are many days of hard work before us; but, alas! our Knights of Labor are things of the past," and: "When matches strike, they generally get fired. Yes, and a gun is discharged if only the hammer strikes." Those disillusioned with the Knights went on to draw a lesson from the strike. Surveying the wreckage of the contest, the quasi-official organ of the brotherhood concluded that "in future movements for the amelioration of our condition as skilled workers in the world's great workshop, we must rely implicitly upon ourselves."[64]

Knights supporters rejected the brotherhood charges, countered that the telegraphers' walkout had been foolishly planned and executed, and noted that the financial backing demanded of the order had not only been extravagant but, within the rules of the organization, illegal. "If they went into the strike with their eyes open, which as intelligent men I presume they did," argued Knights assistant grand secretary Gilbert Rockwood, "they knew well enough that all the assistance they could promptly get from the Knights of Labor would be voluntary contributions"—not the general assessment that the strike leaders claimed was promised and then denied them. Declared John S. McClelland, both a telegrapher and secretary of the Knights national General Executive Board: "Too much reliance altogether was placed upon the Knights of Labor in this case, and too much blame is given them, now that the strike has failed." In private, McClelland was much harsher with fellow operators who had turned against the Knights. "There is a widespread determination to sever connection with the K. of L.," he wrote Robert Layton, "and the d——d asses don't know what for. . . . Too bad they were beaten but we are not to blame, and its influence wont be as disastrous as pictured."[65]

Few members of the shattered union could have shared McClelland's optimism. While the battle may have cost the Western Union as much as $2 million all told, President Norvin Green pronounced his firm's strike losses "the best financial investment ever made by the company," explaining, "General Eckert tells me he will get one-third more work out of a man each day, and that is economy."[66] For those rehired—and many eventually were—the humiliation of defeat included the signing of an ironclad contract, and for some, harassment of varying kinds and degrees.[67] At the main New York office, manager William J. Dealy, assistant manager Thomas Brennan, and assistant superintendent Irwin reportedly inflicted indignities on former insurgents. But the most rarefied gloating came from the company's premier manager. "I'm glad enough to get back," an operator told the *New York Tribune*, "but it breaks me all up when General Eckert comes in the operating room and looks around with that sarcastic smile of his and seems to say, 'Ah! you rascals, are there any more of you with whistles you want to blow?'"[68]

Through all this, the operators still had friends. *Puck* extended condolences with a front-page cartoon that pictured a setting sun tagged "Strike" and a column of bowed and weeping men and women filing into a cave whose entrance bore the sign "WESTERN UNION TELEGRAPH COMPANY. 'ALL HOPE ABANDON YE WHO ENTER HERE!'" A grinning, troglodytic Jay Gould, a club marked "Monopoly" in his hand, was hunched nearby. More forcefully, while taking testimony during and after the strike Senator Henry W. Blair of New Hampshire, chair of the Senate Education and Labor Committee, confronted the Western Union on the operators' behalf. Reminding Norvin Green of his company's great power, the productivity of its plant and employees, "and considering the money that you do make," Blair asked him, "don't you think that you could afford to give your operators more money?"

Green squirmed, smiling. "Well, that is a question—"

"I have that impression very strongly," Blair cut him off, "and now that you have got your own way about it I wish you would just come up and give those boys more money."[69]

Beyond such continuing public sympathy was an even more consoling aspect of the month-long battle: the militancy and faithfulness of the women strikers had been exemplary, and heartening to their male co-unionists. Praise for the behavior of the "girls" was universal. But the movement that John Campbell had hopefully called "a mild sort of revolution" was over, leaving the Western Union's power intact and the operators' attempts to challenge that power hobbled and addled.

The defeat of telegrapher unionism in the Great Strike was in fact but one of several issues that the struggle had raised—issues bearing directly on the kind of society evolving in the late nineteenth century, and on the reactions of contemporary Americans to the flux and conflict shaping their era. Beyond importance in its own right, the strike had also been a backdrop against which the manifestations of an industrializing United States that puzzled, plagued, and haunted its citizens emerged in relief: a new kind of business enterprise so powerful and extensive as to call a continent its domain; a complementary body of employees who wore the middle-class garb of the countinghouse but who adopted the working-class activism of the shop floor; women whom convention assigned a role of domesticity and weakness but who, compelled to earn a living, could display militant resolve; and a clash between a faith in the sanctity of private property and a notion of the public good in the Good Republic that could at times suggest alternatives to the rule of the market. In 1883 all these things claimed the attention and concern of Americans trying to understand and master their times. All of them are still worthy of exploration. What follows is an attempt to do so.

A TERMINAL STATION.

A VILLAGE TELEGRAPHER IN THE EARLY 1870S.
Branch offices such as this, usually in railroad depots, were the most common kind of telegraph facility. The young woman managing this one has given it a suitably domestic touch with the framed picture and climbing plant. Her office is provincial in more than one sense: the weight-driven Morse paper tape register in the center of the table was already a bit old-fashioned by this time. From *Harper's Monthly*, August 1873. Courtesy National Museum of American History, Smithsonian Institution.

OPERATING ROOM, WESTERN UNION HEADQUARTERS 195 BROADWAY, NEW YORK, 1881.

The view is from the City (or Ladies') Department. Chief operators supervise while check-girls nip through the aisles shuttling messages. Faintly visible in the left background are the switchboard and the pneumatic tubes connecting the operating room with the receiving and delivery departments downstairs. Courtesy National Museum of American History, Smithsonian Institution.

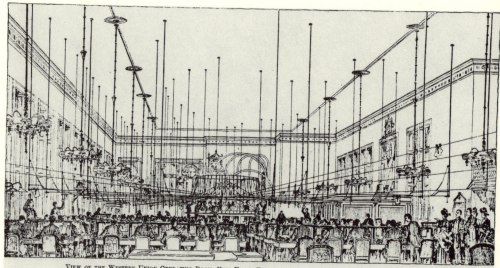

VIEW OF THE WESTERN UNION OPERATING ROOM, NEW YORK, FITTED UP WITH THE LAMSON MESSAGE CARRIER SYSTEM.

195 BROADWAY IN 1887.
The "industrial" configuration of the great operating room is even more pronounced here. The Lamson mechanical message carrier has been installed to augment the speed and reach of the check-boys and girls. From the *Electric Age*, July 1, 1887. Courtesy National Museum of American History, Smithsonian Institution.

Check-girls who Collect and Distribute Messages.—Western Union Main Operating Room, New York.

APPRENTICE IN A PINAFORE.

A check-girl at work in the City Department of 195 Broadway. Such girls (and the check-boys) were usually from working-class families and often went on to become operators. The telegrapher on the left, unoccupied at the moment, is apparently knitting or crocheting. From *Scribner's*, July 1889. Courtesy National Museum of American History, Smithsonian Institution.

WESTERN UNION OPERATING ROOM, BUFFALO, NEW YORK, CA. 1892.
The operators nearest the camera have forsaken the traditional steel-pen-and-
ink-bottle ensemble for the faster and neater typewriter, a trend that began in
the late 1880s. Sounders, no longer mounted on the tables, now sit in ele-
vated resonators visible in the corners of the operators' cubicles. Courtesy National Museum of American History, Smithsonian Institution.

"HAZING A FRESHMAN."

CRAFT CULTURE WITH A VENGEANCE.
The "hazing" of a new telegrapher as amused office veterans look on. From the *Operator,* Jan. 1, 1879. Courtesy National Museum of American History, Smithsonian Institution.

GENTILITY FOR SALE—AND MORE.

Advertisements for the lower middle class. From the *Operator,* July 16, 1883. Courtesy National Museum of American History, Smithsonian Institution.

2

ANATOMY OF
AN INDUSTRY

Our Fathers gave us liberty, but little did they dream,
The grand results that flow along this mighty age of steam;
For our mountains, lakes and rivers, are all a blaze of fire,
And we send our news by lightning, on the telegraphic wire.
                    —"UNCLE SAM'S FARM," POPULAR SONG, CA. 1860

In the great transformation of the United States in the nineteenth century the telegraph and the railroad were in the vanguard, twin enterprises growing up together and in their turn fathering the corporate
economy that would come to dominate the next hundred years. "Industry" seems somehow inappropriate for telegraphy, with its slen-
der poles and fragile wires and its small and intricate plant; more
fitting that the railroads take that description, with their smoky, mus-
cular locomotives and their voracious consumption of iron and steel,
coal and wood, land and men. But the images are deceptive. The capitalist industrial revolution of the postbellum years, Alfred D. Chandler, Jr., has convincingly argued, was one of economies of speed as

much as of scale, and in that the telegraph, like the railway, was indispensable. Wire and rail—often sharing the same right-of-way—knit an efficient national market, economically consummating what had politically begun in 1789. Of equal importance, the telegraph and railroad companies, Chandler writes, "were themselves the first modern business enterprises to appear in the United States." It seems richly symbolic that the establishment of four standard time zones across the continent and a nationwide telegraph strike should have both occurred in 1883.[1]

Complementary partners recasting an atomized, agrarian republic into an integrated, industrial one, railroad and telegraph companies evolved in similar fashion. Both traced a pattern of many small, competitive firms giving way to fewer, larger, and more stable ones. The nature of the telegraph was such, in fact, that the pace and extent of wire consolidation well outdistanced that of the nation's steam roads. No railway, or consortium of railways, ever approached the stature of a Western Union.[2]

After the initial Morse experiments in the 1830s and an aborted government interest in the new medium, the initiative to develop telegraphy fell to private enterprise. In the decade or so following the mid-1840s, venturesome businessmen and speculators such as Andrew Jackson's ex-Postmaster General Amos Kendall, Henry O'Rielly, Ezra Cornell, Cyrus W. Field, Peter Cooper, Hiram Sibley, and others lent their capital and commercial acumen in the race for markets and profits. This first flush of telegraph promotion produced many lines whose hurried and shoddy construction often mirrored equally rickety finances, and promoters devoted a good deal of their time and effort to rate wars and patent squabbles. Wasteful of human and material resources, this "reckless expansion" had nonetheless planted a rudimentary telegraphic grid across the Northeast and Midwest by the 1850s.[3]

But the cost was terrible and the surviving firms, bloodied and sobered, sought peace and stability. They found it in 1857 in a pooling arrangement dubbed the "Treaty of the Six Nations," in which a half dozen of the largest companies (including the recently incorporated Western Union) carved up a vast market encompassing the eastern

United States as far west as Minnesota, Iowa, Missouri, Arkansas, and Louisiana. The treaty prescribed mutual aid and respect for spheres of influence, and also bound the signatories to ruthlessly eliminate or absorb any new competition. But pools among telegraph capitalists proved no more durable than those that their railroading brethren fashioned. By the 1860s the pact had withered, and the Western Union and its principal rivals, the United States and American Telegraph companies, battled to dominate the field. It turned out to be a painful fight whose assaults on dividends forced a growing number of entrepreneurs to consider replacing the rigors of competition with a more predictable and lucrative arrangement. "I know that large holders of telegraph stock are discussing the necessity of relief from present difficulties," wrote the president of the United States Telegraph Company in early 1866, "and some of them say tis only a question of time about our coming together." Within a year the three main contenders had done just that by merging under the aegis of the most aggressive of the firms, which had begun in 1851 as the New York and Mississippi Valley Printing Telegraph Company, and whose name—Western Union—the new company would retain. After this great consolidation, the Western Union was not the only remaining telegraph company in America, but it was already the most powerful and important one.[4]

The clash of raw market forces had much to do with the molding of the new communications giant, but so did the public purse. Eight years before locomotives touched cowcatchers at Promontory Point, Utah, the Western Union and an amalgam of California companies had completed a transcontinental line under the terms of the 1860 Pacific Telegraph Act. The act promised the companies up to $40,000 a year in government subsidies in consideration for which the companies would transmit federal business. Like the contemporary grants to railroads, the Pacific Telegraph Act encouraged the kind of financial easy virtue that marked quasi-public enterprise in the years of the Great Barbecue. The act did make it possible for east and west coasts to talk to each other by wire, but it also redistributed some of the nation's wealth to a small number of resourceful, if not entirely honest, telegraph promoters. The Civil War, too, was kind to the Western Union. It stimulated telegraphic business in general, of course, but it also enlarged the company's wire and cable network by over 14,000 miles of government-built lines in 1866. The official reason for the transfer—that the state was only rightly restoring private property

comandeered or destroyed by wartime necessity—lost some of its co-
gency when it was learned that the gift of wire and poles went either
to the Western Union or to the firms it was about to absorb, and that
General Thomas T. Eckert, late assistant secretary of war, was assuming a high managerial post with that same fortunate corporation.[5]

Despite near monopoly status early in its career, the Western
Union was never free from competition of some sort in the postbellum years, ranging from the pinpricks of small firms to more serious
bouts with larger concerns or consortia. As late as 1878, one writer
counted 132 companies coexisting with the Western Union, most of
them of the small, local, entrepreneurial kind that had typified telegraphy in its first years. Among them, true enough, were scattered enterprises of substance, often ancillaries of railroad systems: the
Central Pacific (142 offices, 212 employees, 4,904 miles of wire), the
Montreal Telegraph Company (1,507 offices, 2,337 employees, 20,479
miles of wire), the Baltimore & Ohio (136 offices, 341 employees,
1,409 miles of wire), or the Atlantic & Pacific (528 offices, 794 employees, 22,248 miles of wire). But more representative of the mass of
companies were such as the New Jersey Midland (19 offices, 19 employees, 160 miles of wire), the Troy and Union Springs (5 offices, 5
employees, 30 miles of wire), the Snohomish Telegraph Company (3
offices, 3 employees, 14 miles of wire), or the South Hadley Falls (2
offices, 2 employees, 1 mile of wire). And peering down on all of
these—with 7,672 offices, 12,224 employees, and 199,022 miles of
wire—stood the Western Union.[6]

The Western Union's growing scope and power, resting in part on
government generosity and the sheer weight of concentrated capital,
was also due to advantageous leasing and franchise arrangements,
most especially those with railroads. The roads needed fast and reliable communications both on and beyond their systems; the telegraph
giant sought rights-of-way easily and quickly accessible to repair crews
(unlike those that meandered along bumpy rural highways or through
forest, field, and swamp), and cheap operator labor and office facilities. Both partners satisfied their needs through the franchise agreements. "By a division of expenses, and a joint use of line and offices,"
the *Boston Herald* explained in 1883, "vast areas of country are made
tributary at a very small expense to the revenues of the telegraph
company, while the low cost of maintenance of the lines on roads so
frequently traversed, and under constant surveillance, is an advantage that is obvious." It was certainly obvious to Jay Gould. "That ar-

rangement," he told inquiring senators the same year, "has given the Western Union a hold upon an immense system which it could not have got in any other way. For instance, today take our 25,000 operators in the Western Union system, if we paid them all salaries . . . the gross earnings of the telegraph business would not pay that expense alone, the salary roll, to say nothing of the maintenance of the lines." More than three-fourths of the nation's railroads had such agreements with the Western Union.[7] The company also profitably leased private wires to bankers, brokers, and other businessmen, and it further bolstered its market position through press contracts, particularly by its intimate ties with the Associated Press.[8]

Thus fortified, the Western Union prospered in the Gilded Age. Between 1870 and 1890, corporate profits, in nominal dollars, rose some 215 percent from around $1.9 million to $6 million; but adjusted for deflation, the company's profits had actually shot up from $1.4 million to $7.4 million, a dizzying climb of 428 percent.[9] The number of offices multiplied too: 3,972 in 1870, 9,077 in 1880, and, by 1890, 19,382 of them.[10]

But accompanying this remarkable expansion and accumulation were spurts of competition and rate cutting, stock jobbing, and mergers, all intertwined with the jarring rhythms of boom and bust. Even during the lean 1870s, the Western Union made money. Noting the "general dullness in every department of business" plaguing the nation in 1874, Western Union president William Orton nevertheless reported a "most gratifying" $1.4 million in net profit that the company had earned within the past six months. Profit rates wavered in the 1870s though and did not reach a 6 percent plateau until the end of the decade. This newfound stability, lasting through 1883, then eroded as the rate slid down to 3 percent, again recovering in the late 1880s and achieving a rough stasis, at around 4 percent, through the 1890s. Dividend declarations (at least from 1873 on) were never entirely suspended, and their yearly fluctuation followed a path similar to that of profit rates over the same twenty-year span. Three times (1875, 1884, and 1885) dividends paid out exceeded net income, and in nine instances (1886, 1888, 1894–1900) the dividends declared covered 90 percent or more of the year's net earnings.[11]

Behind these numbers, in part, were challenges from ambitious rivals. In 1871, the independent *Telegrapher* welcomed the appearance of a pool of Western Union competitors and hopefully predicted that they would provide a "reasonable and proper" contest in the field that would both serve the public through lowered rates and prevent a recourse to government ownership of the wires. The pool's threat passed, but a new and much more serious one surfaced in the mid-1870s when Jay Gould turned his attention and peculiar talents to telegraphy. Early in 1875, using a line linked to western railroads called the Atlantic & Pacific, Gould—with the technical and managerial help of a disgruntled ex-Western Union official named Thomas Eckert—inaugurated a rate war that forced the Vanderbilt interests controlling the Western Union to buy out the A & P three years later. As his most recent and sympathetic biographer notes, Gould "not only managed to dispose of [the A & P] on lucrative terms but also leave Vanderbilt with the impression that he had made a good deal" —which he most certainly had not, since Gould's upstart company, though leeching Western Union dividends and driving down the price of its stock, was itself a shaky concern. Nor was Gould done making good deals. Within a year he renewed his assault on the Western Union, again by manufacturing a rival company, this time called the American Union. As before, the fight hurt the Western Union enough to make its directors come to terms with Gould, in 1881. The settlement this time included another great merger, but also Gould's wresting a commanding seat on the board of the enlarged Western Union, now armed with 90,000 shares of its stock.[12]

Neither Gould nor his newly wrought wire empire was immune from the play of market forces, though. The Baltimore & Ohio Telegraph Company, an erstwhile ally in the battles of the 1870s, was now hostile despite overtures from Gould for a pact. "We are on the brink of a big contest," he warned B & O vice-president Robert Garrett shortly before his 1881 Western Union triumph, "& we fear if we Educate the people to too low rates it may lead to *restrictive legislation* that will hurt *other interests* as well." But the threat of government regulation failed to move Garrett, and he chose to fight the huge company. So did a trio of smaller, though scrappy firms—the American Rapid, the Bankers' & Merchants', and the Postal Telegraph Company—organized in the early 1880s in the speculative frenzy engulfing the industry. And so after thrashing the operators in 1883, the Western Union found itself dragged into a sharp rate war that lasted until 1887. That year, a financially unsound and soundly battered B & O capitulated, and the Western Union absorbed its largest single competitor. By the late 1880s the worst was over, and telegraphy settled into a stable oligopoly of which the surviving Postal was the decidedly junior partner. As it had been since the 1860s, but to an even greater degree, the telegraph business was synonymous with the Western Union.[13]

Important as competition was in the evolution of the industry, more than dispassionate, invisible hands were guiding the pens entering profit figures in Western Union ledgers. Stock watering and financial sleight-of-hand were as much a part of the business as relays and insulators. When Robert Garrett contemplated negotiating a pool with the Western Union in 1885, B & O Telegraph Company president David Homer Bates—who as a senior manager of many years' Western Union service should have known—cautioned that "there are so many bye-ways in the W.U. plan of book-keeping that like Dicken's [*sic*] character who always had a natural suspicion of the freshness of an egg, so I have a natural suspicion of the fairness of W.U. statements that may be offered for the settlement of so important a question." Telegraph firms had an inveterate reputation for waterlogged corporate structures, and none more so than the Western Union. Critics of the great monopoly frequently charged that to maintain dividend payments on watered stock it made up the difference by cutting employees' wages and overcharging the public. In the wake of the 1881 Gould coup, the venerable *Commercial and Financial Chronicle* indicted the merger and subsequent $80 million recapitalization as "another immense stock-watering upon which the people must pay dividends," and other businessmen repeated the allegations during the 1883 strike. Norvin Green denied the charges, but another apologist for the company, E. B. Grant, dismissed the "great but unreasonable opposition to what is termed 'watering' stock" because "watering to any conceivable extent does not affect the real value of the stock."[14]

Shady corporate practices may well have been conducted at the operators' expense in the form of speedups and pay reductions. One student suggests that the combination of watered stock and competition created pressure on the company that prevented a "uniform, rational" rate structure, but he does not explore the obvious expedient that the directors could have turned to: trimming labor costs. Falling operators' salary levels, in nominal dollars, were an unquestioned feature of the 1870s and 1880s. The notorious Sliding Scale of graduated cuts dating from 1876 was such an economy measure, as was the practice of filling vacant positions at $5 or $10 less than the previous occupant had been receiving.[15] The relation between competition and wages may not always have been linear and mechanical, but the imperative to maintain dividends and market power, rather than salary levels, guided company policy.[16]

Corporate consolidation also hurt operators by tightening the job market through eliminating redundant facilities. Looking ahead to the coming Western Union–American Telegraph merger in 1866, General Anson Stager observed that many of the American's force could "be dispensed with, without detriment to the interests of the consolidated company," a clinical judgment with which his fellow board members readily agreed. While the Western Union grew larger and more powerful, operators ultimately remained at the mercy of the market's drift. "The very general suspension of telegraphic extension," noted the *Telegrapher* during the punishing slump of the mid-1870s, "has lessened the usual increase of demand for such [operators'] labor, while until recently, there has been little, if any, decrease in the number of those who are entering telegraphic ranks."[17]

The Western Union frankly celebrated its virtual monopoly as both economically natural and a public good. "Notwithstanding the clamor in regard to telegraphic monopoly," declared the firm's house organ in 1881, "it is the result of an inevitable law that the business shall be mainly conducted under one great organization. "Competition, the editor explained, hindered rather than promoted progress in the field.[18]

This "one great organization" was unique in reach, power, and physiognomy. By 1880, 80 percent of the country's message traffic pulsed along Western Union wires connecting 12,386 offices. Four years later, the company counted some 21,010 persons in its direct or indirect employ, the bulk of them (15,242) managers and operators. That ratio was roughly typical for the firm in the Gilded Age, although earlier the proportion of managers and operators had been a bit lower, averaging 63.7 percent of all employees in the period 1867–79. Most Western Union operators were in fact employees of the hundreds of railroads with which the firm had its franchise contracts. Western Union operators proper—3,629 of them by one tally a month before the Great Strike—made up only about a third of all those sending and receiving the company's business. Likewise, close to 80 percent of all the Western Union offices were actually local railway depots, which, under the franchise system, performed double duty as train stations and commercial telegraph facilities. Rather than fostering weakness and dependence, the farming out of work to the railroads increased the weight and breadth of the Western Union's empire.[19]

At the apex of this huge enterprise sat a board of directors that included some of the best-known and most hated businessmen in America. Jay Gould was foremost among these, of course, having stormed his way into the boardroom in 1881, and his son George occupied a seat as well. A recent account of Gould's career suggests that he was as much a manager as a speculator in his later years, at least with regard to his railroad interests, but there is no such evidence for his tenure at the Western Union. Gould's presence was important, though. So were those of the West Coast robber baron and Central Pacific Railroad president Collis P. Hungtinton, and Union Pacific directors Sidney Dillon, Russell Sage, and Cyrus W. Field (the latter of Atlantic cable fame). At the board table, too, was Western Union president Norvin Green, a Kentuckian who had spent fourteen years as a country doctor "traveling about on horseback, with a pair of saddle-bags, over a pretty rough country," before turning his energies to patronage politics and then telegraph promotion. In evidence at directors' meetings were also New York Central Railroad lawyer and Vanderbilt deputy Chauncey M. Depew, and the dour visage of investment banker J. P. Morgan, who had engineered the Western Union–B & O merger in 1887. And there was also Western Union vice-president and general manager Thomas T. Eckert.[20]

Eckert dwelled in two worlds: that of director and company officer, and that of professional manager and technician. He was of that first generation that guided the industry through its initial phase of competition and concentration in the twenty years or so leading up to the Civil War. In turn operator (and postmaster) at Wooster, Ohio, in the late 1840s, superintendent of a railway telegraph in the 1850s, gold mine manager, chief of the U.S. Military Telegraphs under Lincoln, assistant secretary of war under Edwin Stanton, and then senior manager in the Western Union and its rivals, Eckert eventually assumed the presidency of the great monopoly upon the death of Norvin Green in the early 1890s. His influence (he was rightly reckoned a Gould lieutenant) and success were atypical, but his role in the new stratum of manager-specialists was not. The same was true for another ex-manager and board member in the 1880s, vice-president

John Van Horne.[21] Behind Eckert came a second generation of men who, although too young to have known the rough-and-tumble days of the industry's teething period—a time when promoter Ezra Cornell and his son Alonzo cut poles and sweated alongside their laborers in the woods of upstate New York—were still old enough to have entered the craft during its mid-century boom. Beginning as messengers and operators in the 1850s and 1860s, many would be the managers of the Western Union by the time of the Great Strike. Many were also alumni of the military telegraph service. Colonel Robert Clowry received his honorific in the same way that General Eckert had, and men such as David Homer Bates, Albert Brown Chandler, Charles A. Tinker, and William J. Dealy had all worked government keys during the Civil War.[22]

The military association with the growing telegraph business was more than a matter of historical accident. Because the telegraph, like the railroad, was a form of enterprise so unlike the traditional small-scale ones of workshop or merchant's office, there was but one model, as Harold Livesay notes in connection with the railroads, that could bring rational structure and discipline to the new corporate giants, and that was the military one. Like the army, the Western Union issued a rule book (it went through at least three editions), giving employees detailed instructions for conducting the company's business and their own behavior. Presidents William Orton and Norvin Green both insisted on strict observance of the chain of command within the company. "It would be subversive of all system," Green reminded an employee who had bypassed the regular hierarchy in 1880, "were I to interfere or in any wise make an exception on your behalf."[23] Nor is it surprising that the three great territorial blocks of the Western Union were dubbed "Divisions," or that company directives came down as "general orders" and "special orders," or that operators in larger offices were grouped into "squads," uniformed messenger boys called by number and placed under "sergeants," or that the house organ listed monthly appointments, transfers, resignations, and dismissals under the heading "The Service."[24] Not that the firm's organization was purely a transposed military one. Long before he was called General Eckert, the Western Union's top manager was building and running telegraph lines; that, in fact, was why he had been commissioned. What was likely at work was a kind of managerial dialectic: the army had things to offer those interested in corporate empire building, but telegraphy and railroading, of necessity, themselves spurred managerial innovation. The two fed off of, and influenced, each other.[25]

Beneath the company officers and senior managers spread a pyramid of employees, plant, and offices. The latter included thousands of small-town railroad depots, as well as an urban spectrum, running from branch office cubbyholes to multistory edifices. In 1883, by its own account, the company maintained thirty-nine "principal main offices" across the nation. The New York headquarters at 195 Broadway, with 444 telegraphers on its payroll, was unmatched even by its relatively big counterparts at Chicago (83 operators), Boston (96), Saint Louis (88), or Philadelphia (80), and the same nominal class of office also represented Kansas City (56), Detroit (41), San Francisco (28), Oil City, Pennsylvania (18), and Memphis (13).[26]

Despite such variation, city offices had much in common. The operating room contained banks of instrument tables at which each telegrapher, separated from his or her neighbors by sound-deadening glass and wood partitions about a foot high, sent and received. Message blanks entered the operating room from a separate receiving department, via pneumatic tubes or dumbwaiters in larger offices. Thence they continued, in the youthful hands of the distributing clerks (popularly called check-boys and check-girls), until they reached the appropriate operator's desk. This was the setting in which city-based telegraphers often spent their nine-and-a-half-hour day and seven-and-a-half-hour night shifts.[27]

New (or reconditioned) urban offices were impressive examples of contemporary commercial architecture, and especially noteworthy were the Western Union headquarters built in the mid 1870s and the rival Postal's new facilities that went up almost twenty years later. They even boasted company-run restaurants where, as at 195 Broadway, employees could spend their half-hour lunch break eating fare as plain as crackers and milk or as fancy as roast lamb with mint sauce. Not everyone was pleased with the lunchrooms or the big offices, though. "One of the Girls" in New York complained in 1875 of the restaurant's clatter, slow service, and consequent "scalding our mouths and burning our throats to get through within the allotted time," and went on to condemn prices that, "unless we contented ourselves with living upon soup and a piece of pie," were too steep. An anonymous poet of the 1890s was less concerned with the cost than the taste of the Western Union's victuals, declaring that

> The soup was fat and so was the meat,
> The butter I got was far from sweet,
> The bread was hard; yes hard as a stone,
> I broke two teeth and my left jaw-bone.[28]

The metropolitan offices could also be dirty, unhealthful, or downright dangerous. Tired of having to share his midnight meal with the roaches that swarmed over his desk in the Boston Western Union office in 1868, Thomas Edison exercised his pragmatic genius by tapping current from the office battery to automatically electrocute the invaders. The situation in Boston's operating room was little better over thirty years later, though the operators, less gifted than Edison, could only complain of the foul and close air in the summer and a cloakroom full of vermin "playing leap frog and base ball on broadcloth coats" and "picnicking on the lunches of married men." The complaints were not solely from operators. After an inspection tour in 1870, a disgusted William Orton found the Cincinnati office filthy. "If soap and water are too expensive," he told superintendent Anson Stager, "an occasional broom is still within our reach." At Washington, D.C., in 1893, a huge chunk of ceiling plaster that had "for months past showed signs of weakness," broke the slow and quiet routine of an Easter Sunday morning when it gave way and crashed to the floor, leaving the operator working the Boston wire with torn pants, an eye abrasion, and a very close escape.[29] But the hazards of urban offices were usually more insidious. A Philadelphian told the *Telegrapher* in 1870 of temperature extremes in the Pacific & Atlantic office that had brought illness and death to some of his colleagues. Sixteen years later, the *Electric Age* called the main operating room of 195 Broadway "that consumption breeder." Hale's Honey of Horehound and Tar, a patent medicine, played on such fears with full-page advertisements warning operators, "especially those in large cities," that their calling, more than any other, made them prone to consumption. Commercial hyperbole aside, there was something to the claim. The Western Union–sponsored Telegraphers' Mutual Benefit Association reported in 1876 that "the confining indoor life of telegraphers" made them "particularly liable" to fall victim to the dread disease.[30]

Numerous small offices complemented the larger ones in the telegraphic network. Most were fairly simple arrangements, tucked into the available space of depots, hotels, drug or stationery stores, piers, stockyards, fairgrounds, exchanges, and the like. "The railroad traveler who looks out of the car window at some rural station often sees that the window of the telegraph office is the principal object of interest," an observer noted in 1873. Peeking inside revealed

> the operator at the key, holding a dispatch in her hand, and with the key making strokes which are necessary for its transmission. The line wire connecting with the key passes up the window-frame, and through the wall, to the telegraph poles beyond. Next to the key, upon the broad shelf which serves as a table, is the switch, or cut-off. . . . Upon the wall near the operator are the hooks on which the written message papers are filed after the messages have been sent.

Nattie Rogers, the fictional young mistress of an urban branch office in the late 1870s, catalogued her domain as "a long, dark little room, into which the sun never shines, a crazy wooden chair, and a high stool, desk, instruments—that is all—Oh! and me!" The saccharine 1881 verses of "The Telegraph Operator" limned a similarly unflattering sketch of a kindred office, beginning:

> She sits within her narrow cell,
> A jewel worth a fairer setting.

Cells or not, city and country branch offices made up the bulk of telegraph facilities for the public.[31]

They were a mixed blessing for the Western Union: they spread its wires throughout the nation and undergirded its monopolistic power, but they were also frequently economically marginal on an individual basis. "At many stations the gross receipts are but little more than the salary of the operator," William Orton pointed out in 1869. His successor, Norvin Green, claimed in 1883 that the business of many such offices would not even cover that. Consequently, while professing a desire to serve public convenience by keeping as many branch offices open as was consistent with its stockholders' interests, the company got its operators for them as cheaply as possible.[32] That meant paying minimal salaries and expecting that commissions or the subsidies of others would make up the difference. Telegraphers working under the railroad franchise agreements might take a 10 percent commission on the Western Union business they handled, and if traffic increased to the point where it interfered with their duties on the road, the Western Union would open a regular commercial office in the place. Branch operators without the benefit of a railroad salary were usually less fortunate, whether they worked for the Western Union or other firms. "I am a tel opr at present employed by F.[ranklin] Tel co in Georgetown," an unhappy Washingtonian named Hugh Coyle wrote B & O president John W. Garrett in 1873 asking about a job, explaining, "have an office on commission. it don't pay." They often didn't. "I regret that your compensation should be insufficient to support you," Norvin Green told a branch manager asking for a raise in 1880, "but such must be the case in many small offices. I shall be rejoiced to learn," the doctor added, "that you have coupled your services for the company with some business that will add to your income." That was frequently the expectation in taking a branch office position—it could hardly be otherwise where an operator could look forward to earning $5 or $10 a month on $20 to $25 worth of business —and it was why O. S. Denise combined the branch office he managed in Chicago in 1875 with a cigar store–newsstand.[33] Long hours often accompanied low pay in the small offices, particularly in the ubiquitous railroad way stations that as late as the mid-1890s accounted for about three-fourths of all telegraph posts. Forced to wear many hats as both railway and telegraph functionaries, rural operators working twelve- or even sixteen-hour days were common.[34]

Like its offices, the Western Union's employees were ranked and specialized. Besides operators, the company comprised a myriad of white and blue-collar labor: clerks and bookkeepers, messengers, battery men, construction workers, skilled craftsmen in company-owned work-shops, and the indispensable linemen.[35] Office hierarchies descended from managers to chief operators (the latter roughly analogous to foremen), under whom, finally, worked the squads of telegraphers. Some chiefs specialized. Wire chiefs supervised circuits, ferreting out the various breaks in the line—"grounds," "crosses," and "escapes"—that interrupted service. Their technical expertise made them more prestigious, and upwardly mobile, than the traffic chiefs who shepherded the flow of messages. Status and responsibility also varied with the particular office. The modest little Western Union facility at Harrisburg, Pennsylvania, had chief operator Richard B. Ziegler monitoring the work of seven subordinates in 1883; his counterparts at 195 Broadway each kept watch over eighteen to twenty-five telegraphers.[36]

Operators, too, were subdivided and stratified according to specialty and skill. The aristocrats among them were the press and market report operators, men (mostly) who combined speed, accuracy, and stamina in sending and receiving the copy that filled the nation's newspapers and coordinated its trade. Their salaries were commensurate with their great ability and small numbers. John Taltavall, who until coediting the *Telegraphers Advocate* had been an Associated Press operator in New York, told a Senate inquiry in 1883 that AP men could command as much as $110 to $170 a month—at a time when male operators in large offices probably averaged around $70. High pay and high skill also meant high status. "After working all day I worked at the office nights as well," Thomas Edison recalled of his days as a young country telegrapher in the Michigan of the 1860s, "for the reason that 'press report' came over one of the wires until 3 A.M., and I would cut in and copy it as well as I could, to become more rapidly proficient. The goal of the rural telegraph operator was to be able to take press."[37]

The Western Union had no formal criteria defining exactly what separated first-class operators from those of lesser rank (which, along with charges of arbitrary and unfair personnel policies, was cause for frequent complaint), but there was a rough consensus, at least among telegraphers, about what made for a master of the craft. Operators of the first rank were expected to send or receive thirty to forty words per minute. Mistakes ("bulls") were anathema, as was "breaking" a circuit while receiving to ask the transmitting operator to stop and repeat a word. Neat and clear handwriting that rapidly transcribed the message as the ear received it—with all the constant dipping required, in an age of steel pens and inkwells—was also necessary. Nor was that all. H. S. Smith, formerly chief operator in the Detroit Western Union office, described this bit of mental and physical ambidexterity that first-class skill embraced:

While transmitting it he puts on the number of the message between the
. . . offices, the call for the office, the time sent, his own private signature,
and the private signature of the receiving operator. In most cases that is
done with the left hand, where operators are expert enough to do it. As a
general thing, on all large wires, where there is a large amount of business
handled, the operators are expert enough to do so; in smaller offices they
are sometimes not.[38]

It was in those smaller offices, or in the "City Line" departments of
urban complexes such as 195 Broadway, that the second-class telegraphers plied their trade. "Second-class or inferior operators," the
brotherhood explained during the Great Strike, "have charge of one
or more 'way' wires. Way wires are those which run through small
towns from which the volume of business is not large." Many second-
class operators, for social and economic reasons rather than biological
ones, were female, and the second-class niche was often an occupational dead end. But it could also be a period of journeyman telegraphy in which young operators honed the skills of hand and ear, and
then followed the way wires and trunk lines to the promise of the big
city.[39]

Significant differences in ability, work milieu, and status among operators should not obscure what they held in common: knowledge of a
coded alphabet and the skill needed to send and receive it with some
speed. They were all Morse operators, and Morse telegraphy was a
skilled and labor-intensive affair. Not all wire traffic was. Throughout
the Gilded Age, inventors produced a variety of automatic telegraph
devices meant to convey messages at superhuman pace and volume,
and to do so using semiskilled labor. Daniel H. Craig, in whose automatic apparatus the hopes and capital of the American Rapid Telegraph Company lay, told a Senate hearing in 1883: "This is girl's
labor, and is accomplished by a piano-shaped key-board, which is op-
erated with as much ease and rapidity as a piano key-board. It taxes
the mind scarcely more than reading, at a speed of 35 to 50 words per
minute, and the proper handling of the perforating machine can be
acquired in one or two months." And it would dramatically cut labor
costs. Craig calculated that by using twenty-three low-paid "girls"

rather than thirty-six first-class Morse operators, monthly salary expenses would shrink from $3,060 to $760. The implications of such technological advances were not lost on Western Union officials. As early as 1869, the company's *Journal of the Telegraph* warned its readers that the likely result of an operators' strike would be "invention to make labor unnecessary."[40] But automatic telegraphy never delivered on its promises in the postbellum era. Although some systems, most especially the British-developed Wheatstone, which the Western Union adopted in the 1880s, had limited successful use, the automatics never bested the hand-operated Morse telegraph for accuracy, simplicity, and flexibility. Telegraphy would eventually be automated (and feminized) beginning around World War I, with the perfection of the teletypewriter, but in the late nineteenth century, it remained a skilled craft.[41]

The false starts of the automatic systems did not mean an absence of technological breakthroughs. On the contrary, two such innovations—the duplex and quadruplex—profoundly affected the industry and its operators. Introduced in 1872, the duplex made possible the simultaneous transmission, in opposite directions, of two messages over a single wire that had previously allowed only one to pass. Thomas Edison's quadruplex of 1874 simply doubled the capacity of the duplex; now four messages shared the same line and two-way flow. The economic impact of these inventions is hard to exaggerate. "It costs a telegraph company, which has a line constructed and in use," the *Journal of the Telegraph* explained in 1870, "as much to send a message 50 miles as to send it 500 miles. For while the message is in transmission, no other message can be sent; consequently, all the operators are unavailable although being paid." The duplex and quadruplex did away with this idling of labor and plant, increasing the productivity of the latter substantially. Duplexing or quadruplexing a line added "phantom" wires to the Western Union system: in 1883, the company's mileage, 436,548, consisted of 327,000 miles of actual wire and an additional 109,548 miles (25 percent of the total) of phantom line that the multiple telegraph devices created.[42]

With the potential for boosting traffic volume fourfold, the pressure for increased productivity shifted from capital to labor. And here the advantage of the quadruplex lost some of its edge, for in order to work at maximum capacity and keep eight operators busy, none of the receivers could break the circuit to have a word repeated; if one did, all traffic on the line halted. "The Quadruplex system acts as a police by driving the operators up to their work," a contemporary student wrote. "No man can loiter over his key while seven others are watching him."[43] Intended or not, the introduction of the "quad" was in effect a speedup. From about 1872 to 1882, average costs per message (in constant dollars) for the Western Union steadily declined. Competition and salary cuts had something to do with this, but so did the increased productivity of the corporation's plant and, through the ensuing speedup that the multiple systems induced, the increased productivity of its employees.[44] When things went well, quad operators were productive indeed. On the eve of the Great Strike, the three quad wires connecting Boston and New York carried almost 3,000 messages daily; the ordinary circuits could only claim an average of 300 to 1,000 telegrams in the same period.[45]

The quadruplex and kindred developments touched on the essence of the revolution that telegraphy and the railways were propelling. The high-volume flow, centralization, and thoroughgoing rationalization of a Western Union simultaneously shaped and mirrored the new economic order coalescing in the era. It is hard, a jaded century later, to appreciate how miraculous it must have seemed to someone accustomed to gauging speed by the gait of an ambling wagon or, at the outside, the intoxicating fifty miles per hour of an express train, to place a telegram on the receiving counter at 195 Broadway in New York and know that two to ten minutes later it would appear in Philadelphia.[46] And this was all possible in part because telegraphy, despite its unique form and function, had a distinctly industrial cast. "Busy as it is," *Harper's* noted of the Postal Company's operating room in 1896, "the work presents no confusion and but little noise, for a great telegraph office is one of the best examples of modern industrial organization." With its continuous-flow "production," the large telegraph office, mutatis mutandis, was subject to the same economic imperatives as a steel mill or slaughterhouse. Rather than silly or trivial, Western Union president William Orton's 1875 directive that all employees use pencil holders "to reduce the consumption of lead pencils one half" was akin to John D. Rockefeller's penny-pinching on the cost of oil cans that increased Standard Oil's profits by $5 million a year. Cost accounting was part of the telegraph business, too. Weekly reports went from 388 sample "test offices" to 195 Broadway so that senior managers could monitor the Western Union's corporate pulse. The directors' decision in 1867 to inaugurate reduced-rate night letters may have come from a desire to offer greater access to the wires to the public, as they claimed, but the more compelling motive by far was their realization that "the greatest pressure upon our lines occurs during a few hours near midday leaving them *comparatively* idle during certain other hours—especially during portions of the night."[47] The same rationalizing drive was present twenty years later when, convinced that the nimble feet of check-boys and girls at Western Union headquarters might be improved upon to expand the volume of traffic, the firm installed an overhead carrier system (like those used to convey cash in contemporary department stores) to increase the young clerks' efficiency. Even the company-run lunchrooms had more than paternalism behind them. They saved "a vast amount of time," managers discovered, since it was "cheaper to provide the noonday meal, and thus control the time of those employed at this hour of the day than to permit them to go outside of the building to the neighboring restaurants."[48]

Disciplining the operators' lunchtime habits was not, after all, so far removed from disciplining their work-time ones in the managerial calculus of efficiency and profit. Company regulations and rule books were meant to proscribe as much as to prescribe, to form telegraphers as well as to inform them. Keys, sounders, and white collars notwithstanding, a large operating room was a shop floor, and a chief operator, no less than a mill foreman, embodied constraint and compulsion in the daily world of work. "At your work you must ever take good care," advised a facetious set of "The Rules of '197'" in an operators' journal of the mid-1870s,

> To watch for that grim chief operataire,
> Who has gimlet eyes which are everywhere,
> And cover each man with a ghastly stare.
> Nor must you ever wildly stare
> To gaze on the ladies over there,
> For if you do, you may safely swear
> You'll get reported and "bounced" then and there.
> Work, brothers, work with care,
> 'Neath the eagle eye of the chief operataire![49]

The parallel with industrial workers of the more usual sort must not be pressed too far. The operators and the enterprise for which many of them worked were in many ways in a class by themselves. At a time when most of the labor force carried grease, soil, or coal dust under its fingernails, the hands of telegraphers, if stained at all, were stained with ink.

But operators were employees, too, and their place in an industrial hierarchy and setting would mold their outlook and actions—for many of them, to the extent of collective action against their massive employer in 1883 and a fleeting alliance with a broad working-class movement. Yet outlook and actions take their shape from more than one source. The new regime that the Western Union represented left a deep imprint on the telegraphers, but they also bore the stamp of their origins and their aspirations.

3

THE KNIGHTS
OF THE KEY

The American telegrapher of the late nineteenth century seems a contradictory and perplexing fellow. He set much store by his membership in a "genteel," middle-class "profession," at the same time earning a reputation for being irresponsible and dissolute. He complained how difficult it was to maintain a family in respectable circumstances, yet he appeared to be a footloose young man more concerned with beating boardinghouse bills than sinking roots and raising children. He bemoaned, long and loud, the degradation of his calling and income, but his income may in fact have been increasing, and his Morse skills never suffered the kind of catastrophic assault that unmade such craftsmen as molders, weavers, and shoemakers until well after the turn of the century.

What to make of all this, then—the Gilded Age telegrapher as schizophrenic, or worse, liar? Probably he was neither. Social portraits tend to caricature, and demographic statistics at times obscure as much as explain. But the operators' collective portrait also appears ambiguous because they were themselves, in a social sense, ambiguous. They were among the very first mass white-collar employees, poised between an older order of entrepreneurial capitalism and an ascendent corporate one, between a declining "old" middle class and an emerging "new" one. It was among the nether strata of the latter than most telegraphers found themselves. They were part of a lower middle class in the making.

Most operators were male, single, and relatively young. More concretely, scanning the 1880 federal census manuscript schedules for Baltimore and extracting a sample of 150 operators gives an average age of 25.6 years and an unmarried majority of 66 percent. A similar survey for Harrisburg, Pennsylvania (and a few surrounding villages), among a sample of 93 operators, shows 24.5 years as the average age and a married proportion of only 26 percent.[1] By century's end, telegraphers as a group were becoming older, more likely to marry, and a bit less predominantly male. The census data outlining these shifts are marred by their lumping telegraphers together with telephone operators and their use of crude age categories, but the shifts were apparent enough. In 1890, the proportion of single operators was 65.1 percent; it fell to 56.5 percent by 1900. As for age, by 1900, 41.9 percent were in the 10-to-24-year-old group, and a decided majority—52.3 percent—belonged in the 25-to-44-year-old group. But these were trends, not a revolution, and if there was a typical Gilded Age telegrapher, he was in his late teens or early twenties and unwed.[2] He was also likely to be a native-born white and, at least by 1890 (though probably well before) so usually were his parents. Of the minority of operators born abroad, most were of western European or Canadian origin.[3]

Like his fellow Americans, the late nineteenth-century operator drifted or swam in the period's great streams of migration. "As a rule," the *New York Dispatch* noted in 1874, "telegraph operators are either village bred, or have graduated from the ranks of messenger boys, who are employed in every large city, in numbers ranging from ten to a hundred."[4] Awed by the weight and color of the European exodus to the United States in these years, it is easy to forget that an equally important flow of population simultaneously took place within the nation's borders. Most Americans were "village bred," and most telegraph offices, as adjuncts of railroad lines, were in rural settings. In all probability, most operators were country folk. Norman H. Rugg was. Born in Saratoga, New York, in 1845, Rugg began to learn the craft under his brother's tutelage in 1860 and in three years was managing the local Western Union office, a career cut short by his death in 1871. Mortimer D. Shaw, master workman of the Saint Louis brotherhood during the Great Strike, had been an Illinois farm boy in the 1850s and 1860s until the wires lured him away. When the craft journal *Electric Age* attacked telegraph "colleges" that defrauded would-be operators, it described "a young man, working a thrashing [sic] machine or maneovering a plow" as a common victim of such schools. An operator named George Kinter was the victim of unemployment rather than a swindle when the census enumerator found him in 1880 living in Middle Paxton Township, Pennsylvania, with his father Isaac, a farmer.[5]

Those who entered telegraphy in the bigger towns and cities were often workingmen's sons. The Gorsuch brothers, Zachariah, Jr., and Edward, Baltimore operators in 1880, were the sons of a molder. The father of Francis Jenkins, twenty-one, was a watchman. And these young men were not unique. James Conley, a sixty-two-year-old plasterer, had fathered three boys, one of whom, Samuel, now followed telegraphy. Albert Cooper, a Harrisburg machinist, also had a son who earned his livelihood at the key. It would be surprising if so office-bound a calling as telegraphy did not also attract the offspring of the middle class. George Boyer came from a Harrisburg business family headed by a carriage manufacturer, and the Boyers lived among such equally solid neighbors as a bank cashier, merchants, a physician, and another manufacturer. Telegraphy was likewise an apt choice for Jacob Whiteman, the son of a railroad dispatcher, as it was for Charles Barkman, whose father was a Baltimore commission merchant. But what remains noteworthy, at least among those operators whose fathers' (or male household heads') occupations are known, is how many of them came from working-class homes. If census samples are representative, the proportion was fairly high: among fifty-two Baltimore telegraphers and forty-two at Harrisburg in 1880, the same substantial majority—64 percent—were the children of blue-collar men.[6]

Ethnicity as well as class origins often set city telegraphers off from their largely Protestant, Anglo-Saxon, rural counterparts. The descendents of Irish immigrants in particular appear to have found a place in the new industry in its urban locale. The frequency of Irish names in the operators' journals of the time is striking, although such impressionistic evidence invites caution. But less dubious signs also point to a marked Irish-American presence at the key. "Some of the operators who went out of the offices with members of the brotherhood were Catholics," reported the *New York Times* during the Great Strike, "and according to the rules of their church they were prohibited from joining a secret organization." The same problem occurred four years later, when a revived brotherhood reaffiliated with the Knights of Labor. "Many members of the profession will not affiliate with the brotherhood," the *Electric Age* regretfully noted, "because they imagine the objects antagonize those of the Catholic church." The Catholicism of "many" telegraphers is indirect evidence of Irish origins, but more explicit testimony has survived. Among the fictional sketches that Walter P. Phillips wrote to immortalize the members of his craft, he chose to typify the urban messenger boy who works his way up the telegraphic ladder by a character named Patsy Flanagan.[7] Patsy was more than a figment of Phillips's literary imagination. "The Messenger Boys," one of their number in New York told a labor journal in 1887, "are mostly the sons of hard laboring men, residing for the most part in the 'tough' Eastern and Western quarters of this city. They are almost wholly descendents of Irish parents." That would as well have described the situation of Dennis McLaughlin, a fifteen-year-old messenger in Baltimore in 1880 who lived with his widowed mother, Bridget, a boarder, and three siblings, one of whom, Timothy, was a telegrapher. In fact, of a sample of fifty-two Baltimore operators having at least one immigrant parent, well over half (55.7 percent) were Irish—and this in a city where the German-born outnumbered the Irish by better than two to one. The phenomenon was not confined to one city. Among telegraph (and telephone) operators enumerated in the 1890 census having at least one parent born abroad, the largest single group (36 percent of the total) were of Irish descent; the second largest, the Germans, trailed with 20 percent. Like politics, municipal services, and various skilled trades, telegraphy provided the offspring of Irish peasants a calling and an avenue of mobility. Whether his parents were among the millions driven from already marginal plots by the horrors of the Great

Famine is uncertain, but Thomas Brennan had much to thank telegraphy for. Born Christmas Day 1844 in Ireland, Brennan began as a messenger in New York City at the age of seventeen, went on to become an operator, then a chief, and at forty-two was assistant manager of the huge operating force at 195 Broadway. At a lively stag dinner and musicale that followed a baseball game between New York area operators in 1875, two of their number—Landy and McDermott by name—entertained the gathering by singing "an Irish localism" called "Since Terence Joined the Gang." The *Telegrapher* reported that "they created much merriment by their imitations of the Hibernian element of Gotham." Self-congratulation, as much as self-parody, was at work that evening.[8]

There was truth to the claim that telegraphy provided a rewarding career for industrious and intelligent men. The young operator of the 1880s, looking around him, could find evidence that former Knights of the Key had either advanced within the field or gone on to high positions in other callings. "As I have said," Western Union president Norvin Green reminded the Senate Committee on Education and Labor in 1883, "all our general superintendents and office managers, all the vice-presidents on duty and all the general managers and assistants, have come up from the key." Thomas Eckert had, of course, and so had vice-president John Van Horne, superintendent Robert Clowry, and many others running the giant firm or its competitors. William B. Somerville, press manager and corporate spokesman during the Great Strike, had started as a junior operator at Buffalo in the late 1850s. George E. Holbrook, born in 1857 in tiny Deposit, New York, where he had the benefit of "a fair education in a primitive district school," had ascended to the post of night traffic chief at Western Union headquarters by 1888. His exact contemporary, Brooklyn native Christopher P. Flood, who in 1887 managed the Postal Telegraph Company's New York office, began his climb in 1868 by carrying messages for the Bankers' & Brokers' Telegraph. In 1865, twenty-two-year-old William Joseph Dealy had sent the news, while the rubble was still warm, of the fall of the Confederate capital at Richmond; eighteen years later, he was master of the 444 operators at 195 Broadway.[9]

Telegraphy worked its magic of success on those who exchanged it for a different occupation, too. As early as 1868, the Western Union's *Journal of the Telegraph* offered readers models of achievement by former members of the craft under the heading "How Operators Rise." Marshall Jewell, for one, had risen. The currier's son turned telegrapher won the governorship of Connecticut that year—not, to be sure, without an intervening and prosperous career in business—and would, by 1874, serve as President Grant's postmaster general.[10] Much better known were the colorful careers of Thomas Edison and Andrew Carnegie, both of whom had begun to make their way in life sending and receiving Morse, but others, if less famous, had also used the key as a springboard to higher ground. Theodore N. Vail, who divided his attention between clerking in a New Jersey drugstore and mastering telegraphy in the 1860s, later became the managerial architect of the American Telephone and Telegraph Company. Horace A. Clute's post-telegraphic years embraced success too, though of a more modest sort. A Western Union manager in Harrisburg in the 1860s and a superintendent by 1880, he soon struck out on a dual entrepreneurship, setting up telephone companies in central Pennsylvania and running a Harrisburg livery stable. Richard B. Ziegler, who had been Clute's chief operator in the Western Union office, turned his attention from the wires to the mails when Grover Cleveland appointed him an assistant postmaster in 1887. Others of prominence, locally and nationally, as corporate managers, journalists, politicians, and entrepreneurs, could trace their impressive mobility back to a berth in telegraphy.[11]

Their remarkable success was due to skill and hard work, no doubt, but for most of them, to chance as well: they had the good luck to have been born at the right time. As young men in the 1840s to 1860s, they had entered telegraphy when it was new and wide open. Although brawling and unstable, it was also rife with opportunity, with its proliferation of small firms whose competing poles and wires marched aggressively over the countryside. Mobility in these early years could be stunning. Charles F. Wood was an operator and clerk for the Magnetic Telegraph Company in 1848, chief operator of its New York office within three years, and by 1853, thanks to a fortuitous resignation, was superintendent of the New York & New England Union Company. With the coming of the Civil War, the industry called to prospective operators more insistently still. Thus blessed, the early generations of telegraphers often assumed posts of responsibility as they matured along with the industry.[12]

It was just such men who formed the Old Timers' Association, a group limited to those who had entered the craft from its beginnings through the Civil War. The association, steeped in craft pride and self-indulgent nostalgia, implicitly celebrated the success of the many veterans of telegraphy's formative period. Scanning the backgrounds of the members who showed up for the 1880 annual meeting is illuminating in this regard since, for eighty-two of them, we know the dates of their first telegraphic employment (as messengers or operators) and their occupations as of 1880. Forty-two of them (51 percent) were then managers or superintendents of telegraph lines, seven (9 percent) were chief operators, seventeen (20 percent) still fingered a key as operators or railroad agent–operators, and sixteen (20 percent) were in various pursuits outside of telegraphy. The degree of mobility to management positions is striking enough, but it becomes more so by counting chiefs as junior managers, which then raises it to 60 percent; and if four of the men in outside fields who nonetheless claimed managerial status are also included, the proportion of those who exchanged glass partitions for rolltop desks expands to 64 percent. The Old Timers' Association is not an infallible gauge of mobility, since those most successful and well disposed toward the craft were more likely to join than operators who fell into stagnant troughs or left the key in disgust, but the proportions still suggest a substantial degree of achievement for those who entered the industry when it was young. These were the children of telegraphy's golden age.[13]

By contrast, the 1870s, 1880s, and 1890s seemed the dark age of the craft. What had once looked like a boundless horizon now appeared to be a dead end as opportunities for ambitious young men within the industry shrank. The flush days of the 1860s were barely past when the *Telegrapher*, in 1871, saw the glow surrounding the occupation beginning to fade. "The best and most valuable telegraphers are continually leaving the profession and engaging in other lines of business," declared the editor, "because telegraphing no longer offers sufficient inducement to retain them in the service." Even the Western Union house organ offered little encouragement. Promotion, it admitted, was a sign of success, "but it can not be so to all, for the positions open for preferment are but few, compared with the number of those who consider themselves qualified to fill them." By 1875, the same journal could only console stultified operators with the thought that "faithful performance of duty," although unlikely to raise income or status, was nonetheless a sure sign of "character" and so a source of inspiration to others.[14]

Despite the general economic recovery of the 1880s, prognoses for the occupational health of telegraphy remained pessimistic. The *Operator*, in 1884, thought it "one of the cardinal principles of all parental operators" that their children follow a more promising line of work. The learners' manual that the telegraphic supply house of J. H. Bunnell put out in 1882 made it clear to students that Morse skills alone, without mating them with "other occupations in railway, express and mercantile business," cut them off from advancing "into more important and profitable business" than telegraphing. The next year, no less a spokesman for the industry than Norvin Green flatly said that "a large majority of operators quit the key when they get married and look for something that is better"—a pale recommendation for a career in the enterprise he headed.[15]

Some, of course, did rise in the calling and do well, since telegraph managers had to come from among practical operators. W. R. Holligan, a check-boy at the main Chicago Western Union office in 1873, was its chief operator two decades later. T. J. Condon, of the company's Syracuse office, rose even faster from office boy in 1890 to traffic chief by 1898. A few halfhearted attempts to discern some kind of improvement appeared in the late 1880s. The *Electric Age* spoke of a "decided advance financially" and "promotions of various kinds," which there doubtless were, but they were exceptional.[16] More common was the familiar indictment of low incomes and crippled mobility, repeated into the 1890s—and not only by operators. Postmaster General John Wanamaker took official note of the moribund and demoralizing condition of the craft in 1890. Five years later, economist Richard T. Ely, comparing the situation of American operators under private ownership with that of those employed in the state-run German service, found the contrast "painful" and "really a disgrace to our own country." Walter Phillips, who had himself risen from a key to become general manager of the United Press, threw up his hands in frustration and advised young operators to get out of telegraphy while the getting was good. "It is quite as unreasonable for men to continue to do telegraphic work if their hands and brains are fitted for a higher order of employment," he wrote in 1888, "as it would be for a college graduate to remain as janitor or librarian in the university where he had been prepared, instead of going forth to battle with the dragons which environ the path leading to success."[17]

Quite a few did strike out on other paths. "It has been said that one-third of all the telegraphic operators are continually preparing themselves for other professions," Postmaster General Wanamaker reported in 1890, "and that the other two-thirds are continually thinking of doing so." The proportions may not have been exact, but the sentiments probably were. Medicine held considerable attraction for disgruntled operators. Billy Washburne, a railroad operator in Chicago, was on the verge of receiving an M.D. in 1875. At the time of the Great Strike, Knights and brotherhood activist John McClelland already had his. In Philadelphia another prominent strike leader, Harry W. Orr, alternated practicing dentistry during the day and sending Associated Press report at night. In 1885, the *Operator* recorded five doctors and one dentist leading double lives as telegraphers at Western Union headquarters. The law beckoned as well. "Fatty" Gooding forsook a Chicago key in 1875 and headed west to offer his legal talents to the citizens of Evanston, Wyoming. Others turned to advertising, business, journalism, stenography, technical pursuits, and even the cloth. And David Adams, reversing the usual pattern, packed his trunk and left 195 Broadway in 1885 to try his luck with a ten-acre truck and poultry farm in Ontario.[18]

These desertions meant that telegraphy, like the economy that had spawned it, was changing. Companies that began small grew large to survive—so large, as in the case of the Western Union, as to be of revolutionary dimensions. All the while the individual telegrapher's situation within the company changed too, something that both operators and managers had recognized well before the crisis of 1883. As early as 1870, the *Telegrapher's* editor spoke the truth (though guilty of romanticizing telegraphy's swaddling period) when he reflected: "In the earlier days of the telegraph in this country the employees felt a personal interest in the success of the lines upon which they were employed. They were recognized as being more than mere hirelings; and, although more labor was required than now, it was rendered cheerfully; and, in return, privileges were accorded to them in the way of vacations and similar favors, which are now unknown." All this was indeed past. "With the expansion of the Western Union Telegraph Company to mammoth proportions," he explained a year later, "this custom [of company-subsidized vacation substitutes] was abolished, and employes desiring vacations required to provide, at their own expense, for the discharge of their duties during their absence." Nor would the company foot the bill for an operator's time lost for illness. "No sick list here," a New York operator sarcastically reported in 1874, "since the introduction of the 'Universal Panacea,' called Lefferts' Extract of 'dock.'"[19]

Docking pay and denying vacations, painful as they were, were symptoms rather than causes of the operators' malaise. The fundamental problem had to do with corporate growth and rationalization, with the immense scale of the Western Union, whose inverse was the diminishing power and status of the Gilded Age telegrapher. This was most evident in the factorylike setting of 195 Broadway, of course. It was less so in a smaller office, especially where operators worked alone, yet even there, the overwhelming presence of the communications giant—through salaries and commissions, supervisory hierarchies and the book of rules, and the great wire network itself—was always there. Relations between "officers and men" had never radiated the warmth that golden age myth ascribed to them, though there was a dash of truth in the tales of a premonopoly Eden. The ten operators of the Western Telegraph Company (a Baltimore-to-Wheeling line) who gave their president a gold-headed cane in 1854 presumably felt like "more than mere hirelings." W. W. Shoch certainly must have. Shoch was a B & O Railroad depot operator at Harper's Ferry, West Virginia, who so resented his being transferred there in 1864 that he wrote directly to president John Garrett to complain. His entreaty drew sympathy and a sense of paternalistic obligation from the road's highest officer. "Report," Garrett curtly wrote his superintendent of telegraph. "Why was this change made? Mr. Shoch is a very valuable man, whose courage and faithfulness at Point of Rocks [Maryland] have attracted my special attention and commendation."[20]

But by the 1870s and 1880s the relations between employers and employees were chilling, and markedly so in the nation's foremost telegraph company. "But is not the feeling 'we, the operators, and they, the company,' almost universal?" asked a troubled woman in 1873. Nine years later, *Operator* editor W. J. Johnston sighed that "a feeling of cordiality . . . between all the component members of the telegraphic system, from the highest down," was dead. It seemed to be so at the big Chicago office. "Hearty friendships are rarely formed between the managers and operators," a man there reported in 1881. "There is a high fence of separation to anything like such familiar intercourse, and each side finds a certain kind of pleasurable interest in keeping the fence in constant repair." Company officers and managers had industriously dug postholes for the fence since at least the early 1870s. In the wake of the unsuccessful strike that began the decade, the Western Union's James D. Reid, speaking through the *Journal of the Telegraph*, made plain the shape of things to come: "The telegraph service demands a rigorous discipline to which its earlier administration was unused. The character of the business has wholly changed. It cannot now subserve public interests or its own healthful development without the precision and uniformity of mechanism."[21]

More than one telegrapher complained of being reduced to a machine by the great monopoly,[22] but others spoke of the deteriorating quality of operators, and not everyone agreed that the Western Union was solely to blame. Some operators took their colleagues to task for their lack of industry and ambition, and for indifference to technological knowledge. Pioneer operators had not only been diligent but well rounded; now, telegraphers had become a stunted tribe, many no better than "mere manipulators of a key."[23] It was true that early operators had a varied and often challenging work routine. Particularly in the small offices, an operator was also clerk, bookkeeper, battery man, and as Taliaferro Shaffner explained in 1859, lineman:

> When the line is found to be down on any given section, the operator immediately prepares his implements, and proceeds on horse to mend his line. . . . Being thus prepared, he proceeds at a rapid gait along the highways, through uninhabited forests, or wherever the wire runs, until he finds the place of difficulty. . . . While others are comfortably seated around the fireside, the operator has to traverse forest and wild regions in rain, snow, and hail. Through the cold, chilling blast, he wends his way along the wire thread, anxiously seeking for the break. Solitary and alone, he thus nobly performs his task.[24]

By these heroic standards the pasty-faced young manipulators of a key populating city offices in the postbellum decades looked effete. But there was a way out of their rut, the editors declared, and that was through hard work and self-help, especially self-education in matters electrical. "The electricians, superintendents and managers of the future are among those who are now studying the lessons taught by the JOURNAL and kindred publications," lectured the Western

Union's company sheet in 1876—one year after the rival *Operator* had begun "to drop the gossip and small talk of the profession and to indulge in more serious and practical discussion," as its editor later explained.[25]

Stymied mobility rested on something more complex than sloth and ignorance, though. "There is a tendency which becomes more marked as the telegraph business is extended and developed," one astute craft journalist noted in 1875, "for telegraph operators to become divided into classes or divisions, which are becoming as distinctly defined as though established by authority." Most operators would not be deskilled in the usual sense, but an informal division of labor among them took shape as the wires and corporate structure of the Western Union ramified. The operators' numbers grew, their duties narrowed, and their overall standing fell. Fading, too, were the days when the lines between operator, electrician, tinkerer, and entrepreneur—nowhere better exemplified than in the career of Thomas Edison, who quit his key in the late 1860s—were fluid and invitingly permeable. Electrical engineering, by the 1880s, was becoming less a branch of the telegrapher's art than a preserve of the college-educated upper middle class. Even the fastest press operator, at bottom, was now a "mere manipulator."[26]

This de facto sorting of operators suggests a Western Union drive to rationalize its work force, much as it had rationalized its work procedures with the book of rules, but there was a lot about its personnel policy that remained irrational. Operators, the *Philadelphia Inquirer* pointed out in 1877, "are unfortunately not paid by any recognized schedule or standard of ability, but according to the scarcity of help at the particular time when they were hired, or the favoritism of an official." Asked about his company's system of grading operators' pay, Norvin Green confessed at a Senate hearing in 1883, "We have not any such scale as that," and could only offer a table of salaries, ranging from $30 to $150 a month graduated in $5 steps, with no indications of skill or seniority.[27]

Favoritism angered telegraphers as much as capricious pay scales. Calling for the Western Union to reform its personnel policies by adopting "civil service principles," an 1887 *Electric Age* editorial blamed "cliques and factions" and "those who command the 'biggest pull'" for denying worthy telegraphers the promotions and raises due them. Critics charged that operators doing the same work did not necessarily receive the same pay, and in some instances, the less competent of two men drew the higher salary. That struck some as not only vicious but stupid. Weren't such practices of dubious wisdom, Senator Wilkinson Call of Florida asked John McClelland, in the light of the Western Union's economic self-interest? "Well," replied McClelland, "they do some very funny things in the Western Union office, some things that we cannot understand."[28]

To the extent that the company had an understandable employee policy, it seems to have been much like the one that Walter Licht has found guiding the era's railroads up through the 1870s: a regime of "rules, regulations, and strict hierarchies of authority and accountability established from on high" in which, however, decisions about raises, promotions, hiring, and the like were usually locally made. Western Union rule books contained detailed instructions for conducting the daily business of large and small offices, but not one word about seniority, salary, or grievances. A highly centralized corporation, in short, had a highly decentralized way of dealing with its work force. William Orton, that most rationalizing and managerial of Western Union presidents, did toy with a plan for establishing "an arrangement of the compensation of skilled operators based upon the amount and character of the work performed by them" in the mid-1870s, but he intended it to apply only to some urban telegraphers, and in any case he evidently lost interest in the project. By the late nineteenth and early twentieth centuries, several railroads moved toward more uniform and explicit personnel policies (affecting telegraphers as well as other employees), but the Western Union never offered operators the sort of predictable, graduated career that critics demanded. Perhaps that explains why, at the firm's Syracuse office in 1900, traffic chief T. J. Condon (ten years' service) and night chief W. J. Guilford (twenty-five years) both received the same salary.[29]

Top Western Union managers eschewed a bureaucratic personnel policy, but they could not ignore the question of raises and promotions. In theory, the board of directors ultimately approved all raises. William Orton turned an analytical—and sometimes skeptical—eye on his subordinates' requests for salary hikes in their divisions and districts. "I have approved [$5 and $10 raises] without question," he wrote superintendent Anson Stager in 1875, "but when it comes to adding at one time $15 and $20 to salaries at the rate of $50 and under, it seems to me the rise is unnecessarily rapid."[30] Energetic and painstaking as Orton was in matters of corporate policy and operations (and his genial successor Norvin Green was far less so), he could not single-handedly deal with matters of pay and tenure, and so the fate of a raise, transfer, or promotion usually remained the formal concern of the local superintendent or manager. When George W. Gray wrote Orton in behalf of his son Cyrus, an operator recently fired for sloppy management, the president declined to intervene, reminding Gray that superintendents had jurisdiction over "all the details of our business within their respective districts, and consequently are permitted to employ and discharge operatives according to their judgment."[31]

Not every plea that crossed the presidential desk met with such chaste disinterest. A sympathetic word from the firm's chief officer doubtless colored superintendents' decisions. R. Talcott's chances for a position with the Western Union must have been better than average after fellow Cuba, New York, native William Orton, who also knew Talcott's father, sent an enthusiastic recommendation to a division superintendent. (Orton's desire to do a neighbor a good turn never overwhelmed his business sense, though; he advised the superintendent that since Talcott's wife also needed a job, "you could probably secure the services of two operators by this arrangement on better than usual terms.") Norvin Green could also be accommodating. To a North Carolina congressman asking that one of his constituents, an operator, receive a desired transfer, Green responded that he had passed on his note to the superintendent "with request for favorable consideration, if no controlling reasons to the contrary exist."[32] This was certainly favoritism of a sort. It had limits, of course. Although apparently well disposed toward another operator desiring a transfer, Green told the man's intermediary, Senator Wilkinson Call, that since "we never discharge an operator who is giving satisfaction, or without sufficient cause, he will have to await a vacancy."[33] Much harder to document is how favoritism worked at the lower levels of the firm, where most of it took place. Local managers and superintendents left not even the modest paper trail that Orton and Green did.

Evidence for the operators' complaints about the salary cuts that the Western Union made in the period is less arcane. "Though the wages of most service, and especially of artisans, in the line of manual labor, have greatly advanced in this country," Norvin Green wrote the head of the German government telegraph in 1892, "I think we are not paying quite as much for operators, and certainly not for clerical work, as we did 15 or 20 years ago."[34] In terms of *nominal* salary levels, Green was right; late nineteenth-century telegraphers were losing ground, and saw this as yet another sign—together with the rise of a huge, impersonal employer, narrowed skill ranges and status, and a career ladder whose rungs were rotting and falling away —of the degradation of the craft. Special pleading was always involved in complaints about salaries. Activists tended to cite the lowest contemporary pay levels and the highest of the golden age. True enough, first-class operators getting over $100 a month were not rare in the war boom years (Edison earned $125 in 1865), but how typical they were is another matter. Average salaries appear to have been much less generous. Robert Luther Thompson, a student of the industry's early years, thought that operators averaged $70 to $90 a month during the Civil War. In the riotously inflationary year of 1864, a B & O telegrapher of great value to the company made $50, with the promise of a raise to $60—in contrast to the "ordinary $35 or $40 operator" whom his superintendent mentioned. An Ohioan wrote the *Journal of the Telegraph* in 1868 complaining that insurance fund plans requiring monthly $1 assessments were "unreasonable" for "the great majority of operators," who made only $40 to $60 a month.[35]

Still, the postbellum salary cutting was real, and it came in essentially two forms. The first was the Western Union's Sliding Scale of early 1876, a progressive reduction of all salaries from the president's down to those earning $50 a month—a response, Norvin Green later testified, to the depression of the 1870s. Board member James Milliken had proposed the retrenchment in the summer of 1875, just at the time Jay Gould declared war on the Western Union with his Atlantic & Pacific Company. Gould's attack was a powerful incentive to lower salaries, especially in order to maintain dividends, which the board indeed did, declaring another 2 percent quarterly payment to stockholders at the same meeting that adopted the Sliding Scale.[36]

Besides the immediate prod of competition, the firm's directorate was convinced that its telegraphers were overpaid anyway, seeing their inflated salaries as a lingering financial hangover from the great binge of the 1860s. In late 1875, William Orton reported that his survey of clerks' and bookkeepers' pay in the various commercial, banking, and insurance houses in New York suggested an average "considerably below what is paid by this Company in the various departments carried on in this building. It was the knowledge of such facts," he explained, "that has caused many of our Directors during the past year to ask for a reduction of the wages paid by the company." Exceptions might be made for those especially hard hit by the cuts, but "upon the great majority of the operators, the reduction falls so lightly that complaints of its severity from them seem to me unreasonable." And while Orton assured superintendent Anson Stager that he shared his concern for "the young men who came into our service as boys and are growing in years and necessities, as they are in knowledge of the business, and in capacity for serving us," he reminded him that stockholders deserved justice as much as employees did.[37] The stockholders received their due in January 1876, when the Sliding Scale took effect. A first-class operator at New York making, say, $120 a month took a 10 percent cut to $108; one getting $90 wound up with 5 percent less, or $86. Someone rated at $50, also cut 5 percent, lost $2 a month. "This is, we believe, the first general reduction that the Western Union has made," the crestfallen *Operator* noted when it learned of the cuts, "and, as the financial condition of the Company is just now so prosperous, it was quite unexpected."[38]

The second method used to diminish salaries was more diffuse. "It is a favorite tactic of some telegraph Superintendents," charged the *Telegrapher* in 1870, "whenever a change is made in an office, to fill the vacancy at a reduction from the compensation formerly paid." Thirteen years later, operators still complained of the custom—compounded of pressure from above on local managers and superintendents to institute economies, and the "nomadic disposition" of many operators—that had been chipping away at salary figures. An operator making $80 in New York, P. J. Tierney testified in 1883, might pick up and head for Chicago to take an $85 berth, assuming a post for which his predecessor, before dying, retiring, or moving on, had been getting $90. And on it went, depressing the general level of telegraphic pay. Existing company records support the angry operators' claims. In 1866, at the Harrisburg Western Union office, manager William D. Sargent took home $110 a month. When Horace Clute replaced him five years later, he settled for $100. Clute's successor in 1881, Charles A. Bigler, had to make do with $90, and he, in turn, gave way in 1887 to Emil A. Teupser, who would run the office for the rest of the century—at $80 a month. Sometimes the disjunctures were especially ragged. The same year that Teupser became manager, Amos Mumma, formerly a $45 operator, graduated to the post of chief operator, with the reward of a raise to $50; but the previous chief, Richard Ziegler, had been getting $80.[39]

Whether the Western Union employed this piecemeal scheme or the more dramatic Sliding Scale, many telegraphers felt mightily wronged. To the insult of blocked mobility and decaying prestige, the company added the injury of thinner pay envelopes. One indignant man seized on the current popularity of *H.M.S. Pinafore* to lash out at corporate economies by having "Sir Botelle Porter" sing:

> Of 'lectric knowledge I acquired such a grip,
> That they gave me the efficient managership.
> The boys in the office soon set up a wail,
> For I cut 'em all down on the sliding scale.
> I whittled their pay with a hand so free,
> That now I am a super of the W.U.T.[40]

Oppression did not end with chronic pay cuts, for as the Western Union grew and consolidated, it reduced the number and quality of telegraphic job opportunities. Mergers and takeovers, with one possible exception, consistently threw operators out of work. John Van Horne told a Senate panel in 1884 why, in economic terms, this was so: "In a town of two or three thousand inhabitants one operator can do all the business. If there are three companies there they are just wasting the money on two operators." Branch offices were economically fragile anyhow, but big-city operators also lost out. After the Gould-arranged Western Union–American Union marriage in 1881, the *Operator* reported that while two main offices would still handle New York City business, "a great number of competing offices [would] be closed in all the large cities throughout the Union" to eliminate duplicate facilities. And duplicate facilities employed duplicate operators.[41]

The telegraphers' indictment of Western Union greed and "grinding," of its degradation of a once-fertile occupation into a barren one, had much truth to it. It was in the nature of Gilded Age capitalism in particular that the bloodletting of corporate pioneers in the market would bleed many operators too, and it was in the nature of capitalism in general that the interests and prerogatives of stockholders would outweigh those of employees. But although uncommonly powerful, the company was not omnipotent, and the full story of the craft's decline involved other influences that, while related to the contours of Western Union size and strength, were not entirely dependent on them. This was especially so of the labor market in telegraphy.

During the industry's vigorous mid-century growth, the supply of operators failed to keep up with demand, a trend that national events after the firing on Fort Sumter accelerated. "Immediately after the beginning of the war," John Campbell testified in 1883, "there was quite an increase in the compensation of telegraphers. The Government, of course, was compelled to have a large number of operators." But the war's end slackened demand considerably, and this, exacerbated by corporate concentration, an ongoing influx of recruits because of the continuing appeal of telegraphy to rural and urban youth, and the rigors of the business cycle, made it increasingly hard to find a place at the key.[42]

By the early 1870s there were already signs that the calling's best days were over. Operators who followed Horace Greeley's famous advice could not always squeeze through a frontier safety valve. "It will do no harm to mention, for the telegraphers in the East," wrote a Nevadan in 1870, "that at present there is little or no chance for operators to secure positions on the Pacific coast. There are now many telegraphers here out of employment and 'dead broke,' who are daily passing eastward along the line of the railroad, and even 'footing it,' when not fortunate in getting 'dead headed' by train, and dependent upon their more fortunate brethren for an occasional 'square meal.'" The ensuing depression choked off opportunity even more. An anonymous San Francisco operator spoke in 1875 of "that ever over-flowing evil of going west." Six years later, the general economic upturn notwithstanding, a Union Pacific Railroad man warned eastern Knights of the Key that "the entire Western country is flooded with idle operators, all having flocked West with a mistaken idea."[43] The glut was not confined to the West. William Orton politely brushed aside an 1875 inquiry about a job for a Rye, New York, woman aspiring to a Western Union key, explaining that the company had "a larger number of applicants than we can employ." John Campbell reckoned that the number of telegraphers had "probably doubled" between 1870 and 1883. Whether his estimate was accurate or not, he and virtually all others close to the industry agreed that the craft was overpopulated.[44]

The peculiarities of telegraphy made matters worse. In a job that placed a premium on stamina under high pressure, youth was a considerable asset, and most operators were in fact young single men.[45] But unattached young males were also those most likely to pick up and leave a position, whether to seek higher pay, adventure, or simply a change of scene. The close intertwining of telegraph and railway systems increased the ease and appeal of moving on. The "boys" of the 1860s, Thomas Edison remembered, "had extraordinary facilities for travel. As a usual thing it was only necessary for them to board a train and tell the conductor they were operators. Then they would go as far as they liked. The number of operators was small, and they were in demand everywhere." That demand began to fade, but the peripatetic impulses of young telegraphers did not. Whether such roving inspired the piecemeal wage cutting described earlier or was a response to it is unclear, but once begun, the wandering became part of a cycle of moves and salary reductions. Concluded one journal in 1875, "The nomadic nature of the modern operator makes it an easy matter to reduce salaries aided by the present hard times."[46]

Consequently, turnover was high. An Ohio operator thought that a "majority" of his fellows in 1868 seldom spent more than three to five years at the work. Two years later, "Tina," a denizen of the City Department at Western Union headquarters, counted only six operators out of a standing force of thirty, including the manager, who had been in the office for more than two and a half years. A Buffalo man looking back over the past year commented on the markedly high turnover there. "An examination of the number sheets," he wrote the *Electric Age* in 1887, "shows a large array of new 'sigs' and it is characteristic of the wandering tendency of telegraphers, that out of a force of 75, fully 20 are new people, and an equal number have come and gone with the summer work." Turnover for the long haul was substantial too. Reviewing the course of two decades at the big Chicago Western Union office in 1893, L. K. Whitcomb could only point to himself and six others, out of the sixty-six operators there in 1873, who had persisted on the payroll. In all this, some were on the move from one office to another, others were changing companies, and still others were entering or leaving the field, and reasons as varied as market forces, self-improvement, personal caprice—and perhaps a form of implicit resistance to corporate tyranny—propelled this flow of telegraphers.[47]

Seasonal fluctuations based on trade cycles and summer vacations accounted for some of the movement. Resort areas drew operators to staff branch offices in the hotels to which the affluent fled from the summertime heat and stench of the city. Officially starved of vacations by company policy, operators took them indirectly by working the resort area posts. "As a rule," the *Electric Age* remarked of those about to assume keys at watering places in 1886, "the same persons have filled many of these positions for years, and they still delight in the imaginary vacation." Winter, in contrast, with little if any vacationing (at least in the North) and slackened trade, was doubly harsh for operators lacking permanent jobs. But come spring, unattached Knights of the Key began their seasonal migration, often to the larger cities, where the sheer size of the job market offered some hope, sweetened by the exodus of resort-bound telegraphers. "The inevitable sign of Spring is at hand in the presence of numerous weather-beaten and battle scarred itinerant members of the craft, who invariably arrive in New York about this time of year," announced one journal, inaugurating the season for 1887. But the drifting operators could usually expect little more than a place on a Western Union waiting list and sporadic work as an "extra." As many as three-fourths of the force at the main Chicago office in 1883 were extras, a situation that the district superintendent there, F. H. Tubbs, defended as vital to the workings of large offices, with their great variation in demand. This may well have been so, though it also created a segmented labor force of a minority of regulars and a reserve army of the sometimes employed. In any case, the waiting list remained a feature of the business through the turn of the century. Edward Delaney, who as "De" wrote the *Electric Age*'s humor column, immortalized the waiting list with a parody of Hamlet's soliloquy that, despite the tongue in cheek, is tinged with bleakness:

> To wait or not to wait? That is the question.
> Whether 'tis better to loaf around the building talking
> Shop and other damphoolishness,
> Or to pack up one's trunk
> And leave for parts unknown
> 'Tis a question of great moment.
> The dread of riding in a box car
> Or being dumped at a way
> Station where there are
> No station houses, gives
> Us pause and makes
> Us rather increase our
> Indebtedness to our landlady
> Here, than to seek other
> Parts. With forty men on the

Waiting list, what chance
Hath the fortieth man. Aye, there's the rub.

The depression of the 1890s was a brake on the telegraphic freewheeling characteristic of the postbellum years. "The operators are no longer moving from place to place in their efforts to procure more remunerative positions, which was considered necessary previous to five years ago," reported the *Telegraph Age* in 1897.[48] Actually, the *Age* exaggerated. Operators moved more reluctantly, but they still moved. At the Syracuse Western Union office, with an operating force of around thirty-three through the 1890s, annual average turnover stood at a bit under a third, or 29.2 percent. But perhaps even more important, less than half (44.4 percent) of those on the 1890 roster of twenty-seven operators were still in the office to greet the new century.[49]

More complete records for the Harrisburg Western Union office survive to supplement this tale of operators on the move. Despite its location in a state capital, the office was modest in size (the average payroll contained only eleven telegraphers), but the long span of its records enables us to cautiously generalize about turnover and career mobility in the Gilded Age. The broad contours are not surprising: turnover roughly paralleled the boom-bust patterns of the era. Movement increased in the late 1860s, dropped in the early 1870s, increased again during the recovery of the late 1870s and early 1880s, maintained something approximating a plateau through the decade, and then followed the fall and rise of the business cycle in the 1890s. Over the thirty-four years between 1866 and 1900, annual turnover averaged 43.4 percent. So, as a rule, a little under half of the Harrisburg staff was coming or going each year. Most who passed through the office doors did not stay very long. Taking three years as an average period of minimal stability—one that would enable a messenger to develop into a competent working operator—there were 198 operators (including managers and potential operators in the form of messengers and clerks) who could have remained that long and been recorded within the payroll book for 1866–1900. Of that possible total, only forty-three (21.7 percent) spent three or more years at the place, their average stay covering just under eight years.[50]

Perhaps most who worked at the office could not have stayed and advanced even if will and industry were present; perhaps a place such as Harrisburg was inevitably a way station for most of them. It was for C. L. Laverty, who appeared there in the early 1870s, and whose subsequent career would remain as obscure as most of the others on the Harrisburg payroll had he not wound up as master workman of the Philadelphia Brotherhood of Telegraphers during the Great Strike. Another bird of passage, Leona Lemon, went on to a different kind of prominence. Lemon (despite the first name, a man), born in rural Pennsylvania in 1867, had already bounced around a good deal among keys in his home state and New Jersey by the time he appeared in Harrisburg in 1883. He went on to bounce some more, though ever higher, with the Western Union, the B & O, and by the early 1890s, with the Postal Company, whose Baltimore office he managed.[51]

The Harrisburg records tell little about most of their other inhabitants beyond their fleeting tenure there. They are more helpful on the fate of those less restless—or more lucky. And some of them made real careers out of the Western Union. That was the case with Emil Teupser, the son of German immigrants, who began as a messenger boy in 1864, rose to a clerkship by 1869, and within two years had doubled his salary to $50 and begun to work a wire. In 1872 he became night manager (at $80 a month), a post he retained through the 1870s and 1880s, though his salary fluctuated, dropping as low as $60. But that hardly shook his confidence in his future. He married a Gettysburg telegrapher named Mary Scott in 1877, and hard work and patience were rewarded ten years later when Teupser was appointed manager of the Harrisburg office. There he presided, a plump Teutonic countenance framed in muttonchop whiskers, earning an equally plump $80 a month, for the rest of the century.[52]

Amos Mumma's twenty-four years at the office bespoke impressive mobility too. Young Mumma carried messages at the standard $12 a month from 1874–78; combined his courier duties with telegraphing the next year; was clerking, at $35, in 1881; and then operating, with the same pay, in 1882. The year that Emil Teupser won the manager's desk, 1887, Mumma also received a significant promotion when he became chief operator (and simultaneously got a raise from $45 to $50). In 1890, his salary jumped to $60. Both his position and pay remained the same through 1900. But long tenure at the key did not guarantee advancement. Gustavus C. Catherman was another Harrisburg telegrapher with an extended, stable record. Rated at $60 a month when he first appears in 1885, he was night operator, with salary unchanged, by 1887. And he was still night operator in 1900, and still earning $60, although by then the father of two teen-agers. Harry W. Spahr's experience was even more ambiguous. Born the same year as Emil Teupser (1853), Spahr entered Harrisburg's Western Union service about the same time and way that Teupser did, as a messenger in 1866. He reemerged on the payroll in 1873–78 as a $40 operator. Harry may have tired of the key by 1879, for he was then listed as a clerk, still at $40. But he was back on a wire by 1881, this time at a commission branch office at the local stockyard, where he would spend the next nineteen years. His main source of income working amid the cattle, sheep, and swine came not from the Western Union—with monthly commissions that ranged from $23.61 to $6.73 it hardly could have—but from a stockyard clerkship. This evidently led to better things: Spahr left his father's household, married in 1891, had two sons, and by 1900 the city directory listed him as "Superintendent Stockyard." That was substantial mobility by any standard, but it was not, strictly speaking, telegraphic mobility. What's more, there are two perplexing aspects to Spahr's story. Though rising in the stockyard, he never quit his Western Union branch office, with its paltry commissions; and even stranger, he announced himself to the census enumerator in 1900 as a telegrapher, not superintendent or even clerk of the stockyard—and this in a year when his October earnings on Western Union business totaled $11.10. At best, Harry Spahr's twenty-seven years on a Western Union key had led to success only outside of telegraphy; at worst, his long tenure, though itself unusual, still typified the stagnant careers of so many contemporary telegraphers.[53]

Market forces, corporate managers, and population vagaries were not alone in creating the world of the telegrapher. Like any social group, operators made themselves as much as others made them.

They made themselves as much as the Western Union and its kindred made them in the telegraph office. Whether in urban wire centers or tank stops nestled among pines, all operators had a shared work culture that grew out of the nature of the medium itself. For all its vast scope and industrial organization, telegraphy did not render its work force into ciphers. Even so seemingly rigid and impersonal a form of communication as Morse code, in the hands of its practitioners, was in fact a language spoken in accents. Each telegrapher had a distinctive way of sending that set him or her off from another, and experienced receivers could detect the subtle variations in style as readily as they could the peculiarities of a human voice. But even a novice could discern the personal "signs" (or "signatures") that Knights and Ladies of the Key adopted to identify themselves over the wires. At Detroit in 1875, for instance, an operator named Mills signed himself "Ms" to his colleagues, Singleton became "Si," Miss C. Edwards was "Ce," and Miss A. Edwards went by "Ae." The companies required the signs for their own convenience, but it was the operators who devised them.[54]

Telegraphers developed regular partnerships over a shop floor at times hundreds or even thousands of miles wide. Thomas Edison described how one such pairing took place in the late 1860s: "When on the New York No. 1 wire, that I worked in Boston, there was an operator named Jerry Borst at the other end. He was a first-class receiver and rapid sender. We made up a scheme to hold this wire, so he changed one letter of the alphabet and I soon got used to it; and finally we changed three letters. If any operator tried to receive from Borst, he couldn't do it, so Borst and I always worked together." This was not only clever; it was an informal assertion of workplace autonomy, and operators could be downright proprietary in claiming an exclusive hold on "their" wires. Western Union rule books had to remind operators that it was the company's prerogative to assign wires, and not theirs. But official rules failed to supplant the telegraphers' own unwritten code, and friction over allocating circuits persisted. As late as 1898, the management of one large office struck back with this placard: "Those operators who object to being 'snatched,' as they term it, are reminded that upon entering the employ of this company they were not engaged to work any particular wire or wires, to sit at dead or comparatively idle ones when their services could be utilized elsewhere, and the sooner they realize this the better it will be for all concerned."[55]

The electric bonds of operators working together could be explicitly social. During lulls in traffic along a circuit, L. C. Hall wrote, "stories are told, opinions exchanged, and laughs enjoyed, just as if the participants were sitting together at a club." Press operators were especially given to this sort of gregariousness and banter. Midwestern press men in the 1860s circulated the jokes and stories they had heard throughout the region over the wire, and a small percentage of them wound up in local papers (the vast majority did not, Thomas Edison recalled, because they were smutty). A "very common occurrence" among bored and lonely night railroad operators, one of them reported in 1888, was a game of checkers played on the key.[56] Loneliness of another kind sometimes had a telegraphic remedy. "Many a telegraph romance begun 'over the wire' culminated in marriage," reminisced Minnie Swan Mitchell of her days as a young operator in the 1880s. Ella Cheever Thayer's 1879 novel *Wired Love* built its plot around just such a courtship.[57]

Telegraphers did not always treat each other so tenderly. Thomas Hughes, grand secretary of the brotherhood during the Great Strike, mentioned "petty spites between men working together" that his union had reduced. Letters to telegraphers' journals complained of boorish manners on the wire. "Struggling for the circuit is strictly forbidden," intoned the Western Union *Rules* in 1870—and again in 1884 when the problem had not gone away. Norvin Green had personally rebuked Clara Brown, a Tarrytown, New York, operator four years earlier for the same sort of behavior. "You can never succeed in establishing a position of favor on the lines by fighting over the wires," the doctor wrote her, "or by refusing to work with this or that operator." In at least one case, more than pride was injured. Vexed during "an irritable moment" at the key in 1881, John Cone, of Greenville, South Carolina, managed to insult Reginald de Fevre, his counterpart at Charlotte, North Carolina. The latter demanded satisfaction, and the two met halfway at Gastonia, North Carolina, to settle the matter with fists at 1:00 A.M. The 170-pound Cone triumphed. "It was a hard fight," a correspondent to the *Operator* reported, "and both men were badly punished."[58]

Such violent encounters were rare, but the problem of ill-mannered and arrogant operators was not. Nor did it stem simply from flawed character. Clara Brown's truculence rested as much on her notion of a right to choose workmates as on a prickly personality. But even more, the premium on speed and skill within the craft—valued as much by the telegraphers as by the companies, if for different reasons—engendered tension between operators. One Iowan, ticking off the faults of his collegues, ended the list with "tyrannical and ungentlemanly conduct over the wire, and the utter want of consideration on the part of skillful operators for the feelings and sensibilities of those not so expert." The Western Union rulebook again tells a tale by forbidding what many telegraphers were in fact doing: "The sending operator will regulate the transmission of a message to suit the ability of the receiving operator," it decreed in 1884. The brotherhood's positive influence that Thomas Hughes had invoked was aimed at precisely this problem. "A member of the brotherhood, in sending messages to a fellow-operator," he explained a week before the Great Strike, "sends to accommodate his ability to receive. It is a case of mutual assistance which redounds to the benefit of all."[59] Even with the best of intentions added to company sanctions, it was difficult to avoid the weight and glamor that speed had for telegraphers. In their least divisive form, speed and accuracy found an outlet in organized contests, often with prizes and special categories (old-timers, women, railroaders, and so forth) to insure fair competition.[60] But speed was central to the craft culture, and its manifestations were not always so restrained. Operator jargon was rich in terms dealing with speed: a fast sender could "rush" or "salt" (overwhelm) an inferior one; the latter, apt to "break" (stop to ask the sender to repeat or slow down), bore the contemptuous epithets "plug" or "ham." To leave such lowly status behind as quickly as possible, as "De" made clear in 1883 in "A Check-Boy's Song," was the goal of every budding operator:

> I'll learn to telegraph, if I can,
> Says I to myself, says I;
> I'll be what they call a very fast man,
> Says I to myself, says I;
> I'll rush all the men that work with me,
> Then in the papers my name I'll see,
> Then I'll be a great man, do you see?
> Says I to myself, says I.[61]

Rushing was all the more fun when the victim was a yokel. An 1876 contributor to the *Operator* captured the ethos of the aggressive young urban Knight of the Key this way:

> At work the best man is the best rushaire,
> And must always give his greatest care
> To salting the plugs and making 'em swair;
> You once were a plug yourself, remembaire,
> And now, of course, it's only fair
> That you appear as the revengaire;
> So raise all the music you can in the air,

And salt all from plug to managaire.
Salt, brothers, salt with care,
Salt every country managaire![62]

Salting and rushing were sometimes less sadism than rough-edged camaraderie. This was certainly true of the ritual that the *Operator* dubbed "hazing a freshman." The "freshman" was a novice telegrapher, often newly arrived from a rural district. The hazing might involve sending ludicrous copy to the ingenuous candidate—telegrams addressed to "L. E. Fant" or "Lynn C. Doyle"—but was more often a straightforward salting. It ended, as a rule, when the neophyte, on the verge of collapse or tears, looked up to find himself surrounded by a knot of grinning operators who had been enjoying his growing frustration and discomfort. "If he accepts the situation as a joke, he is initiated," an 1879 account of a hazing explained, "but if he becomes angered, he is still a 'Freshman.'"[63]

However pregnant the rite was with the tensions that divided telegraphers of differing skill and backgrounds, it also bespoke ties that knit a particular set of workers into a national community. Even the ungainly hick operator was an operator first and a hick second. "Country operators," noted L. C. Hall, "when they get leave to come to town, are drawn irresistibly to the city telegraph office. However strange the city may be, in the central commercial office or the railroad dispatcher's den they are sure to find others who speak their lanuage, and with whom they may fraternize and feel at home." They shared occupational ills, such as consumption and operators' cramp (or "glass arm"). And despite the craft's decline, they also shared a sense that their job was one requiring special ability and part of the epochal transformation of America that wires and rails represented. "They were looked upon with wonder as possessing knowledge which separated them from the rest of the crowd," Minnie Swan Mitchell wrote. "Passes to theatres and on all railroads, etc., were always available. This made it possible for telegraphers, with youth and the great wide world beckoning, to give ear to the siren song of adventure. Wherever one stopped he (or sometimes she) could find employment, or, barring that, friends." Mitchell's picture of her youth at the key was the prettified nostalgia of an old woman near death, but it retained some of the truth nonetheless. As late as the

1940s, a young railroad operator in the Midwest could still feel a romance and excitement in working in so huge, complex, and dynamic a network.[64]

Craft community at times took the shape of formal organizations. Some operators tried to buffer the jolts with which a capricious market economy threatened so many Americans by joining friendly societies. The most prominent of them, the Telegraphers' Mutual Benefit Association, with headquarters at 195 Broadway, was actually a quasi-official appendage of the Western Union that enrolled managers as well as operators. In restricted numbers, the Magnetic Club in New York also admitted both managers and operators, where they mixed technological interests and conviviality. Limited to 100 members, the club in 1888 could induce brotherhood activists Tom O'Reilly and John Taltavall, as well as the Western Union's William Dealy, to hear shop talk and break bread in the same room.[65]

More vigorous forms of socializing attracted operators too. As early as 1868, the Saint Louis Western Union office boasted a baseball nine whose captain, J. H. French, also supervised his teammates during working hours as their chief operator. The *Journal of the Telegraph* lauded the team's efforts, judging "an hour or two [of] exhilarating enjoyment in the pure, fresh air" far preferable "than to knock about billiard saloons and bar-rooms till the 'wee sma' hours, as some (I was going to say many) of our profession do." Baseball and lager did mix at a "free and easy meeting" in 1875 at Hoboken, New Jersey, where operators from the Western Union and rival Atlantic & Pacific competed on the diamond, in a footrace, and then repaired to a local restaurant for food, drink, and musical diversion.[66]

The Hoboken revelers' beery waltzing was confined to men, but Knights of the Key often exchanged sweat-stained jerseys for their more accustomed suits and starched collars and, with female companionship, enjoyed the sort of dances, dinners, and entertainments popular in the era. Announcements of telegraphers' hops and balls appeared frequently in craft journals. The Merry Meeting Club, formed by members of Chicago's Western Union force, presented an evening of music, recitations, and tableaux vivant in 1874 very much like the gatherings in other cities that were fixtures of operator social life. By the time of the Great Strike, Brooklyn had an annual telegraphers' concert of three years' standing. The program of the 1883 affair included piano and vocal solos and duets and "humorous recitations" by the ubiquitous "De."[67]

Graver concerns reinforced the sense of a telegraphic community. Through their journals, operators warned one another about dishonorable members of the craft, such as Charles H. Biller, a chronic liar, or the "Dead Beat, Scoundrel, Villain, etc., etc." named Will H. Swan, who in 1887 had left behind him a trail of defrauded merchants and at least one wife with children while attempting to take on another spouse. They also solicited funds for those in distress, as they did for May Harris, an eighteen-year-old orphan from Xenia, Ohio, who, seeking the gentler climate of California to restore her health, broke down when she arrived there friendless. The same impulses lay behind the appeal a decade later, in 1897, for the veteran brotherhood activist Mortimer Shaw, who was by then "a physical wreck and in need financially." But the craft culture also suffused the happier incidents of life. Any operator reading a personals column that announced one of his fellows had been "duplexed" immediately knew a marriage had occurred, and there was no doubt about the meaning of this bit of news sent to the *Telegrapher* from Chicago: "Our friend Mr. Leroy Robinson, Manager of the Northwestern Company's Minneapolis, Minn., office, has had a male *sounder switched* into his family circuit. It was ready for *operating* its lungs April 22, 1875."[68]

Taking the stuff of their workday world and fashioning it into a unique craft culture, the Knights of the Key identified themselves as telegraphers. They also located themselves within a broader social band—that of a "new" lower middle class beginning to crystalize in late nineteenth-century America.

My use of the term "new lower middle class" requires a brief explanation. It follows the taxonomy of C. Wright Mills and others, both in separating the independent "old" middle class of businessmen and free professionals from the salaried "new" middle class of managers, technicians, and lesser white-collar employees, and in ascribing this dichotomy to the emergence of corporate capitalism in the latter half of the nineteenth century. Telegraphers were among the junior members of this new middle class. Recent scholarship has found a significant and growing number of clerical employees in the precorporate era—clerks, bookkeepers, and so forth—occupying desks in the great commercial antebellum cities, employees who, unlike their counterparts of a generation or two earlier, were apt to spend their lives working for someone else. Corporate employees, then, were not the first wave of permanently salaried office folk. But the corporations and managerial capitalism of Gilded Age America *were* revolutionary, and their employees, whatever their affinities with the scriveners of prewar counting houses, were a novel and unique group of people. It is both useful and accurate to discuss the telegraphers as part of a new lower middle class.[69]

Operators identified themselves as part of a class in many ways. Intermittent unionization and the Great Strike were two such expressions. They were very important, but also atypical. It is equally important to examine the more usual and persistent ways in which the operators perceived their economic and social position—to look at their cultural trappings, in other words—for they would act, or not act, based on just such perceptions. Culture is both mirror and prism, reflecting and refracting the material circumstances of class.[70]

The most obvious sign of the telegrapher's self-defined world was his dress. Clad in suit, collar, and cuffs, he stood out amid an American working population still largely composed of farmers, craftsmen, and laborers. One reporter remarked that Frank Phillips, the young man whose famous whistle began the Great Strike at 195 Broadway, "might easily be mistaken for a well-fed doctor of divinity." An operator was apparently indistinguishable from a representative of the traditional middle class: he could as well be a clergyman, doctor, lawyer, or merchant. And these were all callings that evoked sobriety and responsibility, prudence and solidity, thrift, moderation, foresight, and propriety—the qualities, in sum, of the classic bourgeois.[71]

But bourgeois dress did not always mean bourgeois behavior. Some operators displayed an embarrassing disjuncture between their costumes and their roles. The "fast" and irresponsible element among the craft was a frequent and anguished topic in the telegraphic journals of the era, and the reputation was widespread early on. "Instead of the gay, reckless, and fast young men of former days," wrote a New Yorker in 1865, "our ranks are filled by worthy, intelligent, and moral men, many with brilliant intelligence, who are fit ornaments to any class of society."[72] His optimism was premature. Complaints of "ungentlemanly" telegraphers recurred through the remainder of the century. Both on and off the wires, operators were foul-mouthed, and company rule books warned them to watch their language. They packed the air of telegraph offices with the stench of cigar smoke and mottled the floors with the revolting end products of chewing. Things grew so bad at Western Union headquarters that formal decrees banned smoking and "spitting upon the floors or from the windows" of the building.[73]

Jets of tobacco juice sailing from the heights of 195 Broadway onto pedestrians were a poor advertisement for the firm. So were drunken operators. Intemperance was enough of a problem for the Western Union to have a column, "The Dark Side," in its house organ in 1869 listing dismissals from the company for intoxication. Drinking harmed the craft's self-respect, too, and condemnation of rummy operators claimed much space on editorial pages. Especially intractable among telegraphic topers was the "tramp," or "bum", who combined high geographic mobility, chronically low finances, and an addiction to drink. The tramp personified the blighted character often ascribed to the era's telegraphers, and although he was an extreme case, many operators, if to a lesser degree, shared some of the tramp's failings.[74] Even a clean record was no guarantee of future behavior. J. M. Shea, who ran a Philadelphia branch office for the Reading Railroad's telegraph company in 1881, had up to then caused his employers no trouble, but he more than made up for it that year by spending Easter Sunday overindulging in eggnog. It caught up with him on the train ride home when, as his superintendent later reported, Shea "became very sick, vomiting and otherwise being exceedingly disgusting to passengers in the car." As if that were not bad enough, he "showed fight" when the conductor put him off the train at the next station, "called the conductor all kinds of names until the train got out of sight," and, for good measure, "walked from that point to Chestnut Hill and then abused the agent." The year before, a woman telegrapher observed that "operators, as a general thing, are inclined to be fast (the gentlemen, I mean; your pardon, gentlemen, but it's so, and you know it)." Theodore Vail knew it. Although he would one day head a corporate empire even greater than the Western Union, in 1865 he was an ordinary operator in New York. In March, the twenty-year-old Vail confessed to his diary: "Staying up late of nights playing Billiards and drinking lager is not what young men should be doing and for one I am determined to stop it." What young men should or should not have been doing is less important here than the fact that they were young men. That, indeed, accounts for some of the fast reputation that the Knights of the Key earned, for as in other aspects of the craft's fate, large numbers of youthful males made a difference. So did a calling that encouraged frequent movement from place to place. Nor should we forget the pull an urban environment could exert on a country boy starting out on his own. The city, after all, offered a kind of gritty education at the bar rail, pool table, theater lobby, and whore's bed. That was why such institutions as the YMCA had emerged in the first place.[75]

How extensive the fast operator problem was is impossible to say. Not every youthful lapse followed the uncorking of a bottle. "Our night operators in particular, as a general thing, are young, and it is the hardest matter to keep them awake at night," a B & O Railroad telegraph superintendent reported during the Civil War. Even the drinking was not due solely to youth or shoddy character; the high pressure of some telegraphic posts contributed to the tendency to alcoholism.[76] In any case, most operators, even most young ones, were neither wastrels nor sots, but enough were, and the temptation real enough, to prod craft spokesmen to sound frequent tocsins. Some saw the generally worsening plight of their fellows as the logical outcome of dissolute living. "Operators have no right to complain of partiality or injustice in their employers because they do not receive a better salary or a higher position," admonished the *Operator* in 1874, "so long as they spend their leisure hours in the gratification of their appetites and their money upon tobacco, drink, billiards and theatres." A year later, the journal pressed the lesson home by drawing up an itemized budget of "average unmarried operators" in cities, $254.80 of which—22 percent of the total—was supposedly thrown out on liquor and cigars. "Create an independent spirit by having a little money," the *Operator* counseled, "and you will have more real power than if you belonged to a dozen of leagues [that is, unions]."[77]

Charges of thriftlessness were not limited to conservative voices. Socialist and labor activist P. J. McGuire, a staunch friend of the brotherhood during the Great Strike, told a Senate committee that the operators' "impulsive" nature had fundamentally weakened their rebellion against the Western Union because of insufficient funds. "As a class," McGuire testified, "they live from hand to mouth. They dress well and live freely, and they do not generally save much, so that even a week's idleness comes very severely upon them, because they have made themselves accustomed to better conditions than most workers." An *Operator* columnist put it more wryly and succinctly: "It has become almost proverbial that an operator is wealthy only twice a month, the 1st and the 15th."[78]

An amorphous social position compounded a sometimes precarious economic one. Clearly not a worker in the traditional sense, neither did the telegrapher conform to a genuinely bourgeois mold. In his own eyes, at least, what was he?

The terms that operators used to describe their field might provide a clue. The *Telegraphers' Advocate* declared that the "service may now be classed as a profession" because it united "clerical labor" and scientific knowledge. Elsewhere it referred to the "mental labor" of telegraphers. John McClelland described his fellows as "a steady, sober, and intelligent class of workers." Long-term operator Alfred H. Seymour used the phrase "other classes of workmen." John Campbell spoke of "skilled labor of this kind" and "some of the other trades." The word *craft*, with its artisanal overtones, was often used. Telegraphers sometimes spoke of receiving "salaries," at other times "wages." Sifting through these terms demands care, though, since such words as *labor, class, trade, worker*, and *profession* may have carried important nuances that have evaporated with time. But even allowing for that, the variety and imprecision of the terms remain.[79]

It may be more useful to ask how operators viewed themselves in relation to others, since by definition no social class (or the awareness of belonging to it) exists in isolation. Despite what to twentieth-century ears seems a rather free use of words implying working-class status to describe themselves, operators at times consciously, and at times invidiously, set themselves off from blue-collar people. This was certainly so in complaints of inadequate pay. "A telegrapher's work is of the highest order of skilled labor," asserted a Boston operator two days before the Great Strike, "and he receives the pay that would be thrown to an ordinary laborer." Members of the craft, an 1882 brotherhood recruiting circular aimed at railroad operators pointed out, "often find themselves receiving smaller wages than the trackmen, firemen, brakemen and other unskilled labor employed." Remuneration for telegraphers, argued a brotherhood man in Chicago, should at minimum be "equal to the pay of good mechanics."[80] But the difference between operators and regular workers was not simply a matter of pay. Telegraphers were also brain workers. "The telegraphers as a profession," the *Electric Age* assured readers in 1886, "by actual comparison, is [*sic*] vastly superior intellectually to the railroad engineers." One New York operator thought it took "as much skill and a great deal more education to send and receive over the wires than it does to lay bricks or manipulate a jack-plane." Brotherhood leaders John McClelland, Eugene O'Connor, and John Campbell all stressed the centrality of mental facility in the telegrapher's stock in trade—in implicit contrast to the mass of contemporary wage workers.[81]

The operators' relation to the contemporary middle class was another matter. Whatever the subterranean realities, telegraphy was a white-collar occupation, and this was of prime importance. White-collar work did have an undeniable appeal to many seeking a career. Not to all, of course; the son of a labor aristocrat might have looked upon entering a clerkship (rather than following in his father's footsteps) as a distinct loss of skill, autonomy, "manliness," perhaps even income. But others, for whom manual labor had less rewarding connotations, may have eagerly shed overalls for a ready-made suit. "Every farmer father is anxious for his son to have white hands," a North Carolina operator wrote in 1894, "and, not being able to give that son a high education to fit him for a higher life, that son is put in some telegraph office to learn the business." The *Chicago Tribune* judged telegraphy "clean-fingered, genteel" work. John Campbell said that young men were "extremely anxious" to enter the field, thinking it "more respectable than some of the other trades." This notion of "respectable" is tricky. Walter Phillips's fictional Irish-born messenger, Patsy Flanagan, went through a blue- to white-collar metamorphosis in which "he appeared on the evening of his succession to the night clerkship in a white shirt and a collar—a new departure for him. . . . He adhered to his hobnailed shoes for several months; but one day they gave place to 'Oxford ties,' a cravat followed, and so, little by little, the rough boy was transformed into quite a tidy young man." What Patsy actually thought about such a change we can only guess, since a Yankee farmer's son, and not an unskilled Irish immigrant, had created him.[82] Closer to a firsthand account, although hardly uncolored, was the reaction that Andrew Carnegie later set down of his move from a textile mill basement to a telegraph office. The gnomish robber baron fondly recalled that he had been "lifted into paradise, yes, heaven, as it seemed to me, with newspapers, pens, pencils, and sunshine about me."[83]

Few operators would have described their situation as heavenly, but the fact that they wore business dress and were educated above the working-class average placed them, as they saw things, somewhere among the middling strata. "With the amount of intelligence and general information possessed by the average telegrapher," an Iowa Knight of the Key maintained in 1883, "he is entitled to move in the best social circles." And entitled to "just as much respect in ordinary society as a doctor, a lawyer, or a politician," added John McClelland before a Senate hearing the same year. His colleague John Campbell was a bit equivocal, though, when one senator asked him:

Q: How do they compare as a whole, in your judgment, with the men that are made into lawyers, and doctors, and ministers, and merchants?

A: They are probably not equal to that class.

Q: I mean originally, primarily?

A: Well, I don't know. They are probably equal in that way.

Some lawyers, doctors, ministers, and merchants doubtless looked with bald contempt on such as a telegrapher. "Up in Amherst, some of the ginger-pop professors used to sniff a little at my enthusiasm about telegraphy," military operator Thomas L. Somerby wrote a friend in 1861. "They regarded it as a trade and not just the thing for a college man."[84]

How widespread such attitudes were, and how painful they were to operators we cannot know. If telegraphers moved in "the best social circles," they were circles that rarely included well-to-do doctors, lawyers, ministers, merchants, or Amherst College faculty. Some operators, true enough, did occasionally achieve prominence within their communities while still members of the craft, though this was most likely to be the case where the operator was in fact a manager, or the community fairly small. The activities of manager Charles Bigler and chief operator Richard Ziegler of the Harrisburg Western Union office make the distinction between old and new middle class problematic. Bigler frequently appeared in the local press for other than telegraphic reasons. An enthusiastic amateur tenor who sang in vocal groups large and small, he was also a Masonic officer, a member of the Historical Society Executive Committee, and in 1883 the father of ten-year-old Margaretta Bigler, then acquiring her ideas of politeness along with several other "young ladies [who] waited on the tables and gracefully performed their duties" at a Methodist church "tea-drinking sociable." Ziegler's wife, Sarah, very likely owed her polish to similar training, as well as to her high school education, a rarity for most Americans when she graduated in 1867. The Biglers and Zieglers also lived two doors apart, but an even closer bond was the electrical contracting business that both men ran as a partnership in addition to their Western Union positions. By all accounts, these were successful, comfortable, and well-placed men, telegraphers of local prominence and standing. Their world was not, however, quite that of a more representative Harrisburg operator, Harry Selin. Young Selin, twenty-one in 1883, shared Bigler's interest in music, but not his audience. The Sewing Society of Grace Methodist Church invited Bigler to sing at "a most delightful sociable at Dr. Hugh Pitcairn's"; Selin played a xylophone solo at a YMCA "public exhibition."[85]

A fair distance separated the YMCA auditorium and Dr. Pitcairn's parlor. Still, while distinct from the solid old middle class, the social niche that most operators chiseled out for themselves was not spurious. Their work setting did demand a standard of dress. They were "required to make a better appearance than other classes of workingmen," Alfred Seymour said of his fellow operators, "to dress better and to live a great deal better, and they have a little more pride perhaps than the majority of other workers, and their money goes in that way. The business is such," he explained, "that you may say they are on inspection and parade nearly all the time."[86]

The parade did not end at the operating room door, since cutting a suitably middle-class figure involved appropriate levels of consumption in the home as well as respectable attire—providing "a decent living for themselves and their families," as the *Telegraphers' Advocate* put it. But they had to be able to afford families in the first place. Some blamed the high proportion of single operators on the meager rewards of the craft. "Demanding in domestic life surroundings approximating to refinement," wrote the editor of a Boston daily, the young telegrapher had to eschew marriage. Even Norvin Green confirmed the problem, admitting that operators who wed usually left the field.[87]

Those who did have family responsibilities claimed that a telegrapher's remuneration was barely adequate, or even inadequate. As early as 1871, the *Telegrapher* asserted that even the highest-paid big city men could but "barely" provide a respectable living standard for their families, "however modest and moderate may be their aspirations." Craft spokesmen echoed the charges at the time of the Great Strike. Alfred Seymour, a thirty-year veteran of the key and former manager who had cast his lot with the brotherhood, told inquiring senators that his pay gave "only a bare living, leaving nothing to save." Harry Orr and Eugene O'Connor, both family men and first-class operators, worked overtime or moonlighted to augment their $70 and $75 monthly salaries (O'Connor also sublet part of the house he rented to reduce the pressure on his family's coffers). Working "extra" was fairly common. Rated at $60, night chief Catherman at Harrisburg regularly took $10 or more a month home in overtime—which his wife, Nellie, no doubt appreciated as they began to raise their two children. Depot agent-operators supplemented their income through their ancillary ticket and express duties. Still, the complaints persisted. "It is almost impossible for a married man to live by the sweat of his brow in this place," protested a Brooklyn Knight of the Key in 1883.[88]

What a "bare living" or "starvation wages" meant to a telegrapher was not necessarily what it meant to a day laborer or even a skilled worker.[89] Senator Wilkinson Call asked John Campbell whether he meant to say that operators' salaries were "utterly inadequate to the support of a family." Replied the brotherhood leader, "Oh, well, they might manage to get along, but it would be in such a manner that they would not be at all satisfied." John Costello gave the senators an idea of the kind of dissatisfaction Campbell had in mind. At the key since 1869, Costello rented rooms in a Brooklyn house, and rent and necessities, with "no luxuries whatsoever," took $65 of his $75 monthly paycheck. So the $75, one senator asked, was "insufficient" for a couple to live on? "Yes, sir," Costello answered, then adding, "Of course, if I would live in the slums of the city I could live on a little less, but I do not propose to do that."[90]

James E. Smith probably did live in "the slums of the city." Head of the linemen within the New York brotherhood, Smith, who likely earned around $65 a month, packed himself, his wife, and four children into "four little rooms"—at $11 a month—"in a tenement house in a tenement neighborhood." Costello and Smith lived in the same metropolitan area in 1883, both joined the brotherhood and struck against the Western Union, and their incomes were different by perhaps thirty-eight cents a day. But both probably had considerably different ideas of what such words as *decent, insufficient,* and *luxury* meant. The same was true of the Chicago telegrapher and teamster who shared not the same neighborhood, but the same page of an 1884 Illinois Bureau of Labor Statistics survey. They certainly did not share living standards. The operator, a railroad employee earning $90 a month ($1,080 a year), would have been among the elite of the craft.

His family numbered four, he rented a house, managed to save $212 a year, and, the bureau investigator recorded, seemed "well satisfied with his work and general conditions." Whether the Irish teamster whose family profile preceded the operator's was also happy with his lot the interviewer did not say, but he and his wife (and his horse) lived on less than half the telegrapher's salary ($530) in a tenement whose environment the survey judged "poor." Worse off still was another teamster the bureau found, this one a German, whose lesser income of $450 had to stretch even farther to support a wife and six children. Family larders testified to contemporary notions of sufficiency and luxury too. Breakfast at both teamster households consisted of bread and coffee and nothing more; the telegrapher and his family regularly began the day by sitting down to bread, butter, ham, eggs, and coffee.[91]

To put the operators' concerns about incomes and living standards in perspective, we should also ask how they fared, in terms of actual purchasing power, over the postbellum decades. Fixing telegraphers' average nominal salaries during the period is possible, although differences in skill, gender, and location inevitably skew such figures. Still, telegraphers undoubtedly had higher nominal salaries in the golden age of the 1860s and early 1870s. First-class operators received $90 to $125 a month, while all operators averaged around $70. Pay figures then dipped, especially after the Sliding Scale of 1876. The brotherhood claimed national averages in 1883 of $54 for commercial operators, $39 for railroad operators, and $80 to $85 for first-class men. The Western Union gave higher figures for its commercial telegraphers—$65—though it attained the higher average by omitting the various branch and commission operators earning less than the $30 that the company regarded as its minimum regular salary. Two years later, Michigan's Bureau of Labor Statistics found an average closer to the brotherhood's, at around $55 for the state's operators. By the 1890s the figures changed little, if anything declining even more. At Syracuse, an office with a force of around thirty-four through the decade, the salary average for 1890–1900 was only $48.31 a month. Philadelphians working for the Western Union in 1893 did a bit better, with an average of $55.[92]

But economic well-being depended as much on the relative movement of prices as on nominal income. Prices, on the whole, declined in the Gilded Age, and so the figures that appeared in Western Union payroll books must be read in the context of an era of general defla-

TABLE 3.1   FIRST-CLASS MORSE OPERATORS' MONTHLY SALARIES,
WESTERN UNION TELEGRAPH COMPANY, 1870 AND 1883

City	1870	1883
New York	$90–120 ($66.66–88.88)	$80–85 ($79.20–84.15)
Chicago	90–115 (66.66–85.18)	75–80 (74.25–79.20)
Philadelphia	90–105 (66.66–77.77)	75–80 (74.25–79.20)
Boston	90–105 (66.66–77.77)	70–75 (69.30–74.25)
Buffalo	85–105 (62.96–77.77)	70–80 (69.30–79.20)
New Orleans	100–125 (74.07–92.59)	75–85 (74.25–84.15)
Richmond	90–115 (66.66–85.18)	70–80 (69.30–79.20)
Omaha	90–110 (66.66–81.48)	75–80 (74.25–79.20)
San Francisco	90–115 (66.66–85.18)	80–85 (79.20–84.15)

NOTE: The figures in parentheses represent salaries in constant dollars based on the 1910–14 Warren and Pearson series.

tion. When nominal salaries are converted to constant dollars to reflect this trend, the results are illuminating. The briefest way to approach the matter is through a kind of wage biography for first-class Western Union Morse operators in major cities stretching from 1870 to 1883. Table 3.1 is just such a profile, giving nominal salaries first, and then, in parentheses, salaries in constant dollars based on the 1910–14 Warren and Pearson series.[93]

Two things are immediately apparent from the table. First, operators in the lower end of this range ($90 to $105) either held their own or made modest gains in purchasing power through 1883 (and in most cases beyond that date, since the rest of the century showed no appreciable inflation). For those with salaries lower than those shown, gains through deflation could be dramatic. A glance at the careers of three Harrisburg men makes this plain. Virginius P. Smith, who tapped a key there in 1872, rated $40 a month; by 1884, he had graduated to a $60 position, an increase of 50 percent. But in constant dollars, Smith's actual pay went from $29.41 to $64.51, a gain of around 119 percent. Richard Ziegler, chief operator in 1866, took home $75. Although his pay fluctuated through the 1870s, going as high as $90, it had settled down to $80 by his last year in the office, 1886. Nominally, after eighteen years, he had gained but $5 a month, a bit over 6 percent; in real terms, though, the span was actually from $43.10 in 1866 to $97.56 in 1886, a 126 percent rise. Emil Teupser did even better. His 1871 pay as an operator is listed as $50 a month, and by 1887, when he became manager, it had grown to $80, a 60 percent boost. But again, when adjusted for deflation, Teupser's salary had in fact gone from $38.46 to $94.11, a jump of more than twice the apparent rate, at 144 percent.[94]

Conversely, the economic elite of the telegraphers—those making $110 to $125 a month—lost ground. Certainly their actual losses were not as sharp as their apparent ones; dropping from $125 to $85 looks less breathtaking when changed into the constant dollar sums of $92.59 to $84.15. The erosion was nonetheless real, and the high-paid operator's perception of that erosion is important in understanding how Knights of the Key reacted to pay cuts. Harry Orr, the brotherhood activist from Philadelphia, provides a case in point. As a single young man in 1873, Orr earned $90. A decade later, with a family, his salary had fallen to $75, which he supplemented by extra work to earn a total of $85 to $90. In constant dollars, his 1873 pay was $71.42, that in 1883 was $74.25 (or $84.15 to $89.10 with the extra). So in reality he was getting more (though his expenses were certainly more) and not standing still, as he doubtless felt he was. An operator's perception of a diminishing Western Union paycheck was further colored by whether the same operator experienced successive cuts (went, say, from $100 to $90 to $80), or simply found a constricted salary range as he came up through the ranks. Again Harrisburg provides examples. Both Richard Ziegler and Amos Mumma spent many years there (eighteen and twenty-four, respectively) and very likely knew each other. They both made gains in real income, although we do not know whether both may have been disappointed with what seemed stagnation or slow advance (Ziegler left the Western Union in 1886 for an occupational smorgasbord of patronage politics, journalism, and municipal technocracy). But if such disappointment existed, it probably looked different to Ziegler, slipping and sliding from $90 to $85 to $80, than to Mumma, steadily stepping up from $35 to $45, and then, at $50, replacing Ziegler as chief. On the one hand, Mumma may well have known that the year he entered the office as a messenger, 1874, the same chief he replaced was making $90; on the other hand, Mumma was undoubtedly rising in both rank and salary. What his standards were—those of 1887 or the golden age—will have shaded his perception of how the craft was treating him.[95]

In sum, reduced opportunities for Gilded Age telegraphers coincided with mild economic gains in the long run. Also in their favor, if on a regular payroll, was steady income throughout the year, unlike, for instance, the mechanic or laborer limited to working in temperate seasons.[96] Whether operators did so poorly compared to skilled blue-collar workers, as they and their supporters charged, is open to question. In making their case, they overstated craftsmen's incomes. Allowing for variation among both operators and workers, and assuming a single breadwinner, a city-based male telegrapher's salary roughly paralleled or bettered that of a labor aristocrat. A Boston operator paid $90 a month in 1875 was not far above a machinist in the same state earning $840 a year, and closer still to a mill overseer with his $1,000 annual income. Likewise, a Chicago telegrapher in 1884 making $1,080 was in the approximate range of a trunkmaker getting $900. Michigan surveyed 4,135 of its wage earners in 1885 (most of them workers, but including some white-collar categories), and the telegraphers' average of $55.84, though not at the top, was still comfortably above the overall average of $45.46. Complaints about low pay had greater cogency in the case of railway operators. One Kansas compilation from 1887 gave the ordinary telegraphers' average as $43.92, which was better than the section hands' $31.12 and section foremen's $41.40, but not impressive measured against brakemen ($49.30), machinists ($64.25), or engineers ($96.97). The distortions inherent in averaging should always be kept in mind here: a country operator making $35 or $40 and a city laborer with the same pay were not comparable. Difficult to compare, too, was the increase in real wages for telegraphers relative to that for blue-collar employees. Manufacturing real wages, mainly for the growing semiskilled work force, rose 11 percent between 1870 and 1880. The only comparable figures for telegraphers are from Table 3.1, and for roughly the same period, the bottom range of the operator elite averaged an 8.8 percent gain in real wages, while the very top lost 4.2 percent. But for less well-paid operators, the gains would have been greater.[97]

Telegraphers looked around and above, as well as below them, to gauge their income and status. If the $125-a-month clerks in New York City mercantile houses that Alfred Seymour invoked were representative, then most Knights of the Key were indeed underprivileged. And if someone as unquestionably middle class as a high school principal in Cincinnati or Saint Louis is the model, a telegrapher's $75 a month in 1883 paled before the $2,600 a year that those educators received. Although less exalted, a Saint Louis high school teacher easily outpaced most first-class operators with his $1,800 annual earnings. But there was great variation in white-collar income, as a Michigan Bureau of Labor Statistics canvass in the mid-1880s found. One civil engineer reported a substantial $125 monthly, managers averaged $96, commercial travelers $80.38, and agents, $90.72. But bookkeepers and accountants were less affluent with $64.59, drug clerks surely were, averaging only $48.69, which still made them marginally better off than the nondescript clerks and salesmen whose average was only $47.09—all the while remembering the figure for the telegraphers in the same survey, $55.84. Peculiarities of location and situation mediated these figures, of course. Railroad operators usually did less well than their city counterparts, as these average salaries from Kansas in 1887 starkly show:

Flour mill managers	$99.93
Flour mill salesmen	78.01
Flour mill bookkeepers	62.92
Flour mill clerks	49.46
Railroad telegraphers	43.92

But some figures were not quite what they seem at first. Men who taught school in Barnstable County, Massachusetts, in the early 1880s commanded $61.57 a month, close to the operators' national average; but since the classroom, unlike the Western Union, closed its doors for the summer, the teacher in fact got less overall than a first-class operator (and in hilly, remote Franklin County, authorities granted male teachers only $38.89 for a month's service). High school principals and teachers were relatively few in number in 1883, but those who taught in one-room village schools—or telegraphed in village railroad depots—were far less so. On the whole, operators fell within the lower-middle income range of America's salaried work force.[98]

What Knights of the Key did with their money was as important as how much of it they got. We still know little specific about contemporary standards of consumption. We do know that at least by the 1870s, mass-produced goods of a semiluxury kind were reaching the homes of better-off working-class families, and more than a few comfortable mechanics' households boasted a piano, carpets, sewing machine, or cottage organ. Middle-class homes doubtless contained such things too, though presumably in greater abundance and quality. The cliché about the studied clutter of the Victorian middle-class parlor is true. The "typical parlor," one historian found, "overflowed with store-bought, mass-produced objects, carefully arranged by family members: wall-to-wall carpeting enclosed by papered and bordered walls and oilings; upholstered furniture topped with antimacassars; shawl-draped center tables displaying carefully arranged souvenir albums and alabaster sculptures; shelves and small stands overloaded with bric-a-brac and purchased mementos." When operators spoke of maintaining their families decently, they surely had this machine-made bounty in mind, in addition to the neat dress and heavy meals that celebrated their distance from a scarcity economy. The distance was even greater for the young urban bachelors who worked a key. If the representative budget that the *Operator* calculated in 1875 was accurate, a well-paid single telegrapher spent about as much a year on shaves, haircuts, and shampoos as a typical working-class family did to cook its food and warm its home.[99]

Material comfort worthy of society's middle ranks also demanded respectable and "refined" social forms. The stress on sobriety during the Great Strike, although as much tactical as cultural, still meshed with a general urge for respectable behavior—an urge certainly enhanced by the fast reputation that plagued the craft. To help maintain the brotherhood's gentlemanly image during the walkout, an inventive New York member came up with the term *contumist* to replace the harsh and plebeian *scab*. Respectability could easily shade into superciliousness. After the strike, the *Operator* exhorted readers to spurn "trades-union slang and demagoguery" such as that crude work typified. John Taltavall, editing the *Telegraph Age* in the early 1900s, attacked a hostile correspondent as much for his lack of social grace as for his arguments. "That he is slovenly of person is indicated by the fact that the paper on which his note was written is soiled," Taltavall wrote, "and the coarse vulgarity of his closing sentence reveals the under-bred mind, altogether and unerringly disclosing a personality with traits of character which the call of promotion rarely reaches."[100]

"It is a nice, genteel occupation—telegraphing," Jay Gould assured the Senate Education and Labor Committee in 1883. Gould's words, though often suspect, seem nevertheless in a contemporary sense to have hit the mark here. "Genteel," in this context, does not have the traditional upper-class connotation. The gentility of a telegraph operator was not that of an E. L. Godkin or Charles Eliot Norton; such men in fact contemptuously dismissed the sort of decor that might fill an operator's parlor as the bastard offspring of a "chromo civilization." Lower-middle-class gentility was a vague mix that comprised adopting "correct" manners, dress, speech, and striving for "cultivation" and social mobility. It was not simply a matter of respectability—workers, too, had that desire—but respectability in a peculiar, marginal white-collar context. Like any other class, it sought to define itself, to establish its social self-respect. Perhaps that concern with personal deportment and affinity for middle-brow aesthetics that Leon Fink, in discussing Gilded Age Knights of Labor has dubbed "popular gentility," best resembles the mood and mannerisms of the period's telegraphers and those like them.[101]

Evidence of gentility as a telegrapher understood it is sketchy but suggestive. One place to seek it is in the entertainments that operators attended, especially those in which they performed as well. They seem very much like the era's band concerts in their makeup: a few tolerably brief nods to Culture amid a great deal of froth and sentimentality. At an 1893 New York affair, the nine-year-old son of one operator played the perennial variations on "The Carnival of Venice" on violin, William Donovan performed comic songs and sayings, George and Annie Murphy a piano duet, and Lew Smith "created wonderment and was given prompt encores" for his skill at whistling. That same year at the Chicago Telegraphers' Club, Mrs. F. X. Duenwald sang "We'd Better Bide a Wee," J. P. Delaney declaimed "Tim Finnegan's Wake," and Mr. and Mrs. Rogers crooned "Love's Old Song." And if the audience at the 1897 New York Telegraphers' Aid Society concert had to sit politely through Mark Antony's oration, they also got to hear a song from The Chimes of Normandy and, better still, George Leveen, the "negro singing and dancing comedian, of the Western Union force."[102]

We can also find traces of popular gentility in the operators' journals, which up through the mid-1880s contained a fair amount of humorous or treacly verse and prose, often with a telegraphic slant. They contained advertisements as well. By far the bulk of them, naturally enough, were for the paraphernalia of telegraphy—keys, sounders, batteries, technical and scientific books—but there was something beyond this. In the mid-1880s, the *Operator* ran advertisements that seem a kind of relief map of the cultural topography of lower-middle-class America. These are, admittedly, only ads; there is no certainty that telegraphers bought what they offered. But the fact that merchandisers were confident enough to run the displays suggests that the Knights of the Key furnished a likely market for the stuff.

Published three days before the Great Strike began, the July 16, 1883, issue of the *Operator* contains an especially rich collection of these offerings. They fall roughly into three divisions—gentility, self-improvement, and what might be freely called kitsch—and deserve a closer look and an attempt to explain their cohabitation of the same pages.

Much of the gentility literature was of the straightforward, etiquette-book variety, and no less than three such volumes (*Martine's Hand-Book of Etiquette and Guide to True Politeness*, *The Standard Book of Politeness*, and *Genteel Behavior*) solicited the operators' attention and coins. You could acquire kindred graces, too, by buying *Ready-Made Autograph Album Verses*, *Young Americans Letter Writer*, or *Prof. Baron's Complete Instructor in All the Society Dances of America*. Once accepted into "our best society," an operator might enthrall a parlor audience by mastering the contents of *Beecher's Recitations and Readings* and declaiming its "Humorous, Serious, Dramatic . . . Prose and Poetical Selections in Dutch, French, Yankee, Irish, Backwoods, Negro and other Dialects." And when social concerns narrowed to more intimate dimensions, the operator could turn to *Confidential Advice to the Unmarried* or *The Mystery of Love-Making Solved*.

The advertisements also included tools for the autodidact. The *Golden Key to Business Life* contained a wealth of information on the ways of the world of commerce, and its publisher promised that it would "give a Farmer's Boy a Perfect Business Education that would cost $3,000 to get in School or College." *The Golden Key* cost only twenty-five cents. So did *The American Business Man and Bookkeeper's Practical Guide*, which covered much the same ground. Ambitious telegraphers could also send for instruction in shorthand, find out "How to Make $10 a Day Without Capital," and even, if so inclined, "How to Learn the Sense of 3,000 French Words in one Hour."

Those more intent on levity than learning might choose to order *Old Gypsey Madge's Fortune Teller*, or to uncover *The Secrets of Ancient and Modern Magic*. On payment of a dime, operators received the Sensitive Mermaid, a tiny, flexible manikin that, held in the palm, indicated the holder's temperament by its contortions. The Electric Sleeve Buttons moved, too. Containing "figures of Bugs, Turtles, Horses, etc., etc.," or "a ballet girl, who goes through every movement known to the most finished danseuse," these cufflinks, by the slightest hand motions, induced their lively inhabitants to produce activity on the wearer's wrists "both life like and graceful." And on the same page, but in a class by themselves, were the "Advantage or Marked Back Playing Cards"—"such," their seller candidly explained, "as Gamblers use to cheat With."

What seems striking about many of these offerings is the dual emphasis on refinement and mobility. The etiquette books promised, as one of their ads had it, to "enable every person to rub off the rough husks of ill-breeding and neglected education"—husks that had presumably formed in urban working-class neighborhoods or on midwestern farms. For a class drawing upon diverse recruits for an unprecedented kind of employment, with its cultural identity fluid and tentative, the appeal of the prefabricated gentility that these manuals hawked is understandable.[103] The preoccupation with mobility makes sense, too. For a calling whose golden age was past and whose members found increasingly less reason to want to call themselves telegraphers for life, escape from the key to bigger and better things— whether by the methodical study of a commercial primer or the more dubious route of the Paul Brothers Violet Ink Secret—was a reasoned decision. The mobility theme in the ads was pervasive. "Your Manners May Be Your Fortune" topped the copy of one etiquette-book offering, and even pulling rabbits out of a hat had entrepreneurial implications. The magic manual's sales pitch suggestively nudged the reader: "$1,000 a night has been received at the door to see these very tricks performed."

A call for self-improvement could focus as much on edification as on social climbing, of course. The *Operator* had rebuked readers in

1874 for wasting time on idle amusement and trashy literature. Instead, it advised, read Thackeray, Swift, Cervantes, *Harper's*, *Atlantic Monthly*, or the *Nation*; visit historic sites in eastern cities; study scientific principles. "The price of a ticket to a third-class theatre will buy a textbook," the editor pointed out. And there is little surprise in finding the injunctions to refinement and rising in position persisting into the 1890s. It was toward the end of that decade that the *Telegraph Age* began an "educational subjects and historical facts" column containing definitions (and phonetic pronunciations) of foreign or high-toned words, and pocket-size discussions of such diverse topics as aluminum, the Bastille, and Damon and Pythias for its eager readers to absorb.[104]

The mass-produced gentility and self-betterment in the ads (both of which appealed to individual solutions to social dissatisfaction) conform to what we know about the operator's world. But what about the kitsch—how do you reconcile autograph album verses and "hints on carving and wine at the table" with marked cards or the Electric Sleeve Button danseuse and her animal friends?

On one level, you cannot. They are incongruous, even ludicrous. But on another level, their very disjuncture makes cultural sense if they reflect a social reality itself unsettled and contradictory. A class that was yet evolving produced an equally halting and unstable set of cultural forms in which pretentiousness and vulgarity coexisted. Many male telegraphers stood with one foot in a Brussels-carpeted parlor and the other on a free-lunch bar rail.

Such an awkward social stance was confined to neither males nor telegraphers. In 1879, a reform-minded minister named Jonathan Baxter Harrison visited Fall River, Massachusetts, principally to investigate the conditions of the town's workers, but he incidentally left us a telling portrait of its lower middle class as well. "At the principal hotel I met many salesmen and book-keepers from the shops and stores of the city," Harrison later recalled,

> and when there was opportunity I sometimes made inquiries regarding the mill people,—their character and way of living. These gentlemen always appeared to be surprised that I should be interested about the operatives, or suppose there was anything in their life that was worthy of attention. At one time there was considerable excitement among my friends at the hotel on account of the announcement that a "celebrated star troupe" of actors would appear "for one night only" at the Academy of Music. It was to be a variety entertainment, to comprise a play in two acts, songs,

dances, a trapeze performance, etc.,—all of the very highest character. My companions at the table courteously advised me to go. It would be a good opportunity to see the people of the city, as the attendance would be very large. "Will the mill people be there?" I inquired. "Oh, no [with impatience]; they are not capable of appreciating anything of this kind. They have their own low amusements, but this is first-class." I went. The house was filled with well-dressed people of both sexes. The feature of the entertainment which was most to the mind of the audience was a song. A rather pretty girl came out in spangled tights, and sang half a dozen stanzas with this refrain:—

> "So, boys, keep away from the girls, I say,
>   And give them plenty of room;
> For when you are wed they will bang you till you're dead,
>   With the bald-headed end of a broom."

This was "received with great enthusiasm," as the playbills said it would be, and was encored again and again. I looked around over the applauding multitudes; the mill people were not there.[105]

But Fall River's telegraphers may well have been, for their tastes and outlook would have been much like those of the clerks and bookkeepers whom Harrison ironically captured. Important here is the double set of condescensions: of the clerks toward the mill hands, and of the old middle-class Harrison toward the clerks.

Not that old and new middle classes were strictly separate from each other. As noted, frustrated telegraphers seeking other careers did in fact move into business, medicine, law, and the like. There may have been considerable traffic between marginal white-collar work and more traditional middle-class occupations, although the latter may themselves have been on the fringes of the old middle class: dentistry, for example; one of the less reputable medical sects rather than, say, surgery; a pulpit in a plebeian or evangelical church instead of in a more prestigious Episcopalian or Presbyterian one. The fact that Harry Orr continued in telegraphy at the same time that he worked as a dentist suggests how fragile his professional practice must have been.

But the new lower middle class shaped its social character in relation to the working class, too. Many urban operators, though themselves plying white-collar careers, came of working-class backgrounds. John Evans, an English-born machinist living in Harrisburg in 1880, had one seventeen-year-old son, William, who was a book-binder, and another, twenty-four-year-old John, Jr., a telegrapher. The Evanses were a working-class family, and yet John, Jr.'s job and the experiences that he brought home with him every day surely affected all their lives and not just his. This was even more so in the case of a Baltimore family, that of Moses Hollenstein. A German immigrant, Hollenstein's hands were no doubt calloused from decades spent at the shoemaker's bench manipulating thread, awls, hammers, and lasts—in contrast to the softer hands of his three sons, Henry (a store clerk), Benjamin (a clerk in a telephone exchange), and Isaac (a telegrapher). The Hollensteins were perhaps less a blue-collar family than a gray-collar one.[106]

Even when a telegrapher's family was more homogeneous, the sense that social ambiguity attended membership in this new lower-middle stratum remains strong. Popular gentility, after all, was something that both labor aristocrats and office employees shared, along with a constellation of values that embraced notions of honest labor, wholesome leisure, education and self-education, and domesticity. Such a consensus hardly rendered class irrelevant. Far from it. Apparently similar forms meant very different things to different classes. Self-improvement for a skilled worker could mean the sort of personal and community enrichment that the phrase "eight hours for what we will" signified; to a telegrapher or clerk it might simply mean upward mobility or incipient entrepreneurship. Likewise with elaborate etiquette: what an ambitious operator might see as a wedge into a more rarefied social sphere may have evolved within its original bourgeois setting for other purposes. But what the ads in the *Operator* and the clerks and bookkeepers of Fall River and the families of John Evans and Moses Hollenstein suggest is that the lines dividing classes are sometimes more a matter of overlapping no-man's-lands than precise frontiers.[107]

4

DEAR BROTHERS AND SISTERS

Four of the young women operators in the Western Union's main New York office, so the *Boston Globe* tells us, "unable to withstand the excitement," collapsed in a faint as the Great Strike of 1883 began. It must indeed have been an exciting moment. The huge operating room, its 444 telegraphers ensconced in their glass-partitioned cubiucles, had only shortly before been filled with the clattering banality of noontime message traffic. Then a startling intruder—the "prolonged screech from a small pocket whistle"—abruptly cut off the usual sounds and motions. An operator named Frank Phillips had mounted a table in the center of the room and blown the signal, producing a momentary, breathless hush, and then, a catharsis: cheering, clapping, handkerchief waving, and for four hapless participants, swooning as well.[1]

Conventional Victorians doubtless found the incident reassuring. Under the stress of a labor dispute—men's business, after all—members of the gentler sex had succumbed in due form. In retrospect, the passing out seems less a product of feminine weakness than of the mid-July air of the seventh-floor operating room and the ugly, con-

stricting dress in which propriety clad the victims. Yet the "lady operators" of 1883 were passive victims of neither their employers nor the
social order into which they had been born. If they were bound sym-
bolically through their garb to stultifying notions of a woman's place
and purpose, they possessed other potentially liberating ties: to each
other as working women, to the men in neighboring cubbyholes as
shopmates, and to a growing body of employees throughout the nation as members of a heterogeneous class in the making. None of the
ties was neat or complete. Tension between cultural ideal and expectation on the one hand, and the realities of capitalist expansion in the
Gilded Age on the other, engendered much ambivalence and per-
plexity for a restless, adolescent America, and even more poignantly
so for such of its daughters as the striking telegraphers of 1883.

The women's participation in the Great Strike was significant to a
degree well out of proportion to their numbers. Although the walkout had left the telegraphers' union broken and its corporate adversary as powerful and arrogant as ever, something inspiring had
emerged from the events of July and August 1883: the women who
struck had shown remarkable loyalty and determination, an integrity
acknowledged by friend and foe alike. Why had they done so? Who
were these "girls" who spent fifty-four hours or more a week bent
over keys and sounders?

In the nineteenth century, most American telegraph operators were
men, although the percentage of women grew moderately throughout the postbellum years. During the industry's raucous first decade
and a half, a female telegrapher was rare. Emma A. Hunter ably managed a wire near Philadelphia in the early 1850s, while up at Dover,
New Hampshire, "an unusually quick and intelligent girl of 14"
named Ellen Laughton ran an office with equal success. Such women
were exceptional. But by the Civil War, crinoline and copper wire no
longer made for an odd combination. "You know that we—that is,
your sister operators—are rapidly growing in numbers," one woman
wrote the editor of a telegraphers' journal in 1864. He probably
needed little reminding. About four years before, an official of a New
York–Boston line had told Virginia Penny that his firm employed
some fifty women, "only at small offices," and another man familiar

with the business predicted to her that "a corps of operators and writ-
ers, composed exclusively of females," would eventually be commonplace in the industry. So it would, but not for nearly a hundred years.
Still, the number of females at the key continued to rise in the Gilded
Age. When *Harper's Monthly* described a representative country telegraph office in 1873 in the charge of a woman, it felt no need of special
comment. Reformer Frances E. Willard found the sight of "a young
woman presiding over the telegraph in offices and railway stations"
so ordinary in 1897 "that one has ceased to have even a feeling of surprise at seeing them there."[2]

Willard's description of the typical operator as young was true to
life. Like her male counterpart, the female telegrapher was usually in
her late teens or early twenties. Among a sample of 102 women operators living in New York City in 1880 culled from that year's federal
census, the average age was 21.8 years. Native birth was typical, too.
Ninety-two percent of those same New Yorkers had been born in the
United States. They were also likely to be unmarried—much more
so, in fact, than the men. All but four of the women in the 1880 group
declared themselves single.[3]

Exactly how many women were in the craft is harder to know because of the statistical caprices of the Census Bureau and the Western
Union. Not until 1900 were telegraphers tabulated separately, and
before then, statisticians obscured their actual numbers by jumbling
them together with other telegraphic employees or, as in 1890, together with telephone operators. Since most of these other employees
were men—managers, linemen, technicians, clerks, and messengers
—the figures understated the proportion of women, except in 1890,
when the inclusion of the already heavily female telephone operators
had the opposite effect on the outcome. Nevertheless, taken at a suitable discount, the figures in Table 4.1 do give a rough picture of the
small, but growing, percentage of women telegraphers. The 1890 totals are the most dubious, those for 1900 the most reliable, but the
overall trend is clear: the absolute number of women operators in the
Gilded Age rose about twentyfold, and their share of the field increased three times.[4]

Many, perhaps the bulk of them, worked in smaller facilities: isolated railroad junctions or one-woman branch offices in hotels and
other public places. When Jenny Mixsell gave up managing the Western Union's Princeton, New Jersey, office upon her marriage in 1868,
the company simply had her sister Minnie fill the job. Eighteen-year-

TABLE 4.1   WOMEN EMPLOYED IN TELEGRAPHY, 1870–1900

Year	Source	Category	No. (% of total)
1870	Census	Nonclerical telegraph employees	355 (4%)
1877	Western Union	Employees	750 (8)
1880	Census	Officials and employees	1,131 (5)
1886	Western Union	Employees	1,402 (7)
1890	Census	Telegraph and telephone operators	8,474 (16)
1900	Census	Telegraph operators	7,229 (12)

old Lizzie Clapp of Readville, Massachusetts, who sent and received at the local Boston & Providence Railroad depot in 1876, would probably have continued to do so for several more years had lightning not struck and killed her as she sat on a station windowsill during a July thunderstorm. But routine, rather than tragedy, was the lot of most women in such settings. At the time of the Great Strike, Sue Van Buskirk took care of Western Union business at Stroudsburg, Pennsylvania, and three years later, equally typically, Miss N. E. Darcy ran the company's branch office in the very different surroundings of New York's Occidental Hotel. Lady operators could be quite a bargain for their employers. Norvin Green explained in 1883 that "a few girls at some branch offices in small hotels" cost the Western Union only $15 a month, since the hotels agreed to provide the operators with room and board. Nellie Welch, who had "full charge" of the Point Arena, California, telegraph office in 1886, was unusual for her precocity—she was eleven—but not for her occupation.[5]

Traffic in the smaller offices was generally lighter than in the big urban ones, and so the skill demanded of women branch operators modest. Much of the work involved the kind of brief, personal dispatches that individuals, rather than businesses, sent. Carrie R. Wetmore's mawkish "A Message" faithfully reflected her workplace milieu, if not her actual experiences:

> Only a pale-faced woman
> Stood at my office desk,
> With eyes filled full to flowing
> Pleading for this bequest:

If I would send a message,
　A message far away,
To a son who now was dying—
　But the service she could not pay.

An easier pace in the branch and depot offices hardly made them sinecures. The telegraphic drudges of the 1871 poem "The Operator's Lament" were two women who "With fingers cold and stiff / With eyelids heavy and red . . . / . . . sat in their office alone / working for their bread." Ten or more hours at the key was common. Even the Western Union's house organ obliquely confessed that it branch operators were hard worked when it published the ironically titled "Far Niente," which began:

Pretty and pale and tired,
　She sits in her stiff backed chair
While the blazing summer sun
　Shines on her soft brown hair. . . .

It seems such an endless round,
　New York and Boston, and "A,"
Asserting their sharp, quick sounds,
　Throughout the livelong day. . . .
Have patience—the daylight dies—
　You may close your office at eight;
Have patience, tired brown eyes . . .

This legion of the pretty, pale, and tired also served as a pool of talent from which the large urban offices could draw recruits for their growing City (or Ladies') Departments. "Quite a number of places in branch offices are being filled by women," a correspondent from 195 Broadway told the *Electric Age* in 1887, "and several late branch office managers are on the day force here."[6]

Such promotions were relative, though, since women's work in the metropolitan offices usually meant the "light" or "way" wires over which an operator both sent and received slower traffic. The more remunerative and intensive "heavy" circuits (usually press or market reports) involved long stretches of sending or receiving only, and were largely the province of men.[7] Surveying employment opportunities for women in 1883, Martha Rayne found the pace of work in the Ladies' Department of Western Union headquarters moderate, and the atmosphere almost homey. She observed operators not actually working a wire "knitting, crocheting, or sewing, passing pleasantly the interval until the arrival of the next message." The company banned reading while on duty, Rayne continued, "but conversation in a low tone is encouraged."[8]

Others described the urban operating room in less idyllic terms. One "nervous little brunette" on strike in 1883 told a Boston reporter about a life at the key so taxing as to have forced her to take an extended vacation the previous year in order to keep her sanity. "I used to hear the tick of the instrument all the time and could not sleep," she declared. "I think I was going crazy. I used to jump up out of bed and read the messages that I thought were coming all the time." Nor were complaints of high pressure confined to strikers. An operator who thought telegraphy "a nice occupation" nevertheless told the Massachusetts Bureau of Labor Statistics in 1875 that "our girls all come to us looking bright, fresh and ruddy; but it is not long before they lose color, and strength seems to go with it." The female manager of a Ladies' Department admitted the same year that "from 8 A.M. to 6 P.M., with only an hour for dinner, makes too long a day for the kind of work. I am sorry to say that some of our girls eat their lunch in the room, not going out at all."[9]

If they had gone out, they would have done so through separate women's exits, for physical segregation of the sexes was as common in metropolitan offices as the division of work between heavy male and light female wires. Women had their own operating room, as at Chicago in 1869, or sat at their keys primly shielded from roving eyes behind an eight-foot-high "light partition," as at 195 Broadway in 1875.[10] But despite the combined obstacles of company regulations and mid-Victorian custom, mixing inevitably occurred. An anonymous Saint Louis operator, chafing under the restrictions of the gender bar in the local Western Union office in 1883, pouted: "Chief Operator Topliff says: 'Smirking and smiling of lady operators at the gentlemen must cease, and all conversation between the sexes must only be on business.' Thus our dearest privileges are ruthlessly denied us. The Crimes act and the suspension of *habeas corpus* will probably follow next."[11]

Topliff was a man, but the "girls" in large offices frequently worked under the watchful eyes and ears of women managers. Much of this had to do with the growing number of operators within the City departments. In 1869, chief operator Fannie Wheeler of the new Chicago Western Union office had only six young women to monitor, but by 1875, in the New York headquarters, chief operator Frances Letitia Dailey supervised between fifty-nine and seventy-five operators. Within eight years, about 120 of the cubicles there contained women, accounting for over one-quarter of the force, and in fact the proportion of female operators in a large urban office was much higher than their presence within the craft as a whole.[12] Propriety also dictated that such large aggregations of young women be subject to a peculiarly feminine manifestation of workplace discipline. Sometimes discipline outweighed femininity. Lizzie H. Snow, the Western Union's senior female manager through the mid-1870s, was something of a tyrant. "Tina," one of her charges, complained in 1870 of her "absolutism," insults, and peremptory firings "for the most trifling infringements of her ridiculous rules." Snow evidently did a bit of infringing herself, since the *Telegrapher* reported her dismissal in 1875 "for her refusal to submit to and obey certain rules and regulations of the office, which applied to her as well as to the other chief operators." Her successor, Frances Dailey, was more adept at combining corporate discipline and ladylike deportment. She employed "sedulous courtesy" in dealing with her force and demanded that they do the same among themselves. Except for intimates, the obligatory form of address in the Ladies' Department was always to begin with "Miss."[13]

Dailey was part of the female telegraphic elite. In a calling whose opportunities for mobility were fading, the prestige and economic rewards of a managership were even more elusive for women than men. A woman might aspire to a handful of other desirable berths, as press, commercial news, or broker operators. Those working for brokers were especially well favored. Great skill was required, of course, but hours were relatively short (10:00 A.M. to 3:30 P.M. in a typical Wall Street office), pay relatively high ($70 to $90), and working conditions more akin to a traditional mercantile clerkship than the industrial setting of a 195 Broadway. Very few women got that far.[14]

All of them though, like the men, entered telegraphy in one of three ways. Country-born Nattie Rogers, of the novel *Wired Love*, learned her Morse at the village depot just the way that her real-life counterparts did. Others enrolled in business schools, the (sometimes fraudulent) "telegraph colleges," or the Western Union–

sponsored course at New York's Cooper Union Institute. The daughters of urban working men usually followed a third route to the key by working as check-girls and simultaneously apprenticing themselves to the craft. Earning $15 to $25 a month, they carved learning time out of their workdays by alternately taking on each other's messenger duties during practice sessions. May Willets, Annie Boyle, Mamie Gilman, Susie McKenna, and Rosie Uth were the proud spring graduates of 1885 at Western Union headquarters, having passed a competitive wire test and won regular desks in the City Department, leaving their days as check-girls behind them.[15]

After a proper apprenticeship of four or five years, a young woman could possess the skills of a first-class operator. Certainly the very best among the craft included females. Quadruplex circuits were normally "heavy" male work, but women sat at quads too. Miss M. Mason tended Cincinnati's Pittsburgh quad in 1886, while an office mate, Miss Scofield, had "her hands full" on the Indianapolis wire. At the time of the Great Strike, four women in the main Western Union office worked the quad to Syracuse.[16] Josie Reiners, who had "one of the heaviest circuits" at 195 Broadway, was equally capable of assuming the demanding work of a broker's office. So was Minnie Swan, who would emerge as the most prominent woman member of the Brotherhood of Telegraphers. Clara Morley, of Bloomington, Illinois, had a reputation as the "champion market-report operator of the West." Back east, in 1898, the same sort of talent won New Yorker Emma A. Vanselow her second telegraphic tournament prize—hardly surprising for a first-class operator in the Commercial News Department of 195 Broadway. Highly skilled, too, was Beda Louise Arnold (her mother had also been a Lady of the Key), who handled the United Press wire at Bridgeport, Connecticut, from the mid-1880s through the end of the century.[17]

As in Arnold's case, refined Morse skills could see a woman through many years in the craft. Kansas native Christina Barnum, a thirty-eight-year-old widow working a wire in New York in 1880, was still so employed seven years later, sharing the *New York Herald*'s ship news reporting station on Long Island with a male colleague. At age twenty, Laura Moore sat in the City Department at 195 Broadway; twelve years later, in 1887, her employer had changed—she now worked for the B & O—but her occupation had not. Some of Moore's shopmates of the mid-1870s also stayed in the field: by 1884, after nine years, Emma Charlier, Anne McShea, C. Breier, and A. Frazee were all first-class operators, and still at Western Union headquarters. Josie Reiners's enviable skill and reputation in 1886 rested on six or more years spent on a circuit. Miss Sinisbaugh, who rose to be City traffic chief of the huge Broadway complex in 1887, had been telegraphing at least twice as long. The Western Union's top female manager, Frances Dailey, was a veteran of eighteen years' service.[18]

But few women were career telegraphers. The large proportion of them in their late teens and early twenties meant that most left the craft at about the time that they would have begun to master it. In this respect, they were like other contemporary "working girls" who passed those same years as breadwinners, with the frequent expectation that marriage would shortly follow. And so Kate Donovan was triply unrepresentative of her sister operators in postbellum America: a thirty-year-old "manageress" in 1880, she was still a manager six years later—and still "Miss."[19] Even in an occupation already notorious for high turnover, the short tenure of women was axiomatic, and the Western Union shaped its policy accordingly. "These ladies," *Journal of the Telegraph* editor James D. Reid explained in 1870, "in the ordinary course of nature, must in time become the lights and managers of homes." That made it unlikely that they would become the managers of telegraph offices. "Very few of them expect to make it the occupation of a life time," declared Norvin Green in 1883. "They are generally looking forward to a time when they can lay it aside, so they do not apply themselves as the men do." Chief operator O. A. Gurley of the Cleveland Western Union said much the same thing. Women lacked the kind of familiarity with the world of business and its terminology that made a first-rate operator, and they did not bother to remedy their ignorance. But then again, why should they? "With most of them," said Gurley, "it is only something to support themselves until they marry." Unlike many European government telegraph services, the Western Union did not force its women to quit upon marriage. It simply expected that most would do so on their own.[20]

Most did, even when talented and promising operators. As a quad woman at Cincinnati, Miss M. Mason was surely an accomplished telegrapher, but when she became Mrs. Beckett in 1886, she abandoned her craft. "Mrs. B. will continue to work here for a short time," a colleague informed the *Electric Age,* "until she and hubby are ready to go housekeeping." Whatever economic advantage a two-breadwinner household might have had for the Becketts was far less pressing than the weight of culture and convention. Respectable middle-class (and working-class) wives did not enter the labor market. Likewise, the expectation that most young working women would—indeed, *should* —soon marry also guided choices about a career. So, though telegraphy was even more barren a field for women than men, the explanations of Norvin Green and others that spoke of female operators' halfhearted commitment to the wires and wholehearted commitment to matrimony had some truth in them.[21]

The whole truth, however, was more complex and less flattering to Green and his associates. The low salaries and meager opportunities accorded most women telegraphers had as much to do with their performance at the key as did daydreaming about trousseaux and hearthside contentment. Dead-end berths and thin pay envelopes were both cause and result of the high turnover of the "girls." A structural bias that typed certain positions as "woman's work"—and by definition less skilled, less well paid, and less likely to lead anywhere—was not confined to telegraphy. The various clerical jobs opening up to more and more young women in the same period also obeyed economic and cultural imperatives that propelled a cycle of stunted careers. "The conviction that woman's place was in the home served to justify her restriction to lower-level clerical work," Margery Davies notes of the practice. "If women eventually were going to stop working to marry and have children, what was the point of promoting them to managerial or even higher-level clerical positions?"[22]

It was the same with telegraphy. Nor is this a matter of glibly reading the situation through twentieth-century radical and feminist lenses. Discussing the question of women's success within the craft in 1865, Lewis H. Smith, editor of the *Telegrapher*, wrote: "The great fault has been in simply teaching a young lady the rudiments of the business and then cooping her up in a room by herself or with others of her sex, away from all chance of gaining knowledge, or emulating those who are in the first rank. If men and women could change places, how think you the former would come out? If we were hampered and excluded as women have been for centuries, where would be our boasted superiority?" Nearly two decades later, the *Operator's* W. J. Johnston made essentially the same point. "As matters now stand," he argued, "there are no inducements to women to give excellent service. No matter how expert they become, how faithfully they labor, how polite and attentive they are to the patrons of the wires, there is no hope of promotions for them." Their "taking no pride in their work and looking forward to marriage as a welcome means of escape from distasteful drudgery" were hardly surprising under the circumstances, Johnston concluded.[23] Young women had been working and marrying long before the existence of the Western Union, and both the company and young women had something to offer each other. But the Western Union emerged from the partnership with much the better bargain.

It was the rare lady operator who entered the field as a lark. Telegraphy meant serious breadwinning, not diversion or "pin money." For one thing, even mediocre skill was a matter of at least one or two years' training and practice, during which period a student had to otherwise support herself (as the check-girls did while they learned on the job) or rely on the cushion of family, friends, or savings.[24] Either way, learning the craft did not come cheaply. In a society whose women ideally did not work outside the home, the presence of a woman in the telegraph office meant a need to be there.

"A majority of the lady operators in the telegraphic profession are with us from necessity and not from choice," the *Electric Age* noted in 1887. Denying charges that women remained in telegraphy to go husband hunting, a Cincinnatian wrote that most of her sisters "follow the profession of operating for a livelihood." It often meant the livelihood of others, too. During the 1883 walkout, a Boston telegrapher said that "a good many" of her colleagues gave "all they earn from week to week" to help prop up dependent relatives. One New York striker went through an agonizing sequence of resigning from the brotherhood and then rejoining her comrades because she had initially feared for the wages that were the only income for her invalid mother. Predicting on the third day of the strike that the "girls" would soon return to work, the Western Union's William Dealy explained that they were "bound to come back, for they are in financial straits." And after the union's defeat an agitated and indignant Charlotte Smith, head of the Women's National Industrial League, addressing the Senate Education and Labor Committee's hearings in behalf of women operators refused reemployment, told the lawmakers that some had "aged parents dependent upon them for support."

So did Linda Girard. A Philadelphia branch office operator for the Reading Railroad's telegraph subsidiary who found her $30 salary inadequate to meet her family responsibilities, she sent the firm's president a pathetic series of notes in 1883 requesting a raise. "I would not ask you if it were not so pressing," she wrote that January. "The winter is hard & now we have no one to help us & we have to support Mother." Statistical evidence also indicates that female operators were full-fledged wage earners. Among a sample of 102 of them living in New York City in 1880, a solid majority—59.8 percent—were either self-supporting or part of families lacking a male breadwinner as head of the household.[25]

Varying circumstances sent young women into the cubicles of the Western Union. A genuine need to work did not always imply desperate poverty. Empty stomachs and empty coal scuttles at home could force a daughter to learn Morse, but so could perceptions of appropriate comfort and status.

Some salaries did meet needs that were vital. Twenty-two-year-old Georgianna Rodman was the sole support of her widowed mother in 1880. That was also true of Agnes Bradley and Augusta Boyton. The Flanagan sisters, Ellen and Annie, supported their mother—likewise widowed—with the aid of their laborer brother, but all three also had to support another brother who was paralyzed. Nor was a "normal" family, with its breadwinning patriarch, always a sure sign that daughters were spared the rigors of the labor market. For Ellen Ryan, twenty-eight-year-old daughter of an unskilled Irish immigrant, working a wire may have meant meeting the elemental demands of food, clothing, and shelter. Perhaps the same was the case with another New Yorker, Ann Clark. Her father worked, too, but his earnings as a watchman were no doubt low. Ann's salary as a telegrapher could have meant that the Clarks' daily breakfast table contained something more substantial and appetizing than the bread and coffee to which many poor families confined themselves.[26]

A daughter's wage could also augment family income to satisfy important, if less pressing, desires: an upright for the parlor, a brother's education, capital for a family business, or a standard of living commensurate with middle-class or labor-aristocratic notions of respectability. "Jo," a female operator in Toronto in 1875, argued that surplus daughters puttering around the house were simply "a great waste of material," for "if, as is so often the case, their father's income happens to be too small to maintain them in comfort, is it not far better and more sensible for some of them to start out in the world and earn their own living, than to stay at home vainly endeavoring to find some plan of making one dollar do the work of two?" That kind of reasoning influenced the Emerson family in Lida Churchill's 1882 novel, *My Girls*. The oldest of the six children, daughter Cecil, became an operator in order to earn "more than would suffice for her barest necessities" to supplement the wages of her father, a Rhode Island carpenter and Civil War veteran. And the same kind of reasoning may have influenced a real family very much like the Emersons, that of Albert C. Clapp, a paperhanger in the Boston suburb of Hyde Park and also father of six. In 1872, his oldest daughter, Lizzie, then fourteen, began telegraphing in the local railroad depot. Lizzie's wages could have served as a kind of economic insurance for the Clapps—Albert told the census enumerator in 1880 that he had been out of work for a year—but they could also have helped to maintain a way of life for the large family worthy of a substantial Yankee mechanic.[27] Like her two brothers, Mary Sheridan worked a key in New York in 1880, and their three salaries, together with that of their father, a clerk, probably underwrote a thoroughly middle-class existence. In Molly Fitzpatrick's case, her contribution certainly did. Also a New York operator in 1880, her income, and that of her widowed mother as a music teacher, were enough to add a live-in servant to their household.[28]

Retaining the accoutrements of affluence was as important as aquiring them. In the late nineteenth century, the caprices of a market economy could quickly and dramatically change a family's situation. The solidity of the great American middle class was often more apparent than real, and having a daughter capable of working could help to check a family's downward slide. Cindy Aron's study of federal clerks suggests that a small but significant number of middle-class women sought government positions to do just that when sickness, death, or the business cycle rendered male breadwinners impotent.[29]

The same circumstances created lady operators. "In the vicissitudes of life, the changes of fortune and the decrees of fate in our large cities," declared Norvin Green in 1890, "so many young women are thrown upon their resources that it is a blessing to find this new field of employment." Self-serving as always, Green's comments nevertheless described a part of contemporary reality. So did *My Girls*, one of whose characters, Grace Farwell, became a telegrapher after her father, a cotton mill superintendent, had to retire under the pressure of failing health. "Compelled by the failure and subsequent death of her father to support herself, or to become a burden upon her mother," Nattie Rogers, another fictional heroine of the period, also chose the key.[30]

Demographic pressures, too, put women between glass partitions. Even if they wanted to, not all women married. There is evidence that the population suffered an imbalance in the ratio of men to women, and that, as the *New York Times* concluded in 1869, there were "in the New-England and Middle States, for instance, a quarter of a million young women who must support themselves, and who cannot reasonably look forward to any matrimonial alliance which will relieve them of this inevitable necessity." Some women operators did stay at the key rather than count on the certainty of marriage. Apphira Eaton, thirty-seven in 1880 when the census recorded her living with her brother and sister-in-law, was likely to remain single. The same was true of Frances Whipple, also thirty-seven, who boarded alone.[31]

Population vagaries and marriage patterns affected Irish-American women even more than those of other ethnic groups and contributed to a goodly number of them becoming telegraphers. Reacting to the trauma of the Great Famine of the 1840s, the Irish had sharply reduced the proportion of their young adults who married at home, and sent off many others—young women in particular—to seek a better life as emigrants. Conditions in the United States were different, but the new patterns of marrying late or not at all persisted, and it became neither shameful nor unusual for Irish-American sons and daughters to remain unwed. The social and economic consequences were especially important for the women: Irish-Americans were more likely than other white women to be independent, lifelong wage earners. What's more, as Hasia Diner found, they "could take advantage of opportunities in fields like teaching and nursing which essentially required that women choose between job or matrimony." They could also enter telegraphy. In 1900, canvassing female telegraph and telephone operators with foreign-born parents, the Census Bureau reported that a large plurality of them, 41 percent, were of Irish extraction (the next closest, the Germans, accounted for only 16 percent). And among a sample of seventy women telegraphers in New York City in 1880 with at least one immigrant parent, nearly three-fourths of them—71.4 percent—turned out to be Irish. It was no coincidence that the unmarried, thirty-year-old career manager Kate Donovan had an Irish mother and father. Frances Dailey, another prominent woman chief, was very likely of similar background. Telegraphy attracted many Hibernian men too, of course, but a unique set of forces—demography, contemporary history, and culture— explains what sent so many Irish-American women into the craft.[32]

Subsistence and custom were sharp goads, but choice, as well as compulsion, turned young women into operators. The very nature of the calling made this so, since a fairly long period of training and the need for a good common school education restricted entry to the field. A woman did not become an operator with the same speed and informality that she became a mill hand, domestic, or sales clerk. The notion of choice for working women goes beyond the specific conditions of telegraphy. One student of antebellum Yankee mill "girls" argues that they went to work not from dire need but from a combination of having become economically superfluous in their parents' farm households, an attraction to the excitement and variety of city life, and a desire for independence. All were interrelated, and the last seems especially important, since it at once raised the family's living standard (directly or indirectly) and provided a degree of autonomy for the working woman. A daughter's self-sufficiency and choice were more important than they would immediately appear, since status as a wage earner, with its corollary of independence, undermined parental (and, weightier still, patriarchal) authority. This is clear in the case of Irish-American women, with their proclivity for breadwinning and celibacy.[33]

All of this implied choice. "For my part," one operator told an *Irish World* correspondent during the Great Strike, "I can say I could live without the Company, but I have always desired honest work and consequent independence." Asserted another woman in 1875: "It is *not* a choice between telegraphy and starvation. The ability and independence which enables [*sic*] a lady to become a successful operator would gain her a living in a dozen other ways." And the sort of choice and self-determination inherent in being an operator inevitably touched on the question of marriage. Made fatherless, *Wired Love*'s Nattie Rogers "chose the more independent but harder course," by learning Morse, as "she was not the kind of girl to sit down and wait for some one to come along and marry her, and relieve her of the burden of self support." Self-support was a far less burdensome prospect than that of a joyless match to Jo, a Canadian operator in the mid-1870s. "Many women accept the first man who offers himself," she wrote, simply for the sake of securing some one to take care of them, while if they were taught to take care of themselves, they could afford to wait for some one whom it would not be perjury for them to swear to love and honor; or, in case such a one never came to them, they could live comfortable, happy lives alone. I admit, freely enough, that a happy marriage is the best possible fate for a woman, but if she is unable to secure *that*, her whole life should not be a failure in consequence.

Even the clear-headed and free-spirited Jo had to genuflect before prevailing convention: marriage was ideally right for a woman. But the prompting of other forces—family needs and aspirations, folkways, and the desire to control and enjoy one's own life—meant that being a Lady of the Key was right too.[34]

Social origins as well as economic exigencies led a woman into the telegraph office. Operators came from varying backgrounds—more so, in any case, than contemporary mill hands, laundresses, or settlement house workers—but all of them, in entering the craft, were at once making and being made part of an unprecedented social stratum, a new lower middle class.

In contrast, some had grown up amid the more traditional surroundings of rural America. These were native-born, mostly Protestant young women, the daughters of farmers, professionals, small tradesmen, or mechanics. Their antebellum counterparts had flocked to New England's textile mills until speedups and immigrant masses drove them out, and they now held keys where their mothers or grandmothers had held bobbins. What the Massachusetts Bureau of Labor Statistics in 1872 called "intelligent American women,—girls such as today find employment as bookkeepers, telegraph-operators, compositors, teachers, artists, etc.," probably accounted for most of the nation's female operators up through the 1870s.[35] The rural woman operator was a stock character in the subgenre of telegraph fiction. Walter Phillips evoked his native Massachusett countryside by creating Narcissa, the charming but "by no means cultivated" daughter of a farmer's widow who applied her mediocre skills to an out-of-the-way office. The more proficient Nattie Rogers, of *Wired Love*, also had rustic origins.[36]

Nattie and Narcissa had plenty of real models. Lisiades Atherton, a Milwaukee operator equally noteworthy for her skill and her untimely death at nineteen, had begun to send and receive three years before in Hastings, Minnesota. Lizzie Clapp also died while still in her teens, the victim of a freak accident while on duty, but she was otherwise representative of the Yankee "girls" who served as village operators. Her father Albert, a Massachusetts native, and her mother, Louisa, born in Maine, no doubt raised Lizzie with injunctions to piety, hard work, and sobriety, for she belonged to the local lodge of the Good Templars, and several members of that abstemious order, "in full regalia," took part in her funeral cortege. Happier to relate are the experiences of two other small-town telegraphers, Fannie and Julia Wheeler. Residents of Vinton, Iowa, they probably learned the craft in the late 1860s from their father, W. H. Wheeler, station agent at the local depot. Julia, the younger sister, took care of the Vinton office, later quitting to attend school, but Fannie, perhaps more talented and certainly more ambitious, rose to successively higher positions and bigger towns: first to Waterloo, then to Chicago (where she headed the Ladies' Department in 1869), and then on to Omaha. By 1875, with "a responsible position at a good salary," she called San Francisco her home.[37] Fannie was significant not only for her typically native, rural origins and her atypically rewarding career, but also for her cityward movement. Although some, like Julia, remained country operators, the nature of the medium, inextricably part of the "metropolitan corridor" of industrializing America, made telegraphy an implicitly urban occupation, and Fannie joined millions of others drawn to the nation's growing population centers. The new lower middle class of technical and clerical workers that included operators was really an *urban* middle class.[38]

Those who had begun operating in the railway stations of drowsy hamlets mingled with city-bred women in the large metropolitan offices. Like many of the newcomers, some came from native, middle-class backgrounds. New Yorker Emily Sutherland, twenty in 1880, lived with her widower uncle, a bank cashier. Eliza Edward also lived with an uncle while she worked as an operator; he was a stationer. As with female government clerks in this period, the association of a relatively desirable form of women's work with those of middle-class origins makes sense.[39] Probably into the 1870s, urban operators were as likely to have such a background as their country sisters. But by the time of the Great Strike, if not earlier, a large proportion of the telegraph "girls" in the cities were the daughters of workingmen, often from Irish families.

Part of the evidence for this is impressionistic. In 1869, for example, the *New York Times* noted that the Cooper Union's free telegraphy course for young women had been a response to "the late strikes of the working classes." Such schools, whether legitimate or fly-by-night, attracted a working-class clientele. When the *Electric Age* reprinted exposés of fraudulent "colleges" in the late 1880s, the typical victim was a shopgirl who had imagined telegraphy as an escape hatch for her and "an invalid mother from a dirty sixth-floor tenement apartment."[40]

Part of the evidence is inferential. By the late nineteenth century, second- and third-generation Irish-American women were eschewing the menial jobs that their immigrant forebears had settled for and, in swelling numbers, entering professional or semiprofessional fields: in hospitals as nurses, in classrooms as teachers, and in offices as stenographers, bookkeepers, clerks, and "typewriters." For the most part, they came of working-class parents, and their achievements, along with those of their brothers, meant that their ethnic group had "arrived"—as did the success of the several Irish-Americans who won important mayoralties—and its contribution of recruits to a middle class undergoing recasting was significant. The cultural dimensions of this I will explore below; important here are the origins of women plying white-collar pursuits. One such pursuit was telegraphy.[41]

To this soft evidence of impression and inference I would add some hard data. From among a sample of forty New York operators whose father's (or male household head's) occupation in 1880 I could determine, 65 percent were blue-collar men, evenly divided between skilled and unskilled (or semiskilled) workers. Not surprisingly, the second largest group of fathers (22.5 percent) were white-collar employees: clerks such as the fathers of Sarah Weeks and Ellen Spencer, or Maine-born Bella Stover's stepfather, a traveling agent. But the large percentage of craftsman or laborer fathers remains remarkable. So does the Irish element. Over half of the fathers (52.5 percent) were native Hibernians, and if Irish descent were the criterion, the figure would surely be higher. Peering into the households of some of these women shows this mixture of class, ethnicity, and generation at work. We do not know what Mary Hickey's immigrant father's occupation was, since he was laid up with pleurisy and so, to the census taker, simply "at home." But Mary helped to support the family, as did her two sisters and two brothers—a book folder, dressmaker, shipping clerk, and, like Mary, a telegrapher. At fifteen, Louise Finigan may still have been a check-girl, but her brother was already a full-fledged operator, and both of them supplemented the earnings of their father, a shoemaker by trade. Mary Trenamin's link with Ireland, telegraphy, and the working class was through her father, a thirty-seven-year-old lineman. If May Sheridan's father hoped to see his children do better than he had as a janitor, he must have been pleased that she and her two brothers had all learned their Morse and now had a place at the key. Ellen Gartlony's father was dead, and his occupation once he arrived in America remains a mystery, but both Ellen and her brother were operators. Nineteen-year-old Elizabeth Pollard was also fatherless. Although she was born in England, her parents were Irish, and by 1880, she joined two brothers in the telegraph office (one an operator, the other a clerk) to provide for their mother and two siblings in school. Anne McShea's only brother had progressed so far as to announce himself as a "broker" to the census enumerator. Anne, of course, was an operator. She and her brother left the house each morning to enter a world of work far removed from that of their father, an Irish-born streetcar driver.[42]

Since most employments open to females were physically demanding, dirty, stultifying, and ill paid, white-collar work was especially attractive. True, telegraphy was not easy, and its women suffered from a discriminatory salary structure, but it contrasted favorably with factory, laundry, domestic service, and the various retail clerking positions. It was, in short, "a nice occupation, and better than standing in stores or working in mills," as one woman described her vocation in 1875.[43]

Operators took more home on payday than the average working woman. With a few exceptions, they were among the best paid of their sex. In 1869, the *New York Times* found telegraphers, at $10 a week, in the same range as schoolteachers, compositors, and wood engravers. They were not so fortunate as actresses ($15) or editors ($18), but better off than book folders ($8) and hoop-skirt makers ($7), and much better off than paper box makers ($5) and live-in domestics ($2.50). At the time of the Great Strike, operators still ranked fairly high as female wage earners. One Boston survey gave a telegraphers' average weekly salary as $6.87, which approximated those of copyists ($6.78) and bookkeepers ($6.55), fell behind that of nurses and proofreaders ($9.50), but well outdistanced those of cap makers ($4.42), cotton mill operatives ($3.94), and cash girls ($2.02).[44]

Prestige, as well as income, was higher for lady operators. Telegraphy demanded a general education above the average.[45] Its workday milieu required standards of dress and deportment unusual in the experience of most female breadwinners. It was appropriately feminine because it savored of domesticity. A woman compelled to earn a living, *Godey's Lady's Book* had decreed in 1853, should be guided toward "all in-door pursuits" since "these harmonize with her natural love of home and its duties, from which she should never, in idea, be divorced." Telegraphy fit easily enough into that scheme. Little wonder, wrote the Western Union's James Reid in 1870, that "so simple, so clean, so apparently domestic" an employment as telegraphy should draw on women. And it was as respectable as it was domestic. Not only did Frances Dailey allow her force at 195 Broadway to do needlework between dispatches, but she made "Miss" mandatory in the operating room, much as it might have been in any polite setting. "It does not soil their dresses," Martha Rayne reported, "it does not keep them in a standing posture; it does not, they say, compromise them socially." Telegraphy was a genteel way for a young woman to earn a living.[46]

This was gentility of a new kind, though, no longer within a patrician setting, but tracing the cultural ambit of an emerging stratum of "brain workers." As with male telegraphers, the experience of the women reveals the uncertainty, contradiction, and synthesis that marked the gestation of this new class.

Three forces molded the operators socially. The Western Union did, of course. Like its wire network, the giant corporation was unprecedented. But the operating room also partook of the traditional world of the countinghouse: the "boiled" shirts and frock coats, the inkwells and ledgers, the "Mr." and "Miss" that imbued employees with a standardized reserve and dignity. This was all old middle class, at least in form—corporate discipline was as much a motive as mercantile courtesy in Western Union rule book prescriptions for gentlemanly language and behavior. Second, some operators had come out of that same old middle class: daughters of rural middling families or the city bourgeoisie who settled (or perhaps fell down) into telegraphy. They brought their past with them into the office. The third influence came from the working-class neighborhoods of urban America where check-girls and their older sisters grew up and continued to live during their tenure at the key. Representing a significant part of the new work force, these women were sensitive gauges of the tensions that class formation involved.

In a sense, they were neither working class nor middle class, or perhaps they were simultaneously both. Entering telegraphy from working-class homes involved mobility, but not necessarily upward; moving sideways was possible, too. Still, working-class women did entertain notions of moving "up." Irish women, for example, were a crucial link between their largely working-class backgrounds and the realm of the middle class. "Observers both within and without the Irish communities," notes Hasia Diner, "agreed that women in families, as wives, daughters, and sisters, brought the family 'up,' civilized them by introducing the manners and accoutrements of the middle class." It was no easy task, for Diner adds that "Irish men resented this effort to make them over into refined Americans." The working-class "girl" who became an operator might have to fight a constant cultural tug-of-war with her family, and perhaps with herself, too.[47]

But not always. The lower-middle-class world of the telegraph office sometimes converged with existing blue-collar values rather than jarred them. Labor aristocrats could accept their daughters' entry into clerical work both because it kept family living standards comfortable and because ideas of proper appearance, behavior, and taste were as much a part of the respectable working-class home— what Leon Fink aptly christens "popular gentility"—as of the middle-class one.[48] But convergence was not stasis. Between blue-collar father and white-collar daughter, a dialectic was creating a gray-collar family.

Augusta Killian, a New York telegrapher in 1880, belonged to such a family. Her German immigrant father was a stonemason, and, like him, two of Augusta's siblings had working-class occupations: one brother as a streetcar driver, and one sister as a silk factory hand. But another brother, who worked in a store, inhabited the same lower-middle-class cosmos as his operator sister. Laura Moore's father was a painter, and her brother followed the same trade. Yet her sister, a saleslady, shared Laura's nebulous position of being of, but no longer in, the working class. In Louisa Cummings's case, her two sisters were dressmakers, but her brother was a lawyer's assistant. As office folk, he and Louisa would have had a good deal in common—at least much more than with their father, an Irish immigrant who worked in the unambiguously blue-collar setting of the janitor. Cultural instability, if not tension, was inherent in gray-collar families. Thomas P. Getz's 1889 vaudeville ditty "Since My Daughter Plays on the Typewriter" had a troubled working-class paterfamilias declare of his white-collar daughter:

> She cries in her sleep, "Your letter's to hand,"
> She calls her old father esquire;
> And the neighbors they shout when my daughter turns out,
> There goes Bridget Typewriter Maguire.

Or Bridget Telegraph Maguire.[49]

An impression persists that many operators struck a precarious social balance as children of the working class and pioneers in a new mass middle stratum. Hewing to standards of feminine reticence and refinement was part of this. Such behavior was not simply a sham or mindless aping of middle-class forms. The piano solos that several New York women strikers played aboard an excursion steamer during the walkout had doubtless first been performed amid the gewgaws and polite silence of someone's front parlor. After the defeat, Charlotte Smith, the reformer who had taken a number of unemployed women telegraphers under her wing, told a Senate hearing that she could not discuss their plight in detail "because very many of them would feel it very keenly if their names should be mentioned." When they did speak, they chose their words carefully. "The ladies are among our most earnest members," declared one brotherhood man in New York, "but they do not like the word 'strike.' They think it sounds more dignified to say 'resign.'"[50]

Dignity and refinement found expression in appearance, too, for dress is a prime statement of social position—or of one's perception of one's social position. Respectable dress was required in the telegraph office, of course. And as Martha Rayne reported in 1883, dressing up to her occupation could nearly bankrupt a young operator: "Her office dress, even if she made it herself, will take eight dollars out of her pocket-book; her bills for other clothes, for shoes, for hats —well, it is easy enough for her to expend ten dollars every week in the year, and her salary is not nine dollars." Most probably did make their own wardrobe. One of the force at 195 Broadway, noting that "lady operators of this office are among the most tastefully attired working women in this City," explained "that in many cases the very skill and taste so displayed are the production of their own brains and artistic fingers. Many of them could testify to 'burning the midnight oil' for this purpose, and that, too, after a long and hard day's work at the key."[51]

The elegant exterior that belied an operator's economic fragility sometimes hinted at a cultural fragility to match. A *Boston Globe* reporter described a striker he interviewed as "tastefully dressed," with "a parasol and satchel in her hand." He continued: "No one would have taken her for a telegraph operator, simply because there is nothing distinctive about an operator that a casual eye can distinguish. To the trained observer, however, there are certain characteristics that are unmistakable." What were they? He never shared them with his readers, but he seemed to imply that the operator's clothes had been "off" in subtle details that in effect hung a sign around her neck saying LOWER MIDDLE CLASS. On the street, the daughter of a surgeon or Presbyterian minister would not have taken the telegrapher for one of her own kind.[52]

The world of the women operators bespoke a peculiarly wobbly gentility in other ways—and not always due to working-class origins. Those without family, or who struck out on their own, often lived in boardinghouses. Such places varied, of course, but there seems to have been much of the socially nebulous about them that resonates so well with the lower-middle-class universe of nineteenth-century America. The Hotel Norman, in which *Wired Love*'s Nattie Rogers rented a room, was not actually a boardinghouse, but its environment was probably similar to that in which many young operators like Nattie passed their evenings. Nattie's back room was surrounded by a dreary montage of "sheds in greater or less degree of dilapidation, a sickly grape-vine, a line of flapping sheets, an overflowing ash-barrel," "the dulcet notes of old rag-men, the serenades of musical cats," and "the strains of a cornet played upon at intervals from nine P.M. to twelve, with the evident purpose of exhausting superfluous air in the performer's lungs."[53]

Even the noon meal posed a problem for an operator's cultural integrity. Despite middle-class dress, operators often kept down expenses by bringing their lunches along with them, as might an ordinary working man or woman. The imperfect fit between tasteful dress and plebeian dinner pails was no trivial point. Dorothy Richardson (herself not an operator), who had grown up in a middle-class home in rural Pennsylvania, recalled that while job hunting in New

York City around 1900, she put propriety before nourishment, skip-ping lunch, "which I could have had done up for me at the boarding-house without extra charge, but which my silly vanity did not allow me to carry around under my arm." But for many operators—less proud or less firmly middle class in the old mold—toting a lunch box was no problem.[54]

Speech, too, indicated the social limbo in which a telegrapher often lived and worked. Very little from the mouths of contemporary La-dies of the Key survives, unfortunately, but one Boston woman did talk to a reporter. She was the same "tastefully dressed" operator whose clothing contained arcane signs of her social place. And so, I think, did her speech:

> "The truth is," she remarked, "that although most of the lady operators are willing to cooperate in every way to bring about the just demands of the strikers, they rather hang back from public demonstrations."
>
> "Why?"
>
> "Well, I suppose because most of them are well-bred women with con-siderable refinement. They have to be to make good operators. I don't know any other reason."

And a bit later:

> "But you will generally find that the girls employed as operators are bet-ter off then almost any other class of women who have to earn their living because," she added, "having acquired a good education, and coming from respectable families, they are not apt to be so extravagant or foolish as some others."

The affirmations of refinement, respectable families, good education, and of proper feminine reticence have a slightly strained, almost defensive quality. Likewise the determination to distance operators from "extravagant" and "foolish" others—presumably overdressed factory women. Not that she did not sincerely believe herself to be refined and well bred, and act accordingly; but the refinement of the gray-collar world was new and tentative, and so eagerly, even over-eagerly, asserted.[55]

The same kind of tension surfaced when someone momentarily strayed from the bounds of refined speech. The *Electric Age*'s Edward Delaney ("De"), in "A Lady Operator's Reverie" of 1887, sketched the supposed random thoughts of a bored young woman working a key at Western Union headquarters. "Gracious," she muses at one point, "how I use slang here, lately. I must quit that, it's not ladylike." Disgusted by the tobacco chewing of a male co-worker, she tells herself sarcastically, "He'd be a nice man for a refined girl to marry, wouldn't he?" Still contemplating matrimony, she thinks further on: "There ought to be a law to make all rich men marry poor girls and all poor men marry rich girls. Then there would be an equal division of property. Ain't that a Henry George idea, eh?" The point is not that the cynical and conservative "De" knew what female operators thought or felt, but he does draw a plausible picture of a preoccupation with refinement and of grammatical lapses and bits of slang that he could have genuinely observed in working with some of these women.[56]

Nor is he the only witness. In 1879, the *Operator*'s correspondent from 195 Broadway icily complained that "the ladies who, in their anxiety to be considered up with the times, stoop to the use of slang, make a most deplorable mistake. To hear them utter the now familiar 'way off,' with an ease that denotes constant repetition, produces a feeling of disgust in those who make the slightest claim to refinement of feeling. It is bad enough for a man to come to this, but there is no excuse whatever for one who pretends to be a lady." Slang was not in itself an unfailing guide to class origins, but many telegraphers were freshly minted "ladies" from blue-collar homes. Their dress, speech, and mannerisms, if sometimes awkward, were signs of having to straddle a line between two social worlds. Members and makers of a new lower middle class, they were in flux and sui generis.[57]

"The brotherhood have induced so many of the young women to join them," John Mitchell remarked a few days before the Great Strike, "that the title of the organization might well be changed to 'The Brotherhood and Sisterhood of Telegraphers.'"[58] Mitchell was right, but less because of the sheer numbers of women operators who became unionists and strikers than for the behavior and commitment of those who did so. Part of what makes the 1883 walkout important is the disproportionate role that its female actors played.

In the broader context of Gilded Age telegraphy, women were likewise far more important, in their male counterparts' eyes, than their numbers alone warranted. With less than chivalrous motives, many

Knights of the Key focused attention and concern on the women: attention on their small but growing share of the field, and concern that they would undermine the salary structure and turn what had been a promising new vocation into one as ill paid and feminized as the needle trades. This did not actually happen until well into the next century, but the fears were reasonable enough, given the state of the craft in the postbellum years. The number of operators, male as well as female, rose at the same time that opportunities declined. Nominal salaries shrank, and "plug factories" (telegraph "colleges," whose purpose was to mass-produce telegraphers) seemed as ubiquitous as corner saloons. What's more, women were invading the traditionally male bailiwick of the office as clerks, secretaries, and "typewriters," and taking much less money to perform those jobs. The same was true of telephony, which, unlike telegraphy, was heavily female almost from the start (the telephone, like the typewriter, was "gender neutral," and so easier to cast as women's work at its introduction). Feminization proceeded unevenly throughout the late nineteenth century, but it was a plausible threat to male telegraphers.[59]

And so they often viewed the women who shared their calling with ambivalence, if not downright hostility. As early as the 1860s, some tried to tack a NO GIRLS ALLOWED sign to the craft's front door. "What operators should do to protect themselves from 'hard times,'" wrote one in 1864, "is to keep the ladies out of the National Telegraphic Union, and also as much as possible off the lines." The next year, the NTU virtually followed his advice when its convention refused to adopt a clause explicitly welcoming female members.[60] Antiwoman sentiments persisted through the 1870s and 80s. Men charged women operators with poaching in the male preserve of wage earning and, by swelling the reservoir of operators, degrading the status and well-being of the craft. Even the egalitarian impulse of 1883 failed to erase such attitudes. "We have shrunk from saying anything that might wound the feelings of any of our sister operators," a Washington man told the *Telegraphers' Advocate* in 1885, and then went on to inflict just such a wound. Another accused the women who remained in the business of being self-defeating, since by doing so they had "reduced their own prospects by reducing salaries to a point where men cannot marry." Such arguments usually included the corollary that woman's place was in the conjugal home and not the telegraph office. An 1887 letter to the *Electric Age* predicted that the competition between male and female telegraphers, and ensuing falling salaries, "if followed to its legitimate conclusion, will break up the marriage state and result in what? community life, polygamous life or barbarous life?"[61]

Real and imagined corporate policies stimulated these fears. Managers did see advantages in using female operators. They were cheaper to begin with, and easier than men to keep that way because docile and tractable. They were also more honest and reliable. Lady operators seldom, if ever, slipped a hand into the office till or showed up for work with a hangover. "As regards expertness, quickness of intelligence, and faithfulness to duty, they are unexceptionable," the *Boston Herald* pointed out, "and were it not that comparisons are odious, it could be borne out by statistics that women as managers and operators in small offices are better bargains for the company than men." Those fearing a female invasion did not confine the danger to branch offices. "It is understood," a member of the Buffalo Western Union force wrote before the Great Strike, "that the policy of the manager now is to fill all vacancies with ladies—at about one-half the price formerly paid, of course."[62]

Men invoking the female threat frequently linked it with the "teaching," or "student" problem, and the proliferation of plug factories, whence the flood of operators depressing the salary levels apparently came. A plug factory much despised by men was the eight-month course at the Cooper Union Institute in New York City. Begun as a joint venture of the institute and the Western Union in 1869, it mixed philanthropy and corporate self-interest. "There are but few of our offices . . . at which it is practicable to educate women," William Orton explained on the eve of the school's opening, "and we have found that such education as has been afforded at seminaries and 'commercial colleges' does not make practical operators." But the course at the Cooper Union would, arming its alumnae with the skills of the key as well as some knowledge of record and bookkeeping and the care of batteries. The potential of the school was explicit from the start. The institute's first annual report declared that "the experience of the telegraph companies has gradually but surely convinced the managers that their interests would be greatly promoted by the substitution of women for men in the greater number of offices." They were undoubtedly right, but such a transformation was easier said than done. The school ran at least through the early 1890s, by then turning out perhaps eighty graduates a year, funneling them to summer branch offices to assist the regular lady operators (without pay), and then assigning them to the shorter circuits in 195 Broadway. Knights of the Key fervently cursed the Cooper school, but it probably hurt female operators more than males.[63]

Far less alarming to the operators who pointed in horror at the stream of young women clutching plug factory diplomas in their hands was the possibility that the companies would combine women with machines to strip the men of their skill and jobs. The keening over the craft's demise seldom made connections between technology and the "woman question." This is surprising, partly because the occupation was so suffused with the technological, and partly because the relationship between technology, skill, and labor costs was no secret. Even in the golden age of the 1860s, the *Journal of the Telegraph* quietly threatened operators contemplating labor activism with retaliation by mechanization of the craft. It was also clear that such mechanization envisioned cheap female labor supplanting that of costlier skilled males. This is exactly what eventually happened, beginning substantially in the World War I era, with the increasing use of the teletypewriter. But until then, a combination of technological dead-ends and the high turnover and low mobility of women within the craft (the latter two cyclically reinforcing each other) insured a continuing majority of male operators.[64]

Plausible threat though the women seemed, not all men blamed them for the woes of the calling. Some combined sympathy with paternalistic gallantry, like the Frederick, Maryland, man who appealed to his colleagues in 1868 "as fathers, husbands, brothers, and as *men*" to welcome the lady operators and so spare them the alternative of the "repugnant positions" that working women often had to take. Less generously, some chided the women for their supposed faults —like the operator who wrote during the Civil War of their "overbearing and uncourteous manner of transacting business over the wires," affected style of sending ("clipping"), and poor penmanship—but still accepted them as craftmates. When "Susannah," a New York operator, asked the *Telegrapher's* editor whether she could join the National Telegraphic Union "without marrying one of its members," he assured her that "no gentleman will dare refuse you admittance if you meet the requirements." In the ensuing two decades, others also spoke up in favor of the women. "I regret that women are *obliged* to compete with men in the struggle for existence," wrote James P. Kohler, a Henry George disciple, in 1887, "but I do not blame the women." If hard times had fallen on the Knights of the

Key, it was not due to the women in the field but "to a maladjustment of economic conditions and the monopoly, by a few, of those gifts which the Creator intended for the use of all."[65]

The most vigorous defense of the women coincided with the rise of the brotherhood and the Great Strike of 1883. The bill of grievances that precipitated the walkout demanded "that both sexes shall receive equal pay for equal work," a tenet that had become brotherhood policy at the union's founding 1882 convention. Within a year it was a shibboleth among activists. "On the subject of grading the operators according to ability on the salary lists, without regard to sex," the *New York Times* reported five days before the strike, "there is a unanimity of feeling among the male operators that is surprising. 'Equal pay for equal service' is an expression that frequently falls from the lips of the men who are most earnestly enlisted in what they call this crusade of reform."[66] As good Knights of Labor, Brotherhood men were bound to condemn the wage disparity since the order held all "producers," regardless of race or gender, to be equal. Confronting the Western Union with the equal pay demand, a leading Boston operator explained, had come "from a sense of justice to the lady operators, who are as much overworked and underpaid in their departments as the men."[67]

It had also come from a calculated appreciation of the dynamics of the labor market. The clause in the brotherhood's 1882 declaration of principles that limited members to passing on the craft to a "brother, sister, son or daughter" was as concerned with reducing the number of operators as affirming the equality of women. "We do not object to women learning the business and getting positions as operators," said a New Yorker, "but we do object to their being employed at half the pay received by men." If that were to continue, "the men would soon have to make a living at something else."[68] Corporate officials read much darker motives behind the union's equal pay principle. "The demand that both sexes shall be paid the same for like service looks to the driving of women labor from the ranks," snorted General Eckert. Vice-president F. H. May, of the American Rapid Company, dismissed it as "a hit against the girls." The reason, they claimed, was that the women, consistently less skilled than the men, were they granted equal pay, would be sacked in favor of the equally expensive but much more productive males.[69]

One of the very few things on which the brotherhood and the companies agreed was that women got far lower salaries than men. The general range for women operators was perhaps $25 to $60 a month. The elite of broker and commercial operators reportedly got $70 to $90, but much more typical were the rural posts paying $30 or $40, or the summer resorts where board might augment a $30 salary. Duty in a large urban hotel branch office could mean $40 to $50 a month, but the small hotels usually offered only board to match the $15 that the telegraph company paid.[70] Yet it was in relation to men's salaries that those of the women took on their significance. Explaining the mechanics of what telegraphers loosely called the "sliding scale" form of wage cutting, "an intelligent-looking girl, who agitated a fan quite nervously as she spoke," told an *Irish World* correspondent that "a male operator with $80 a month being discharged or his services discontinued, one of our sex—our pay being much lower—will be ordered to take the vacant place, and although we are able to fill the duties of the absent one, we will not get the salary belonging to that particular post but only the half of it which we had in our original position." She probably exaggerated the differential, but it was still substantial. John Campbell guessed that it was somewhere between 25 and 35 percent. The Western Union's Walter Humstone put it even higher, at around 50 percent, a figure with which at least one activist agreed. Others cited examples approaching the 100 percent disparity that the fidgety young woman had claimed. Such cases doubtless existed, as did indeed those in which women's salaries were about average for the office, as they were at Syracuse in the 1890s, but both were rare, and the 50 percent advantage for men seems to have been the rule. In terms of averages, this meant $54 a month for men and $36 for women, using the brotherhood's national figures, or, with the Western Union's, around $65 and $43, respectively.[71]

The question of pay inevitably led to that of ability. Here, too, there was a good deal of agreement between brotherhood and corporate spokesmen: women, on the whole, were inferior operators (it was over whether those few who *did* do work equal to men were underpaid that they wrangled). Both antagonists shared a belief in the inherent physical inability of women to work the heavy wires. In such first-class assignments as market reporting and news dispatches, Eugene O'Connor testified in 1883, female operators "could not be relied upon," for "the nervous system of women would not allow it." Norvin Green concurred, saying at the same Senate hearings, "I doubt whether they have sufficient strength, because operating a heavy wire is pretty trying work," an argument he repeated nine years later with the claim that "sending requires a heavier pressure and stronger wrist" on long circuits than on way wires. Veteran telegrapher Thomas Edison supported the equal pay demand, but still thought women unable to match men at the key. "It requires the commercial instinct and judgment to be a strictly first-class operator, and women don't have those qualifications and can't acquire them," he explained.[72]

But commerce was hardly an instinct, and wiser observers than the Wizard of Menlo Park pointed out that training and culture accounted for the mediocrity of most Ladies of the Key. Women were poor operators, one of their number wrote in 1876, because they were lazy, and that made it all the more disgraceful, since "no other business offers greater scope to an intelligent, conscientious, go-ahead-active woman" than telegraphy. If women would only apply themselves, "there will be fewer 'bulls' credited to us, and we shall be the recipients of fewer sneers and hypocritical condescentions [sic] from our brothers." The brothers could certainly be unkind. "I wonder why it is male operators are more patient with each other than with us, poor daughters of Eve," mused one in 1864. "Don't we need gentleness, forbearance, and all the other virtues to get along with some of them, I should just like to know?"[73]

High turnover (and corporate policies that perpetuated it) and social conventions that made it unlikely that a woman could "talk oil and stocks and machinery and trade as fast and as well as the men" explained their generally low skill level, not genes.[74] Some flatly denied the inferiority charges. "A woman can do as much as a man in this business, and do it as well," a female manager said in 1875, "but does not get the same pay for it." Discussing branch office managers during the Great Strike, the *Boston Herald* concluded: "Selfish superintendents may talk of a woman's proverbial inaccuracy, her impressionable nature, her energy, that displays itself by fits and starts, her sudden attacks of fatigue or depression, and they may draw fancy pictures of business arrested or stopped altogether by a wholesale abandonment to flirting and gossiping, yet her whole record in the telegraphic service is a most emphatic and eloquent denial." Branch operator Linda Girard thought her service worth more than the $30 that the Philadelphia, Reading & Pottsville Telegraph Company paid her—which was $25 less than the office's other operator, presumably a man, received. "If I did not feel competent to earn a higher salary, I would not ask it," she wrote the company's president, "but I have several times, when my associate Opr has been absent taken entire charge of our office, for 14 hours at a time. Fifteen [*sic*], or even ten a month more to the Reading Co would be so little, to me so much," pleaded Girard. One woman turned the usual sex bias on its head during the Great Strike and claimed that her sisters were more accurate telegraphers than the men. "We've kept an account of that," the "blonde little lady, with blue eyes and a vivacious expression" told a reporter. "Men always try to know what the message means; women only try to know what it says. They stick to the text and they're oftener on the safe side."[75]

They also stuck to the brotherhood, which actively sought their support and championed their cause with the equal pay demand. The *Springfield Republican* thought it noteworthy "that the young women among the skilled operators who are out, are given leading places in the councils, and their 'rights' are recognized as equal to and the same as those of the men." In consequence, feminists lauded the union. Lillie Devereux-Blake, president of the New York State Women's Suffrage Association, addressed a strike meeting and thanked the brotherhood for its egalitarianism. Boston papers reported "several women well known in public movements" raising money for the strikers because of the prowoman clause. Henry George, who had many reasons to cheer on the brotherhood, included the equal pay demand among them. More conservative voices also found the union's stance on the women praiseworthy. It was "absolutely just," declared the *New York Times*; "a species of 'women's rights' that all will subscribe to in time," predicted the *Cleveland Plain Dealer*; something that "will not be disputed by any just person," concluded the *New Orleans Picayune*.[76] Traditional labor union usage took on expanded meaning during the walkout. When the local assembly of Oil City, Pennsylvania, sent a message of solidarity and encouragement to the Chicago strikers, it began, significantly, "Dear Brothers and Sisters."[77]

How many lady operators this egalitarian crusade attracted is unclear. In an inherently confusing situation, news accounts suffered further from the self-serving information that company and union provided. Accounts of the numbers of women striking, and of their proportion within the brotherhood, are contradictory and nearly impossible to sort out. Take the case at Boston on the first day: the *New York Times* had "all but three" of the female Western Union force quitting, but the *Boston Herald* reported that only four had struck, "some of them shedding copious tears, but whether of joy or sorrow it is difficult to determine." It is just as difficult to determine which figure was correct. At the time of the strike, Eugene O'Connor thought 300 to 400 Ladies of the Key involved, but ten years later, John Taltavall claimed much more grandiose numbers of 7,000 men and 1,000 women fighting the Western Union. If the reports during the affair are any guide, women were less likely initially to walk out than men, but once they struck, they outdid the men in tenacity.[78]

Appropriately feminine reticence explains why some women stayed at their posts. A Canadian Knight of Labor remarked in 1883 (not in connection with the strike) that the order's secrecy was a boon to recruiting women because it "allowed them to avoid public notoriety and protected their modesty." But striking was neither private nor modest. One New York operator, although a staunch striker, raised the same point. Unhappy with their condition, she and her sisters had nevertheless "submitted uncomplainingly to this treatment sooner than undergo the notoriety of blazoning it before the public, and we would, I believe, still labor under it did not the strike opportunely give us a chance of amending our condition." Perhaps such restraints influenced the twenty "girls" at 195 Broadway whose planned walkout on July 23 never took place. Fear of unladylike self-assertion, deference to male managers, financial need, and tactical errors of the brotherhood contributed to the reluctance.[79]

Women not only failed to strike, but scabbed against the brotherhood. Some were part of the reserves that the Western Union drew on from its branch office force. Some were graduates of the various plug factories, including the Cooper Union school, who found a sudden demand for their services in what was normally a depressingly tight job market. "The stream of applicants for situations was a steady one, made up largely of girls," a New York journal reported the first day. The "improved condition" at the Boston Western Union office about a week later was supposed to be "due to the women operators now employed by the company." How important women scabs were in the eventual defeat of the brotherhood is not certain. They did furnish a ready supply of strikebreakers, but apparently few were taking over the vital heavy wires. They were probably a cause, but not a crucial one, of the union's collapse.[80]

Female renegades appeared, too. At Cleveland, the local assembly expelled Anna Read and Anna Wyman for not having followed their comrades out of the office. Later, it did the same to Kate Skinner, who had been out for twenty days and drawn $20 in strike pay before she and three others turned "traitors." In New York, Hattie Wilkins was one of five women included on a *Telegraphers' Advocate* "black list" of those "who thought it more honorable to be bribed by the Western Union Telegraph Company than to stand by their obligation to an organization which was established by themselves for their own benefit."[81] It was also possible to betray the Western Union, though. Under the pressure of overwork, some either broke down or, like the young woman who had been "compelled to work with the key in her right hand, while she held a sandwich in her left," not only quit her instrument but joined the brotherhood. And some, while remaining at work, secretly provided the union with reports on conditions inside the operating rooms.[82]

But it was the unequivocal enthusiasm, support, and loyalty of women strikers in 1883 that impressed contemporaries and was a matter of such frequent comment as to become a virtual cliché. Their model dedication even won the respect of a couple of senior Western Union managers. Almost two weeks into the strike, press agent William Somerville admitted that "but one lady operator" had forsaken the union, "and she came back just after she struck." After the defeat, Walter Humstone called the small number of women apostates "very creditable to the female portion of the brotherhood."[83]

Propriety and modesty did not mean modest backing for the brotherhood's struggle. "In talking with the strikers the girls generally speak more determinedly than the men in regard to fighting the thing out to the bitter end," the *New York Tribune* reported. "We are out for business," declared one spirited woman, proudly noting that "not a girl who was a member of the Brotherhood flinched" when the whistle blew. Another was said to have vowed to her manager to "fight with pickaxe, gun, sword, and pistols if necessary" before yielding to the corporation. At a New York strike meeting, John Mitchell produced a note "from one of our sisters" which read: "Great inducements were offered to me yesterday to go to the main office, and it gave me great pleasure to refuse. Whether it will harm me I cannot say, but I don't care." Someone shouted, "She's a good one," and the audience cheered in agreement.[84]

Carrie Gettings was a good one, too. Despite threats from her superintendent, she refused to transmit Western Union business in her

Tallahassee, Florida, office. Farther north, in Georgia, a company official acknowledged that the La Grange and West Point offices— managed, respectively, by Misses Parrott and Chisolm—were the only ones shut down in the state. Northern "girls" showed equal grit. Although in need of a job, Mamie Edwards of Detroit rejected a local manager's plea to scab and work "dishonorably." After the collapse at Cleveland, Miss Ruth E. Pumphrey and Mrs. E. W. Collins declined their male colleagues' suggestion that they be given preference in rehiring since, as one of them explained, they had "done no more than behooves honorable operators."[85]

If anyone symbolized the militant young woman telegrapher of 1883, it was the worthy forewoman of the New York local assembly, Minnie E. Swan. "She is a very bright, intelligent young lady, and apparently highly respected and esteemed by her associates," the *Times* noted. She was also highly skilled. The year before, Swan had been part of the Cincinnati Western Union force and, while on a visit to New York, decided to move there, winding up in the B & O office. By June 1883, eager for a more rewarding outlet for her talents, she quit the B & O and took a key in a brokerage house.[86] Her telegraphic accomplishments made her unlike most of her sisters; but she shared, and expressed, their determination to beat the Western Union and their devotion to the brotherhood. "The brotherhood need fear no desertions from my flock," she assured a strike meeting. "If the men remain as firm as we are we will never dip our flag, but will go back to our posts with flying colors. We went into this battle to win, and we will fight to the bitter end." And if worse came to worst? "You will find that in case of defeat the girls will not be the first to give in."[87]

Swan and other "girls" backed up their words with deeds. Their behavior bucked up male spirits even as the strike passed into August and its outcome appeared increasingly dubious. A dispatch from Cleveland noted that the absolute loyalty of the local assembly's fifteen lady operators "tends to bind the strikers more closely." From Brooklyn, a heartfelt message simply declared: "The ladies, God bless them, will mark our prosperity and success by their example." More specifically, the *Irish World* pointed out how "the gentler sex in this great strike have, by their energetic and earnest action set an example to the men which must have been of the utmost advantage in inspiring the latter with courage and resolution to carry on the fight. A noticeable and gratifying feature of the struggle is the good order and sobriety observable at all the meetings." More than once, Boston women were supposed to have kept a large number of their wavering brothers from breaking ranks and scrambling back to the office. And when the end came, some ex-strikers did join a Western Union–bound stampede—in contrast to the women. "Elsewhere, as here," reported the *New York Times* on the day of capitulation, "the lady operators were the last to yield and apply for reinstatement."[88]

Some of them had difficulty in getting their jobs back, at least initially. About fifty in New York and an indeterminate number in other cities found managers turning them away when they applied to return to work. Brotherhood partisans immediately accused the Western Union of carrying out a vendetta against the women for their outstanding loyalty as strikers. Charlotte Smith, who had taken the part of the unemployed women, addressed the Senate Education and Labor Committee's hearings "in behalf of these noble women who are told by this monopoly that they cannot go back to work." John Mitchell charged that the Western Union had made a special effort to blacklist the neediest of them "as a punishment and warning to others. . . . It is terrible to think that this powerful corporation is getting revenge in such a manner." The powerful corporation had a different story. Since most women were second-class operators, and since there were so many such inferior operators crowding the labor market, it had been easy to quickly replace most women strikers. This was probably true. There was a chronic oversupply of female candidates for the less-skilled wires in the era. "We do not employ so large a percentage of female clerk's [*sic*] as they do in Europe and have constantly more female applicants than we can give places to," Norvin Green told a Norwegian woman seeking an operator's job in 1884, "but very few of them are first class operators. Applicants of that grade generally find situations very soon," he added. But few of the ex-strikers were "of that grade." Not that the Western Union wasn't vindictive; it had kept a blacklist for years, and intimidation and harassment were hardly unknown in its offices. The company treated prominent activists as dangerous enemies, and it is no surprise that the subsequent managerial careers of John Campbell and Thomas Hughes were in the rival Postal Telegraph Company. But women were at a disadvantage in an already tight job market, corporate terrorism notwithstanding.[89]

In any case, no one disputed the women strikers' fidelity to their union vows. If defections are any indication, they put the men to shame during the Great Strike. It remains to ask why this was so.

It stemmed in part from a sense of gratitude and a desire to reciprocate the consideration that the brotherhood had shown in its equal pay demand. Despite nods of editorial agreement from the *New York Times* and its like, economic parity for women hardly reflected the so-ʿial consensus of the day. As District Assembly 45 of the Knights of Labor, the telegraphers' union honored the order's pledge that neither race nor sex would be tolerated as significant divisions among producers. It is reasonable to think that the women operators felt heartened and grateful for this support and returned the compliment in kind.

Beyond gratitude, pride also moved them: conscious of themselves as breadwinners, they were eager to hold up their end of the struggle as good trade unionists. "They say girls can't keep a secret," one of them told a reporter at the first strike meeting. "I think we have kept this secret pretty well. The girls are fully as enthusiastic as the men in this matter." In a similar, if earthier vein, prominent labor leader P. J. McGuire told a brotherhood gathering, "If you men are half as good as your women you will come out all right. I have seen women hold out better than the men and when the men weakened I have seen the women lick 'em." As full-time wage earners, women such as the operators were more inclined to assert themselves in workplace affairs. Daniel Walkowitz has suggested that women from households lacking a traditional patriarchal head—as perhaps a majority of the telegraphers came from—may have been more likely to actively champion their rights as workers, filling in, as it were, for the absent father.[90] And all the more so if they were Irish-Americans. "Within the marketplace," Hasia Diner discovered, "Irish culture allowed women to be assertive and, if need be, to defy Victorian standards of respectable feminine behavior. This aggressiveness can help to explain the extremely active involvement of Irish women in the American labor movement." In such cities as New York and Boston, this surely was part of the reason for the lady operators' bristling performance.[91]

But the telegraphers were also creatures of a society in which women, at least ideally, were allotted a sphere and role of their own. It embraced hearth and home, purity and morality, nurture, cooperation, reticence, and refinement—a sphere that, given the crucible of the capitalist marketplace and the industrial workplace, could produce a powerful but ambivalent mix.

A decided moralism permeated the women operators' activism. "I appeal especially to the ladies," brotherhood spokesman Thomas O'Reilly declared at the first strike meeting. "Set us a good example and we will follow it." Six of the women present, in spontaneous chorus, exclaimed, "We will," and indeed they did. After the strike, a female operator recalled how, "when there were signs of weakening two or three of us girls mounted the platform and said that a man with a spark of manhood would not go down to Number 195 [Broadway] and accept blood money so long as a girl remained out. That kept them firm." Manhood meant strength, womanhood *moral* strength. Woman as a moral force in the telegraph office long predated the Great Strike. Male operators and managers spoke of the elevating influence that the women had on the craft. "I smoke, and frequently sit with my feet upon the table," confessed one Knight of the Key in 1875, adding, "Yet, were ladies present, I should do neither." The year before, the *Operator* had asked the women "for further aid in putting down the numerous disgraceful habits and practices we men have fallen into—intemperance, profanity, chewing tobacco, the use of low slang, slovenly personal appearance, untidy instruments and desks, disorderly offices, even dishonesty—and they will not disappoint us if suitable opportunities to make their influence felt are afforded them." So it was not surprising that in 1883, too, they should provide moral leadership. Minnie Swan called a basket of pond lilies sent the women operators a symbol of "the purity of their cause." And when the Western Union plied its male scabs with free cigars, the worthy forewoman remarked, "We girls don't smoke, you know, and so Western Union cigars don't tempt us"—implicitly equating the feminine and the delicate with the loyal and the incorruptible.[92]

Like the telegraph office, the strike had become a transfigured domestic sphere in which women served as the stewardesses of morality and constancy: where the world of defection, of bribery and betrayal, and of the renunciation of brotherhood and sisterhood were kept outside the door just as the mistress of the Victorian household shut out the world of work, competition, and profanity.[93]

It is ironic, but not unusual, that the very stuff of Gilded Age society and culture could simultaneously undermine itself. Late nineteenth-century American society, like the economic system that shaped it, was freighted with internal contradiction.[94] By being good and moral women, the telegraphers became active and faithful unionists and, in their way, militant workers. From the Western Union's point of view, they had certainly become bad employees. The dialectic at work here is far from clear-cut, and the women doubtless suffered tension and ambivalence in these halting explorations of new roles. Nor should we read too much into the record of the lady operators during the strike. Their actions still fell largely within the bounds of acceptable female behavior. If they trooped out on strike with their male co-workers in defiance of corporate power and avarice, they did so by chastely using the separate women's exits and stairways.[95]

But understating the significance of the new ground traversed in the summer of 1883 would be equally foolish. The Great Strike had threatened more than the prerogatives of the Western Union. By walking off the job, the women telegraphers had been doubly insurgent: for opposing their employer as labor opposing capital, and for bucking the hierarchy and patriarchy that the massive operating room represented. Men led the strike, it is true, but they also led the Western Union, and the women's exemplary dedication to the brotherhood, at least in part, rested on its professions of egalitarianism. The "girls" had chosen to assert themselves as both workers and women. Daughters had become Sisters.

5

KID-GLOVED LABORERS

The operator who took part in the Great Strike was atypical. Most telegraphers in late nineteenth-century America shunned union membership. So did most Americans. What's more, most Americans earned their daily bread with plows or hammers, not pens or brass keys. And their bosses—for most Americans worked for someone else—were unlikely to be large corporate ones such as the Western Union.

Yet it would be wrong to conclude that the Brotherhood of Telegraphers and its 1883 strike were simply ahead of their time, a historical fluke, a colorful episode of no more than antiquarian interest. They were not. The operators, the brotherhood, the strike, and the Western Union were very much part of the Gilded Age. The striking telegraphers had a significance that their numbers alone fail to convey, something that their contemporaries in business, in the press, and in the labor movement well understood. The white-collar corporate employee was still unusual, but the much-discussed "labor question" was not. The union hall was exotic territory to the average American, but the terms *monopoly*, *soulless corporation*, and *the wages system* were familiar enough.

The brotherhood's ties to the Knights of Labor were all the more important since the Knights were at the center of the worker and reform upsurge of the 1880s. A generation of younger historians has challenged past interpretations that dismissed the Knights as a pack of myopic and anachronistic bumblers, arguing instead that the order represented a rich and diverse "subculture of opposition" to an ascendent corporate capitalism. At times radical, at times ambivalent, the Knights of Labor was an indigenous mass movement responding to the economic and social shocks of the era. In its best moments, it offered alternatives to a system resting on exploitation and greed.[1] Between the brotherhood and the Knights, and the contemporary labor movement as a whole, there were solidarity and hopefulness, but also tension, resentment, and division. To dissect telegrapher unionism in the 1880s is to dissect the America in which it grew and withered.

Collective action for self-help and self-protection by telegraphers predated the brotherhood by almost twenty years. In the midst of the Civil War, operators met in New York for three days in November 1863 and created a National Telegraphic Union (NTU) to further their interests as a "profession." *National* is a key word here, for the war (and subsequent Reconstruction) had a marked centralizing influence on the country. Three national labor unions had emerged in the 1850s, but thirty-one appeared during the 1860s and 1870s.[2] Sectional conflict, the reintegration of a chastised South into the Union, and an increasingly powerful and activist federal government did much to make labor leaders think nationally. So did the shifting economic emphasis from local to national markets. And no industry better represented that crucial change than the telegraph, no firm better than the Western Union.

On the whole, the NTU was a cautious outfit, very much in the mutual benefit society mold, providing members with sickness and funeral payments. The union set lofty and conservative goals for itself: "upholding and elevating the character and standing of our profession" (understandable enough, given the craft's fast reputation), "promoting and maintaining between ourselves and our employers just, equitable, and harmonious relations, and advancing the general interests of the fraternity" throughout the nation. But the fraternity did not include everyone in the telegraph office. At the 1865 convention, delegate Merrill of Maine pointed out that it would be in the NTU's interest to admit clerks and cashiers into the organization—to move, in effect, toward industrial unionism. J. J. Flanagan, representing Louisville, demurred, refusing to even dignify a clerkship with the word *profession*. "A clerk has nothing to do with our business," he declared, "he is employed by the parties to keep books; and most every man can be a clerk, if he can write, read, and cipher a little; but you have to study some time, and practice much, to become a skillful operator." Not all skillful operators necessarily passed muster. A prowoman membership motion at the same convention—introduced, let it be said, by J. J. Flanagan—went down to defeat.[3]

For the rest of its brief life, the NTU remained exclusive, timid, and aloof. It displayed no interest in the national labor congresses of the late 1860s that drew representatives from other unions. NTU president James G. Smith went so far as to say in 1864 that an operator's salary was a purely private, individual matter. Yet within a few years, a growing number of telegraphers found this constraint and rigidity less and less tenable as conditions within the industry began to change.[4]

For many, the change was for the worse. When the war boom slackened, so did the demand for operators. Increased message traffic of war and commerce had attracted new talent to the key. Telegraphy's "genteel" image and promise as a new and expanding industry encouraged an influx of would-be operators. At the same time, the Western Union took on its monopolistic configuration: absorbing smaller firms, and growing large, impersonal, and nationally powerful. Such paternalism as had existed in the smaller telegraph companies was fast declining.[5] So were the bankbook balances of some Knights of the Key. Around 1868 the Western Union began cutting salaries as corporate concentration proceeded, inaugurating the practice of filling vacancies at consecutively lower pay.[6]

All the while the NTU did nothing. Disgusted and eager for action, a number of New York City members, with the example of the locomotive engineers in mind, formed the Telegraphers' Protective League in September 1868. By the following May the league's head, grand chief operator Ralph Pope, claimed local branches ("circuits") of the TPL in eleven large cities.[7]

Like the NTU, the TPL was exclusive, courting "all worthy operators" who worked the nation's wires. But there the similiarity ended. The league was secret. It had to be, since its members worked for employers of unprecedented power. And until it achieved "sufficient strength to warrant protection to every member," it would remain secret. The TPL was no friendly society, either. "We do not propose to relieve the sick, nor bury the dead, but to place the fraternity in a position where they will be able to take care of themselves," a clandestine recruiting circular explained. Most important, the league talked tough. There were no encomia to the shared interests of labor and capital or, as there had been at the 1864 NTU convention, gushing thanks to the country's telegraph mamagers "for the spirit of magnanimity and justice they have shown toward their employees." Telegraphic realities were different now, and the TPL coolly spelled them out. Strong organization by telegraphers was but an expression of "the same regard for self interest as [that of] other persons who control their own capital and their own labor." Organization would make operators "independent of the dictation of all telegraph companies," would counter the "whims and prejudices of magnates placed over us, many of whom are our inferiors in every respect," and enable the craft to "elevate ourselves from our present level." Toughness was not necessarily radicalism. The league grudgingly accepted the large-scale contours of telegraphy and the corporations that carried it out. But it refused to equate corporate employment with impotence. On the contrary, telegraphy's "very peculiarities enhance our facilities for self protection; and while in its nature it must ever be controlled by a vast capital, its foundation rests in our hands. Each individual operator is a component part of the great system, without which the commercial interests of the country would be paralyzed, were our services witheld for a single week." There was much of the later "pure and simple" trade union outlook here: recognition of antagonistic class interests, organization to exert direct economic pressure to win concessions, and the absence of explicit long-term goals for social change.[8]

By 1870, the league felt strong enough to take on the Western Union. The incident touching off that year's strike involved a confusing shuffling of salary rates in San Francisco that left one operator, league secretary L. N. Jacobs, $5 a month poorer and fighting mad. Company and union worked out a compromise, but the Western Union evidently reneged, firing Jacobs and another activist for good measure. After a second failed attempt to negotiate, the TPL backed up its San Francisco members and struck against the company on January 3, 1870.[9]

More underlay the walkout than the unhappiness of two West Coast operators and their $5 loss. The cumulative change as the corporation expanded—the growing sense among operators of estrangement from their employers, the degradation of their calling, and the diminution of their station—had turned many of them from the benign good fellowship of the NTU to the militance of the TPL. Salary levels were sinking in the late 1860s as the pool of operator labor rose in alarmingly contrary motion. This was not the whole story, of course; deflation could mask actual gains in income despite nominal reductions in pay.[10] But men and women act on perceptions of reality, and many telegraphers perceived "growing evils which now hover about us, and threaten dire disaster in the future," as the TPL's circular put it. And so operators coalesced around the league and, perhaps emboldened by a business cycle upturn by 1870, squared off against the great monopoly.[11]

For the Western Union's part, the paring of wages had to do with market forces. Though uncommonly powerful and growing ever more so, the company faced stretches of competition that likely dictated wage policies in the years leading up to the 1870 strike. A. C. Lewis, president of the Cincinnati TPL local, told the *Enquirer* that the corporation had "determined to make up the amount lost by the recent reduction of tariff [the rate customers paid to send telegrams] out of the operators' wages." Lewis was probably right. Average charges per message steadily declined through the late 1860s, and although average costs per message followed a roughly similar downward path in the same period, they bumped upward between 1869 and 1870, putting pressure on the company to make cuts somewhere—perhaps in salaries. Net corporate income likewise fell in the last two years of the 1860s, another sign that the tempo of salary reductions may have quickened as the decade drew to a close.[12]

On top of all this, by 1870 the Western Union must have been keen to extirpate the labor union that had infested its offices, and no one more keen than general superintendent Thomas T. Eckert. One later account had Eckert offering to break the strike posthaste if his superiors gave him free rein. They presumably did, and the general applied his talents to the job at hand. Espionage—nothing new to a former assistant secretary of war—may have been part of his strategy. A copy of the league's "Confidential Circular" has survived in what was once part of the company's archives, very possibly because a stool pigeon within the union forwarded it to management. It bears the ink superscript

Respectfully referred to Hon Wm Orton President for his information.

Tho⁵ T Eckert

which suggests that the general had an inside line on the TPL. Or it may have been a war trophy, captured or surrendered after the strike. In any case, Eckert and the company triumphed over the league's insurgency that winter, though not without sustaining as much as $100,000 in losses. Officially abandoned by the union on January 18, the walkout had actually failed after a week.[13]

League weakness as much as Western Union strength accounted for the quick collapse. Although the union had organized nationally, there were still lots of operators and ex-operators, particularly during the slow winter season, in need of work. Railroad telegraphers, with their peculiar concerns, were another obstacle to unity. Worse still were the union's pallid finances and sloppy organization (perhaps that explains how a secret flyer came to rest on superintendent Eckert's desk). Nor could the league find much support outside the craft. A few progressive trade unions offered money and resolutions, and at least one major newspaper, the *New York Herald*, scored the Western Union for its monopolistic arrogance, but they were unusual. There was little sympathy shown for employees thought to be paid well above the average worker, and who, more ominously, were part of a secret, coercive organization—"not, be it observed, an open and above-board trades' union or protective society," an indignant *New York Times* pointed out.[14]

The Western Union meant to keep the league in its grave. One way was to silence its de facto mouthpiece, the *Telegrapher*. "I am not now prepared to forbid the taking of that Journal in any of our offices," William Orton wrote his senior managers a month after the strike, "but persistence in doing so will not be considered evidence of friendship for the Company, nor of respect to its officers and superintendents." Within a year, Eckert's protégé, David Bates, had banned the *Telegrapher* from the Philadelphia main office. The company also drew up an ironclad contract for employees who wished to return to a key, instituted a blacklist, and resumed its cutting of salaries. Contrition was no guarantee of being taken back, though. "I hope that the regret you express for your act of folly is sincere," Orton lectured a former striker, "but you must remember that others beside you who now find themselves out of employment also suffer from this most cause-less and unprovoked combination against us." Although the TPL was smashed, not everyone despaired. Reviewing the year's events in November 1870, *Telegrapher* editor J. N. Ashley spoke of the "compar-ative peace and quiet between the employes and the managers" after the dust of the strike had settled. Then, looking ahead, he bright-ened: "For some time to come at least there will probably be no organized or concerted action among telegraph employes, but as there is and has been for some time a scarcity of good telegraph oper-ators, there is less necessity for this than heretofore." Ashley proved to be right about the first point, but about the second and third, dis-tressingly wrong.[15]

For many operators the 1870s were a time of drift, fatalism, and the occasional chimera of salvation through competition among the tele-graph companies. The industry itself was far from stagnant. The in-troduction of duplex and quadruplex systems increased the pace and quantity of the nation's message traffic remarkably. More than ever, the wire network both served and stimulated a continental market. And more than ever, one firm dominated that network. The Western Union not only survived a decade of severe depression but grew and generally prospered. Between 1870 and 1880 the company's roster of offices, wire mileage, and net income better than doubled, while its share of messages handled increased over threefold. This was an im-pressive achievement indeed.[16]

From the telegraphers' point of view, that was precisely the prob-lem. Western Union growth and vitality seemed locked into an eco-nomic formula whose logic inversely demanded the degradation of those who, with wrist and ear, created the company's wealth. The Western Union, it bears repeating, was not a true monopoly; it did have to weave and duck when competitors stirred. But the cumula-tive and long-term trend was for such rivalry to lessen as the huge concern absorbed or disposed of challengers. And during all this, op-erators found it an increasingly cold, intimidating, and ungrateful patron for whom to work. Unhappy telegraphers called the firm a nursery of tyrannies great and petty. An acid 1879 caricature of chief operators ascribed to them "a strong tendency to cringe and fawn upon those who are a few steps higher up on the ladder, and a . . . brutal disregard for the rights and feelings of the unfortunates who are compelled to recognize them as superiors, though in reality they are such only in name." The *Telegrapher's* correspondent in the Chicago main office reported in 1875 that the local management kept a running tally of the operators' errors in "the *little black book."* Even darker was the Western Union blacklist, a corporate fixture by the time of the Great Strike. The company had little tolerance for those it found threatening. Ulster-born W. J. Johnston, a branch office manager in New York, devoted part of his energies to editing and publishing the *Operator*, an independent craft journal that, like Johnston, was conservative in tone. But not conservative enough for the Western Union. In late 1875, superintendent A. S. Brown wrote Johnston that his journalism interfered with his duties, and that he had to decide between the company and the *Operator*. Johnston chose the *Operator*. Eight years later, a Buffalo telegrapher described his city's new Western Union office as "one of the finest in the country," but added that the discipline in the place was "worthy [of] the Czar of all the Russias."[17]

Galling, too, were the various corporate economies—whether under the pressure of competition or to pay dividends on watered stock—that shaved company expense accounts and employee payroll accounts. Outright salary cuts accomplished this: recall the trauma of the 1876 Sliding Scale, or the successive $5 or $10 reductions that accompanied the thump of a new arse settling into an old chair. So did a merciless eye on shop-floor costs. No real-life manager matched Sir Botelle Porter's Pinaforesque boast of how

> Ingenious were the methods I did devise
> To lessen my expenses and save the supplies.
> They all wasted blanks at a terrible rate,
> So I made 'em take their telegrams down on a slate.
>   The company praised my economee,
>   And appointed me a super of the W.U.T.

But complaints about "the cutting down of supplies, both in quantity and quality," were far from lighthearted. Nor was there anything amusing about a personnel policy that lacked a uniform scale of grading and promotion, and that tolerated, perhaps even encouraged, the arbitrary and the irrational.[18]

Speedups, through general "grinding" and perhaps through the technological imperatives of the duplex and quadruplex, made the 1870s grimmer yet for many telegraphers. When W. J. Johnston spoke of "the antagonistic feeling at present" between operators and the Western Union in 1878, he expressed a craftwide consensus. Removing the antagonism was not simply a matter of removing Jay Gould and Thomas Eckert. Neither, in fact, was entirely to blame for the operators' grief in the decade. Gould was not even connected with the company until his 1881 conquest (ironically, when he set up his rival American Union Telegraph Company as part of his strategy to capture the Western Union, operators welcomed the prospect of a competitive jolt to the industry's giant). Eckert, though anathema to many for his performance in 1870, left the firm in 1875 after longstanding tension between him and William Orton broke out into an open feud. He would return in triumph, as Gould's man, but not for six years. In short, the great monopoly had earned the loathing of so many of its employees quite independently of any one manager or director.[19]

Loathing did not automatically mean resistance and rebellion. By and large, operators of the 1870s either quit the craft or suffered in silence; they did not band together to fight back as they had at the beginning of the decade. Hard times cowed them, no doubt, as did the sheer power of the Western Union, and the depressing prospect of a poor labor market impoverished further as swarms of newcomers hopefully descended on telegraph offices. High turnover, the fickleness of youth, and a white-collar disdain for anything that smacked of the union hall hindered collective action as well.

This somnolence was not universal. Barely a year after the TPL debacle, W. W. Burhans, a veteran of the league's fight with the Western Union (which won him a place on its new blacklist), called on his fellows to once again organize. "Why, today," he wrote, "we telegraphers stand alone, as the one class of workingmen of the world's numerous branches of industries and callings, that are making no effort to protect our labor or elevate our profession." Airing grievances through a journal such as the *Telegrapher* was fine, Burhans said, but no substitute for a union.[20] The *Telegrapher* cautiously agreed. J. N. Ashley assured his readers that he had no use for "communists or agrarians" and saw no inherent "antagonism between labor and capital," but he did accept the need for a union—and one that might, as a last resort, legitimately defend its rights with a strike.[21]

Such exhortations must have had some effect. On assuming the editorship of the *Journal of the Telegraph*, F. J. Grace was forced to admit that the "mass of employes do not exhibit that confidence in the Company which the Company deserve at their hands," and invited restive operators to air their reasonable complaints in the *Journal* so that "perhaps, in a friendly way, an apparent wrong might be made right." Operators evidently had other ideas, for in the fall of 1872 the *Journal* printed the constitutional preamble of a "Telegraphers' Association" formed earlier in the year. Although the association declared itself "earnestly" opposed to strikes, the Western Union would have none of it, and the *Journal* warned operators to avoid the union. Most probably did, and the organization soon dropped from sight.[22]

But the longing for a union persisted as long as corporate depredations did. When news of the impending Sliding Scale salary cuts broke in late 1875, discontented voices again talked about collective action. Combining self-interest, republicanism, and topicality, a Washington, D.C., telegrapher reflected that "the coming year of 1876, the one hundredth birthday of our independence as a nation, would be a most fitting and appropriate time for an organization expressive of *our* independence as a fraternity." Others, in midwestern and southern cities, gathered to protest the reductions. They established links with the press, held meetings in Western Union offices, and used company lines to coordinate their campaign of remonstrance—all of which, William Orton noted, "impressed me most unpleasantly." Worse, operators at Peoria had sent the Western Union's directors a petition vowing to "do all in our power to have our salaries adjusted so that each man will feel that he is not a slave to monopoly." That declaration Orton judged an "undisguised insult" to the board, and one to which it would surely respond by summarily firing the petitioners. "In view of the fact that slavery has been abolished throughout the rest of the United States by action of the Government, I am unwilling that the Western Union Company shall be held responsible for its longer continuance at Peoria," Orton wrote superintendent Anson Stager. "And if these 'slaves to monopoly' do not succeed in escaping before the subject is considered by the Directors, I incline to believe that their emancipation will then be promptly declared." His irony was more apt than his ire. The worst that the Peoria rebels had threatened was to "find other employment, and leave the service" if their demands were rejected. Early the next year the Sliding Scale duly went into effect. The proposals for a union to counter it did not.[23]

Quiescence and conservatism were in any case more typical. "Alcatraz," a San Francisco operator, wrote dejectedly in 1871 of the apathy and selfish individualism that undermined the commonweal of his West Coast colleagues. W. J. Johnston strained to find reason for optimism wherever he could or, failing that, counseled his readers to endure. "There is no remedy that we can see at present to arrest the downward course of salaries," he confessed in 1875, "so, Micawberlike, we must wait for something to turn up, or for a return of good times." Six months later, when the Sliding Scale left the craft stunned, Johnston advised operators to submit gracefully, and not for a moment entertain the folly of striking for redress. Besides, he added, things could be worse; other corporations had made even deeper wage cuts. Telegraphers in the nation's capital heeded his words. "The men took it very quietly," a local man reported. "No one thought of such nonsense as a strike, which would be a grievous error, but on all sides is heard the resolution to leave the business as soon as possible."[24] Johnston later even reminded his readers not to let their narrow self-interest obscure the broader picture; after all, Western Union stockholders had rights, too:

> We should bear in mind, always, that many of the shareholders are not any richer than the average operator, and less capable of reviving a broken fortune. Many of them are helpless widows and orphans, seamstresses and day laborers who have their little hoard invested, and they look for dividend day just as anxiously as we do for the "first" or the "fifteenth," with all that that implies. If the dividend fails them, they are as much embarrassed as we would be if the company "passed" our salaries once in a while.

This sort of understanding was remarkable, indeed saintly, from one whom the Western Union had hounded out of a job only a few years before. The *Journal of the Telegraph* could have hardly put it better. Yet Johnston was quite sincere, and quite in character, when he hopefully welcomed the ascension of Norvin Green to the company's presidency in 1878 as an opportunity "to promote a better feeling between the operators and officers" of the great concern. Dr. Green, less given to an equanimous view of things, would soon disappoint the conservative editor.[25]

In gauging the response of telegraphers to their occupational decline in the 1870s, we need to look beyond editorial jeremiads, union organization, and protest meetings to something far more elusive and diffuse, but perhaps far more typical: informal resistance and struggle.

Recent scholarship suggests that workers in various settings, through understandings among themselves about what constituted a fair day's work, sought to maintain their autonomy and self-respect in spite of employer and managerial pressure to produce more and more quickly. The craftsman's "stint" marked off his notion of a reasonable amount of work and a comfortable time in which to do it. His "manly" bearing signified a refusal to let dependent status as a wage earner erode his fundamental equality, as a republican citizen, with his wealthier boss. Such a worker met the foreman's officious stare by stopping work, putting down his tool, folding his arms, glaring back, and refusing to continue until his shop space was once again his own. When the compulsive managerial pioneer Frederick W. Taylor set out in the 1880s to shatter the informal quotas that machinists had set for themselves, "ingenious accidents were planned," he later testified, "and these happened to machines in different parts of the shop, and were, of course, always laid to the fool foreman [Taylor] who was driving the men and the machines beyond their proper limit."[26] Informal resistance could be more oblique, as in the case of workers who struck with their feet. Textile mill operatives in antebellum New England, when conditions favored them, used the threat of picking up and finding a more congenial position to bolster their market power. The famous high wages of the Ford Motor Company likewise reflected high turnover as much as high productivity.[27]

Telegraphers adopted the same kinds of defenses and sense of prerogative. They were, of course, a unique class of workers. Unlike, say, coopers or smiths, operators were not artisans with a long-standing (if not unchanging) craft tradition created within the small shop. The wire and railroad corporations had created telegraphers as an occupation in a way that they had not created the carpenters or painters that they employed. Yet operators still developed notions of fair work loads and conditions, as had other and older crafts. According to Norvin Green, stints among operators existed on the eve of the Great Strike. "Ever since the brotherhood was organized," he told a reporter after defeating the union, "the operators were formulating their demands, and too many concessions were already given them. I do not refer to open demands, but silent understandings, as, for instance, a certain amount of presswork was to constitute a day's work. No such rules were posted, but they grew up. That will be effectually done away with now." But the practice persisted. Arguing for the adoption of a piece-rate system in 1898, a telegraph manager pointed out that "'Soldiering' would be a lost art" after such a change— strong evidence that restricting output on the wires was an established convention. And ten years later, James T. McDermott, who combined the roles of operator, Commercial Telegraphers' Union activist, and U.S. congressman from Chicago, explained at a Senate hearing the difference between young operators eager to please their employers and rise in the craft and veteran hands: the neophytes were "sometimes suckers enough to send fifty messages an hour."[28]

Staking out an informal claim to a certain wire or work partner was also a challenge of sorts to corporate power. The Western Union rule that "no operator is entitled to work upon one wire or instrument to the exclusion of others" was really a confession that many operators felt so entitled. And the same sense of a shadow management from below comes from operators in the 1890s angrily denouncing being "snatched" from their accustomed keys.[29]

Telegraphers unable to choose their assignments or restrict their output could still thwart their employers by botching the traffic they had to handle. Noting the incidence of mistakes in messages along Western Union lines in 1874, the *Journal of the Telegraph* testily declared:

> Errors, for which the Company is sometimes sued, and operators dishonored, we more than half suspect are not always errors. By their very peculiarity they seem to us, as we occasionally study them, more of the nature of crimes, either against the Company or companions in labor, and from which both suffer. The suspicion may be false. We cannot help that. What we do know is that the power of operators to annoy and destroy is vast and fearful.

It was a power they never relinquished. As late as 1907, John Taltavall (by then in his reactionary phase) castigated striking operators for a campaign of sabotage "by methods familiar to the craft." How exten-sive this kind of subterranean struggle was, and how much the pecu-liarities of the job helped or hurt it, are less clear. Craft pride, after all, rested on speed and accuracy. A machinist, to take a well-known ex-ample, could be both a first-rate craftsman and frustrate his employer by slow and methodical work; a first-class telegrapher really could not. That very pride in fast and letter-perfect sending and receiving caused tension between operators—the "petty spites between men working together" that brotherhood secretary Thomas Hughes pledged his organization would end by encouraging the best opera-tors to have more consideration for their less-skilled fellows. Telegra-phy was also a high-pressure calling, all the more so after the duplex and quadruplex innovations of the 1870s, and complaints about mis-takes may have reflected sheer overwork as well as covert resistance.[30]

The possibility that telegraphers used mobility from office to office as a kind of informal struggle demands an even more cautious read-ing. Like stints and sabotage, it surely existed. The managerial despo-tism that plagued the Ladies' Department of the Western Union's New York headquarters in 1870 elicited the militant declaration of "Tina," one of its force, that "however much the walls of 'N' office may be gilded, our plucky American girls won't stay there long un-less 'Our manager' ceases to insult and trample on them." And teleg-raphers *were* on the move; but this seems to have worked against as much as for them, since the infamous successive reduction scheme, if not caused by high turnover, did exploit it. The marked turnover of operators, as noted, grew in part out of the youth of many at the keys and the configuration of the national wire and rail network. Job dissatisfaction and the high-pressure atmosphere doubtless quick-ened the flow. In a sense, getting out of telegraphy altogether was a form of resistance, too. But conscious and systematic attempts to regulate the telegraphic labor market were confined to union or company.[31]

Near the end of the 1870s, telegraphers began to think again about more orthodox forms of self-defense. A letter to the *Operator* from "Radical" in 1879 spoke bitterly of corporate oppression and wasted careers, and then drew what seemed to him the obvious conclusion: organize. "It depends entirely upon ourselves," agreed a second man a month later, "whether we receive porters' compensation or the compensation due to the responsible positions we occupy." The mood spread. "'In union there is strength,'" another operator reminded his colleagues the following spring. "Act on this motto, or forever stop whining about hard times."[32]

They did start to act. By 1881, several groups had formed around the nation. The Telegraphers' Mutual Union (later renamed Telegraphers' Union) claimed 150 members in the New York metropolitan area that summer, and a Brotherhood of Telegraphers (as yet unconnected with the Knights of Labor), hailing from Chicago, boasted an equally large constituency. Both groups' avowed aims were self-protection through conservative means—strikes, for example, were explicitly rejected by the New York group, and very likely by the Chicago brotherhood as well.[33] But militancy was in the air. In mid-summer 1882, operators at the Denver Western Union office, disgusted by general conditions and especially by the policies of assistant district superintendent Bennett R. Bates (brother of David Homer Bates), struck for a $10 raise and other demands. The strike failed after two weeks, but it at once focused and stimulated a growing sense of self-empowerment and solidarity within the craft. No union had sanctioned the walkout, but the Knights of Labor–affiliated United Telegraphers of North America, based in Pittsburgh, expressed sympathy with the action and asked its members not to scab against the Denver men.[34]

The talk was now of organization and resistance on the broadest scale. Jay Gould's 1881 takeover of the Western Union, moving the corporation closer to being a true national monopoly and a worse nemesis of operators than ever, whetted the mounting appetite among telegraphers for a national trade union. Nowhere was the new hunger for activism more evident than the editorial page of the *Operator*, where W. J. Johnston—who only four years before had been patiently defending the widow and orphan stockholders of the Western Union—mused in 1881:

Operators are apt scholars, and a little consolidation of their own might not be altogether a drawback. Telegraph organizers [i.e., entrepreneurs] are men with an exceedingly keen eye for the almighty dollar, while telegraph operators may be defined as a class of men disorganized and helpless; and, if "consolidation" is such a fine thing for the former, there can be no harm in the latter indulging in a little of it too.

And not just organizing. "The right to strike is one that operators undeniably possess, in common with all other workers," Johnston wrote months later.[35]

At about the same time, workers outside of telegraphy were also thinking about combining for protection and advancement. What had begun in 1869 as a secretive cell of nine Philadelphia garment cutters was, by 1882, a growing nationwide labor and reform movement that welcomed unskilled day laborer and aristocratic craftsman, black and white, woman and man, brain worker and hand worker—aiming to unite, in short, all wage workers in a common cause. "The solidarity of labor was fast becoming an economic reality if not a psychological fact," wrote Norman Ware, "and it was the business of the Order to make the organization of labor fit the conditions of work."[36] That order—the Knights of Labor—promised to meld the economic self-interest of working-class America with the broader vision of transforming a competitive, acquisitive, and exploitative society into a cooperative commonwealth. And Knights membership, although fluid, was clearly increasing. Singly, in pairs, or as entire locals, wage earners trooped into the expanding order. The general economic improvement after the depression of the 1870s no doubt encouraged workers to organize, as did a growing resentment of the "soulless corporations" that were remaking the Republic in ominous ways. Labor was on the move.[37]

So the new interest in telegrapher unionism coincided with a national labor renaissance. The Pittsburgh chapter of the United Telegraphers of America, which John Campbell and Thomas Hughes had organized in March 1881, was the first operators' group to join the Knights. Along with its associated chapters in other cities, the UTA formed one wing of craft activism, while the rival Chicago-based brotherhood, with no ties to the Knights, made up the other. By early 1882, both were talking about a single national body to match the power of the Western Union. But more than geographical distance separated the two groups. The Windy City operators found the rhetoric of the UTA uncomfortably radical. A brotherhood member explained that the phrase "securing to ourselves of a proper share of the wealth we create" was "unmistakably a communistic formula of expression," and one that the Chicago men feared would endanger their own organization's goal of a "full, amicable and harmonious settlement of relations with our employers." Nor were they happy when the UTA spoke of seeking "more of the leisure which rightfully belongs to us, so that we may have more time for social enjoyment"; that, a brotherhood correspondent sniffed, "would probably lead to a misinterpretation of our highest purposes."[38] With apparently irreconcilable differences but a common desire to weld a national union in their own images, the two camps issued calls for founding conventions, which duly met—within five days of each other—in March 1882.[39]

Between the conventions and the following summer, much reconsideration, consultation, and horse trading must have taken place. Perhaps Pittsburgh and Chicago were not the polar opposites they had seemed. Exactly what went on between the two factions is unclear, but their differences had narrowed (or the desire for a single national union had broadened) enough for them to unite, very likely in the summer of 1882. The new union bowed to UTA precedent by linking itself with the Knights of Labor, as District Assembly 45, but it was to bear the name Brotherhood of Telegraphers of the United States and Canada. The union adopted a motto, too: *Alterum alterius auxilio eget* (roughly, "One needs the help of another").[40]

The officers and organizers of DA 45 quickly got busy: recruiting along the great web of telegraph and railway lines, devising a "wire test" (a kind of telegraphic password) and a set of ciphers to conduct union business safe from corporate eyes, holding a national conclave, and hammering together a platform of principles and goals. The results of the organizing drive were impressive. Two days after Christmas, 1882, the brotherhood's chief executive, district master workman John Campbell, reported that DA 45 now comprised almost 5,000 brothers and sisters—600 in New York, 150 in Boston, 125 in Baltimore, 110 in Quebec, 100 in Chattanooga, 40 in Kansas City, 25 in Milwaukee, the same in Omaha, 35 in Mauch Chunk, Pennsylvania, and on it went. By May 1883, Campbell claimed 120 local assemblies within his district, with some 8,198 members (out of an estimated total of 22,200 operators in the United States and Canada). There were hitches, of course. In some areas willing railroad operators remained outside the brotherhood simply for want of an organizer to properly initiate them. But the union's growth was generally steady and encouraging.[41]

Brotherhood supporters found an unprecedented hopefulness and self-respect abroad among the craft. The new union, a Philadelphian wrote the *Telegraphers' Advocate* in June 1883, had "brought about a better feeling among the men than ever existed here before. It has paid sick benefits or supplied 'subs,' for quite a number of its unfortunate members; buried one member; settled many disputes; frowned down petty jealousies; united the commercial and railroad operators; and in fact has been the means of more general good for the operators of this section than anything ever before started in our midst."[42] Not all were so appreciative. Two members of the Baltimore local assembly, Adrian Grape and George E. Dunning, had not only fallen six months behind in dues, but after suffering suspension for it, they turned on their late co-unionists and threatened to furnish the Western Union with privileged information about the brotherhood. The assembly, in response, expelled them.[43] They were not the only errant telegraphers plaguing the brotherhood that summer. By June 1883, enough members were demanding withdrawal cards from the union to move John Campbell to issue an angry warning about this flurry of desertions. And it all had to do with the pending bill of grievances.[44]

Promoting good fellowship and elevation of the craft had been important aims and achievements of the brotherhood, but a fundamental cause of the telegraphers' ills—the policies and power of the Western Union—remained. Dealing with the huge firm had been on DA 45's agenda from its first national meeting in October 1882, when delegates drafted a bill of grievances for the membership to ratify. The brothers and sisters approved the bill in May of 1883, and this set of demands, in revised form, the union finally presented to the telegraph companies in July. Its rejection precipitated the Great Strike.[45]

The Western Union's decision to resist and break the brotherhood revolved around the matter of recognition. "It is plain," the business journal *Bradstreet's* noted during the walkout, "that the real issue between the striking telegraphers and the Western Union and Baltimore & Ohio companies is the recognition or non-recognition of the Brotherhood." It was plain to Robert Garrett, who could not even stomach an indirect agreement with the union. And it was plain to Norvin Green, who frankly told a Senate inquiry that his company's recognition of the union would have had "fatal" consequences. Dr. Green knew a fatal infection when he saw one.[46]

Consequently, the Western Union ignored the brotherhood's pretensions to represent its employees and set out to kill the union. A Philadelphia operator recounted how the company had begun distributing forms to employees "asking them if they were satisfied with their pay and hours of work, and questions of like nature," in order to ferret out brotherhood troublemakers. This may well have caused timid operators to hesitate to join, or even withdraw from, the union. The "cowardly and treasonable" renegades that alarmed John Campbell in June were probably responding to increased Western Union intimidation.[47] The brotherhood, in turn, bolstered loyal members, expelled or disciplined less worthy adherents, continued to recruit, and, for frightened or wavering operators, drew up this oath:

> I, the undersigned, recognizing the necessity for telegraphic organization, but not wishing at present to become actively identified therewith, do hereby express my sympathy with, and voluntarily pledge myself to refrain from in any way interfering with any movement that may be instituted by the Brotherhood of Telegraphers of the United States and Canada, for the advancement and elevation of the fraternity.[48]

Thus fortified, DA 45 presented its bill of grievances to the Western Union and the other firms, expecting at best a compromise settlement of some kind, and at worst a sharp but short strike. Enthusiasm for the contest varied. Operators in the New Orleans Western Union office told the *Picayune* that they had no serious complaints about their situation, "save the matter of Sunday work," but added that as good union members they would respect the majority decision and join any strike. Brotherhood men at Harrisburg said much the same thing. Reluctant or ardent, around 8,000 telegraphers honored their pledges and quit their keys on July 19, 1883.[49]

At the outset, the Great Strike looked very much like a brilliant coup for the brotherhood. Over three-fourths of the Western Union operating force, by one later reckoning, had deserted the company, and the company was sorely pressed. It wrung as much work out of its remaining operators as was humanly possible, hired scabs to augment them, and succored them all with praise, tobacco, money, and food (what John Campbell later contemptuously called "4 for a quarter baker's pies").[50] But for the first two weeks of the battle, none of this could stop reports of Western Union business badly delayed or mishandled, of more strikers "captured" by the brotherhood, or of its rivals conducting negotiations with the union, one of which (the American Rapid) made its peace with the insurgents while another (the B & O) continually thought about doing so. Nor could the Western Union do anything about the manifest sympathy of so many

Americans for the young operators' cause. The popular sanction of the strike was a powerful component of the brotherhood's high morale.

High spirits among strikers and antimonopoly catcalls from the public could not in themselves break the Western Union, though, and by early August, the attrition had begun to tell on the brotherhood. To regain the shock and momentum that had marked the union's campaign in the first week, brotherhood leaders decided on a mass callout of railroad telegraphers on August 6. It failed, and it marked the turning point of the Great Strike, which lingered another two weeks, and which, despite brave talk at union meetings, increasingly looked like a victory for the great monopoly. "The operators had the sympathy of the public from the outset," John Taltavall reflected a decade later, but "sympathy did not feed the hungry." It also failed to move the tergiversating Robert Garrett of the B & O to come to a tacit agreement with the brotherhood against the rival Western Union— an alliance that John Campbell had hoped to effect until the last day or two of the walkout. The combination of brotherhood defections, exhausted resources, and corporate hardiness forced the operators to give up. On August 17, after nearly a month, Campbell sent out an official order calling off the strike. Pressed and depressed, he added a personal postscript to the formal message sent to the New York local assembly:

> Messages pouring in so fast I can't possibly come up. Read this letter at 3 o'clock *sharp* and make an effort to have the ladies go back first.
> The scrawley manner in which this is written will indicate my feelings.
> J.C.

They were feelings that thousands of other telegraphers shared that day as they sat in union halls or shuffled back to offices to reapply for their desks.[51]

The Western Union lost no time in cleansing its lines of the brotherhood. As in 1870, those wishing to regain a key had to sign an iron-clad oath. Prominent unionists were spared that unpleasant choice; the company simply blacklisted them. At work, other ex-strikers suffered harassment. General Eckert's second victory over operator insurgency seemed every bit as total as his first.[52]

But not quite. Although the brotherhood was certainly destroyed and humiliated, things were not exactly the same in the operating room. The company apparently conceded a reduction in hours (from nine and a half to eight and a half hours for day shifts and from eight to seven and a half hours for night men) and rearranged the work month so that it now contained twenty-six days and not, as previously, thirty or thirty-one. (According to one operator's claim, this in effect meant a gain of $10 to $20 a month.) Even more significant was another man's assertion that the strike had resulted in more dignity accorded telegraphers by management. "We were formerly spoken to as if we were a lot of animals; but we can talk to the chief operators without falling on our knees," he told labor journalist John Swinton, "and the manager will even hear our complaints, so that we can have some self-respect." If true, then the Western Union's triumph was an uneasy one. The company had broken the power of telegraph unionism, but it now appreciated its potential.[53]

Such improvements helped to ease the lot of operators as individuals, although it is not at all clear how extensive the concessions were, nor how long they remained in effect. They certainly did not reverse the fortunes of the craft as a whole. And in no case could they repair the mistrust, rancor, and disillusionment that the strike's failure created within the labor movement. The brief life and death of the Brotherhood of Telegraphers had been the first nationwide action by a Knights of Labor affiliate. Both operators and Knights were stung by the loss, and both now traded insults and accusations over the episode.

The telegraphers shot first. As early as August 11, a Boston operator, noting that financial support to the brotherhood did not meet what he believed the Knights leadership had promised, wearily concluded that the order had "gone back on us." Six days later, with the fight all but officially conceded, the *New York Times* found the Knights "openly denounced" by local brotherhood officers. With the strike's formal end, anti-Knights vituperation became common wherever telegraphers gathered. Another dispatch from New York reported operators and linemen milling around 195 Broadway muttering "many harsh things" about the order. Union partisans impatiently waved away suggestions that the brotherhood shared some of the blame for the collapse. It was not the failure to call out press and railroad operators that lost the strike, Eugene O'Connor explained; rather, Knights officers "who either were lax in their duty or else did not realize our critical position" had bungled the strike. As condemnations of the order went that August, O'Connor's was restrained.[54]

Promises and money were the immediate source of the telegraphers' wrath. John Campbell later claimed that the Knights General Executive Committee, meeting with the brotherhood's leaders at a New York hotel four days before the walkout, had given the operators "every assurance" that "in the event of a long strike the Brotherhood would receive the heartiest support, moral and financial, from the Knights of Labor. Although there was nothing in the general laws of the Knights of Labor that would warrant the levying of assessments," Campbell admitted, "it was mutually understood that if necessary an extraordinary appeal would be made to the whole order for financial aid." That appeal was sent, but only after the brotherhood's position had irreparably deteriorated. Worse, the man responsible for the delay was John McClelland, secretary of the Knights General Executive Board, and also a telegrapher and brotherhood member. Local Knights and labor unions had done their best to aid the operators, but the failure of the Knights leadership to coordinate a national strike-fund drive—and especially the failure of McClelland to act— had defeated the brotherhood as much as the Western Union had. Or so went the telegraphers' argument.[55]

The Knights version of the story differed markedly. The telegraphers, McClelland countered, had been overconfident, had acted rashly, had informed the parent organization of their plans at the last minute, and had only requested fininancial aid if the strike turned out to be a prolonged one. What's more, McClelland pointed out (as did other Knights defenders at the time), the order had no legal right to levy strike fund assessments on the general membership; the brotherhood's expectations of such support had been as groundless as its boasts of adequate resources. In his memoirs, ex-grand master workman Terence V. Powderly recalled the strikers' youth, brashness, inexperience, and superficial grasp of the ways and goals of the Knights. They had surprised him with their ill-conceived decision to strike and assured him of victory within forty-eight hours. He, in turn, had urged them to call off the strike and take on the telegraph companies when their organization, funds, and the timing were favorable. The brotherhood, Powderly concluded, had only itself to blame for the catastrophe of 1883.[56]

Who was right? The Knights seem to have had the better case. Clearly, the brotherhood was a green union. Its leaders were impetuous and, given the task they faced, reckless. Samuel Gompers, who certainly knew his way around a picket line, told Senator James Z. George of Mississippi after the defeat:

> GOMPERS: This strike has another instructive feature. It will teach the telegraphers this, that if they are desirous of holding out for a long period and fighting a concern of the magnitude of the Western Union Telegraph Company they will have in time of peace to prepare for war.
>
> GEORGE: They will have to have a treasury, you mean?
>
> GOMPERS: They will have to have a treasury.

P. J. McGuire, another seasoned trade unionist sympathetic to the brotherhood's cause, called the operators "impulsive and quick" and chided them for having gone into the contest with virtually empty pockets.[57]

It is also true (as even Campbell later conceded) that the Knights could not constitutionally order members to support a strike, although it is unclear whether the operators expected the Knights' appeal to be mandatory. The call for voluntary aid did finally go out in late July, and the Knights General Assembly evidently gave the operators $2,000 beyond the $1,640.65 that the appeal drew. Leaders such as Powderly doubtless took the matter of voluntary relief seriously. "Do all you can to aid the Telegraphers," the grand master workman wrote a Saint Louis Knight the day after the collapse.[58]

All the principals in the affair later publicly defended their actions, and their accounts—none more than Powderly's—were self-serving. Such testimony invites skepticism. But letters written during the strike survive, and they also suggest a brotherhood both ill prepared and less than enthusiastic about sharing its plans with the Knights national leadership until the last minute. On July 10, assistant grand secretary Gilbert Rockwood told Powderly that although the brotherhood's officers had been huddling in New York for a week, he still had no idea what the telegraphers were up to. In the middle of the strike, Powderly wrote grand secretary Robert Layton of his private fears (which contrasted with his public confidence) about the campaign: "I am sorry that they didn't acquaint us of their intentions before they went out, it would have given us a better opportunity of getting ready to assist them." Campbell's telegram of capitulation on

August 17 bore little surprise for Layton. "It's all over and our prediction as to its ultimate end has been verified," he wrote Powderly the next day. "No time for regrets. Lets up and at them."[59]

The Knights were not blameless. John McClelland was a bit vindictive toward the defeated operators. "Go steady on the Telegraphers," he coldly advised Robert Layton on August 22. "A number of victims will be made but they should be looked after individually. . . . I will hold what money I am now receiving as a nucleus of a fund for the relief of worthy victims and am sure they will not be allowed to suffer. Let it wait until I see you in Pittsburgh, about August 30th."[60] The order's configuration was also at fault. Shortly after the defeat, the *Atlanta Constitution* reported from Pittsburgh that local glassworkers, already disgusted with the strike policy of the Knights, withdrew from the order to form independent unions on hearing of the brotherhood's fate. For many, the Great Strike's failure raised serious questions about the official Knights doctrine on striking and the order's efficacy as a labor union.[61]

Bitterness and mutual recrimination over the lost strike would last at least three years, but the brotherhood renounced its affiliation with the Knights of Labor within three months. Operator revulsion for the order was widespread, though not unanimous. Toledo's master workman M. W. Russell assured Knights headquarters that operators there wanted to stay in the order and requested permission to reaffiliate with another district assembly. From Washington, D.C., Robert L. De Akers warned Powderly of the "knaves" and "fools" among the craft trying to turn operators against the order through "misrepresentation and calumny," and spoke of the need to oppose such "evil influences . . . so that the telegraphers may be saved from their enemies—and themselves."[62] But most operators were inclined to dump the Knights and go it alone. From now on, the *Operator's* W. J. Johnston cautioned, avoid the "sanguine agitator" and act on your own. "There is no bond of sympathy between the various unions which will not snap," a Saint Louis brotherhood officer glumly concluded, "under the strain of a very light weekly assessment made upon non-strikers for the benefit of strikers."[63]

After the brotherhood divorce from the Knights of Labor, telegrapher unionism led a shadowy and marginal existence. Hints of reorganization and resurgence persisted for more than a year after the Great Strike. In early 1884, John Swinton reported that a telegraph manager had smugly told him that the operators were thoroughly demoralized and incapable of action. "Well," Swinton winked at his readers, "let them think so." By the spring *Swinton's* had operators "quietly organizing throughout the country," adding that the linemen had persevered and were still union men. Came summer, the paper quoted one telegrapher promising an offensive by a rejuvenated brotherhood that would catch the company at its most vulnerable, during the presidential convention in Chicago. The assault never came off, but talk of operators organizing and biding their time continued through 1885.[64] They had good reason to bide their time. Operators' unions, a Chicago Knight of the Key explained, were actually very much like telegraph companies: "When [the companies] are young and weak, they are very good to their employes . . . but as soon as they begin to get a little power they commence to put on the thumbscrews. In like manner, the operators' organization should be 'good Indian' while it is young, and when its teeth were cut it would then be time enough for it to try to bite."[65]

With or without unions, militancy on the circuits did not entirely vanish. Indignation over the Western Union's refusal to restore extra pay for overtime in 1885 set off a scattering of protest meetings, threats to strike, and actual walkouts—possibly inspired by the Knights of Labor's successful bout with Jay Gould's midwestern rail system that spring—that, at least in Chicago, restored the overtime.[66] Whether any sub rosa union was involved in this spurt of rebellion is impossible to say. Perhaps there was, since by 1885 a new organization, the Telegraphers' Union of America, was proclaiming itself heir to the old brotherhood. Its chief, Edinburgh-bred Tom O'Reilly, had been a British government operator until the Western Union lured him to the United States in 1882 to help inaugurate its Wheatstone department. A Knights lecturer and organizer as well as a veteran of the Great Strike, he personified a continuing, though tenuous, link between the craft and the order. Eventually his interests would tend more to the latter than the former as he assumed the editor's chair of the *Journal of the Knights of Labor* from 1888 to 1893, but in the mid-1880s, his concern was to cautiously resurrect the brotherhood. The TUA, of necessity still a secret body, had begun in early 1885 and held its first convention in Chicago that summer. Its general health, O'Reilly declared the same year, was "very encouraging and highly satisfactory."[67]

Optimism was sufficient by 1886 for the TUA to formally rejoin the Knights and once more bear the name District Assembly 45, Brotherhood of Telegraphers of the United States and Canada. "We rejoice over the fact," John Swinton declared, predicting that the reaffiliation would strengthen both the craft and the Knights. The *Electric Age* was likewise pleased, calling the alliance "the master stroke in organizing the entire telegraphic fraternity." For those with unpleasant memories of 1883, the *Age* stressed the federal structure of the order, and for those who feared that Knights membership meant that "Mr. Powderly will be our ruler," it assured them that he would indeed not "while Mr. O'Reilly has the rein of government." Almost exactly three years after the Great Strike, the reborn brotherhood claimed 3,000 adherents and some thirty local assemblies, such as the one in Brooklyn where, the *Age* reported, the first meeting's initiates included "a fair sprinkling of lady operators." The New York linemen too, following their old leader James Smith, were again under the Knights' aegis. Determined to avoid the mistakes of the earlier movement, the brotherhood offered a fraternal hand to operators along the rights-of-way and declared the interests of commercial and railroad telegraphers "identical." The perennial talk of elevating the craft now seemed less an incantation than a probability. "Those who set to work with thorough good will," proclaimed an 1887 brotherhood circular, "seldom fail."[68]

Goodwill proved inadequate to underwrite a new national operators' guild. In rough parallel with the eclipse of the Knights of Labor, DA 45 decayed and disappeared sometime in the late 1880s or early 1890s. The brief enthusiasm and subsequent neglect that attended the revived brotherhood were linked to the order's fortunes, since the Knights' acme, 1885–87, was also the period in which the second brotherhood came and went. The peculiar circumstances of the telegraph industry were at work, too. Even as the Knights bested Gould in the railway strikes and attracted hundreds of thousands of new members, the brotherhood remained secret, wary, and weak. If the Western Union was vulnerable as it entered into its last serious stretch of competition with the B & O and others in the mid-1880s, it was still formidable enough to make operators think twice before signing union cards. And so, together with stories of discontent and clandestine organizing among the craft, there were signs of demoralization and stagnation. Reporting a 20 percent salary cut and layoffs for Western Union employees in Louisville in 1884, a frustrated John Swinton snapped, "What is the matter with this trade? Do they have to be weak-kneed because their first effort at freedom proved a failure?" An unfavorable labor market helped to keep them docile, of course; the memory of an abundant reserve of strikebreakers was fresh in the minds of many operators.[69]

After the excitement and expectation over the second brotherhood peaked and receded, prognoses for the craft again turned uniformly pessimistic. The operators' world of the late 1880s and 1890s looked very much like that of the 1870s: too many operators and too few keys, no mobility, low pay, and the inescapable tyranny of the Western Union. Complaints about apathy in the face of degradation became commonplace on the editorial page. The typical operator hit by a salary cut, said the *Electric Age*, "lets off his steam of indignation against the companies, upbraids his associates because they are not in a position to resist . . . and overlooks the fact that reductions are possible only because of his indifference." Indifference and conservatism went together. "When radical remedies are proposed," a telegraphic militant pointed out, "the timid crowd shrinks back into slavery, stricken with terror by the sacrilege." Chronic inaction, warned a Chicagoan in 1887, was sure to nourish fatalism among the craft to the point where "our grievances will become part of our nature, and be accepted as a necessity by many."[70]

As in the 1870s, some lamely suggested that operators use their journals to air grievances and expose wrongdoing. The journals themselves mirrored the decline of activism and the diminishing attractiveness of the occupation. The independent sheets of the 1860s through the 1880s had offered a mix of craft news and gossip, material on unions and broad reform movements such as the Knights and Single Taxers, as well as technical articles. Though the magazines were aimed at the industry as a whole, their labor and reformist concerns were noteworthy. But toward end of the 1880s, and especially by the early 1890s, the journals largely discarded the earlier interest in activism and become increasingly "electric"—compare the titles, for example, of the *Telegraphers' Advocate* and the *Operator* with those of their successors, the *Electric Age* and the *Electrical World*. Part of this reflected telegraphy's slipping behind telephony and electric power as the nation's technological vanguard industry; the later journals appealed to a managerial and technical audience, paying little, if any, attention to operators or unions (the *Telegraph Age* of the 1890s was an exception, although its editorial stance under John Taltavall had moved so far right by the 1900s as to have degenerated into apologetics for the Western Union). Even the amateur prose and verse that filled the old journals, so resonant with the popular gentility that surrounded the craft, gave way to ever more schematic diagrams and turgid columns of technical description. One veteran operator surveying the period 1890 to 1910 could recall no more than six telegraphic poems that had appeared in the electrical press during those years. The craft's subculture shriveled much as the craft's status did.[71]

Strictly speaking, operator unionism in the nineteenth century did not disappear with the second brotherhood's passing. Railroad men had formed the Order of Railway Telegraphers in 1886, an organization that, like the conservative railroad brotherhoods it closely resembled, managed to wrest grudging tolerance from the companies and a modest but stable place on the roads. Commercial operators found things tougher. An Order of Commercial Telegraphers, formed in 1890, led a moribund existence through the decade that included organizational splits and rivalries, defalcating officers, and, as a last resort, an incarnation in 1897–98 as a kind of annex to the Order of Railway Telegraphers. Not until 1907 would another national body, the Commercial Telegraphers' Union of America, coalesce to make war on the Western Union—disastrously, as it turned out.[72] But the American political economy and labor movement of 1907 were appreciably different from those of a quarter century earlier. The confluence of organizational vitality, interest in making common cause with other victims of the "wages system," and excitement in asking bold questions about the status quo belonged uniquely to the brotherhood of 1883 and its Great Strike. Never again would whether and how telegraph operators joined the labor movement be so important.

So significant an apparition as the brotherhood demands a closer look. If it reveals so much about its time and place, we should ask what it was all about. Superficially, its quick growth and quick collapse rested on pent-up grievances, youthful ardor, raw leadership, meager funds, and a powerful foe. True enough. But what of deeper strengths and weaknesses? What were the parts—ideological, cultural, and human—that the brotherhood comprised as a whole? And what sort of whole was it?

To begin with, the brotherhood expressed the collective self-identification of an occupation. Since the organization accepted clerks and linemen too, it was not actually a craft union. This is important, and I will return to it. But the brotherhood was primarily an operators' union, both in emphasis and membership. Its very name betrayed the predominant interests within the organization of those who worked with key and sounder for a living.[73]

The brotherhood was also an expression of craft pride. I say "craft" (as did many telegraphers) although the word, with its connotations of the artisanal workshop, is really inadequate to describe the world of the operators. Socially part of a new and fluid lower middle class, they were unprecedented. So was their calling. Nothing comparable to telegraphy existed before the mid-nineteenth century. The Industrial Revolution had created telegraph operators, as an occupation, ex nihilo. It was up to the operators themselves to likewise create a sense of craft, of profession, from scratch.

Telegraphy had a workaday craft culture, of course: the operators' "signatures," the regular partnerships over the wire, the special terminology, the hazing of "freshmen," and all the rest. This was not a professional culture in the way that the old free professions possessed well-defined and fenced-off fields of practice (although, as Paul Starr's deft study of physicians shows, even so apparently long-established and revered a profession as medicine had in fact struggled to forge its occupational identity and stature in the nineteenth century). Nor was it comparable with that of the various branches of engineering. They were closer to the telegraphers in their industrial genesis, but by the 1880s engineers were combining an increasingly favorable economic position with a consciously wrought professional culture that embraced a sense of collegiality, public service, self-regulation, social exclusiveness, as well, naturally, as specialized knowledge. The emergence of the American Institute of Electrical Engineers in 1884 is a clear sign of the distance that separated the new professionalism from those like the Knights and Ladies of the Key. At its founding the AIEE membership was limited to "inventor entrepreneurs, college-trained engineers, physicists, teachers, managers from the communications and electrical manufacturing industries, and a sizable contingent of telegraphic electricians," and within a few years it would discard the last group as too plebeian.[74]

If not professional in the rarefied way that doctors and engineers were coming to define the term, telegraphers did organize with a set of occupational criteria in mind that went beyond the arts of the key. A certain repertoire of skills marked a telegraph operator, but ideally, a brotherhood circular argued, so should "knowledge and worth." Both in and out of unions, those concerned with the sinking status of the craft frequently spoke of the need to "elevate" telegraphy. In part, this had to do with the fast reputation of the operators who criss-crossed the nation leaving the telegraph offices behind them suffused with a whiff of nicotine and alcohol. Organizing, a Chicago man argued in 1884, would raise the general tone of the occupation "so that it would once more be an honor to be known as an operator, instead of, as now, almost a disgrace." Parallel sentiments were behind the temperance clause that graced the platform of the reorganized brotherhood in 1886. And partly, the talk about elevation reflected a less than generous urge to set telegraphy off as not only respectable, but *more* respectable than some other pursuits—the occupational counterpart of the lower-middle-class striving for "gentility." W. J. Johnston told *Operator* readers that organizing to police the indiscriminate access to the craft that was degrading them would protect their salaries, "purify the profession, and lift it above the level of the common store clerk."[75]

Quantity as much as quality determined the overall health of the craft, though, and the brotherhood accordingly embodied the inveterate desire to tame the telegraphic labor market. By sharpening and tightening the terms of apprenticeship—by even establishing a uniform system of formal apprenticeship—activists hoped to reverse their occupational decline. Fewer and better operators, sifted and refined through guildlike regulations, would raise the market power, income, and status of the telegraphers.

The Gilded Age labor market generally had been unkind to operators, and the peculiarities of demography and the industry made a bad situation worse. High turnover, seasonal fluctuations and the waiting list, and above all, too many men and women calling themselves telegraphers had depressed the level of salaries and, through admitting incompetents, the esteem of the craft.

A loose network of mutual help existed along the nation's rail and wire grid, but the brotherhood meant to create a formal scheme, patterned on the trade union practice of issuing members traveling cards, to regulate the continental flow of operators. Those leaving their local assembly received a "transfer card," which they surrendered when they affiliated with a new assembly. The union also hoped to check tramping by issuing general advisories to members seeking work, as it did in one case by relaying the plea of a local assembly that unemployed operators not accept positions on their employers' railroads at salaries that would undercut them.[76]

Issuing transfer cards and circulars reined in peripatetic brotherhood members, but the problems of the labor market extended well beyond local assembly halls. Operators saw a set of twin demons behind their decline: the Western Union, of course; and the "teaching" (or "student" or "college") problem. As early as the 1860s and as late as the 1890s they decried the free and easy opportunities available to anyone wanting to find a place at the key. Local managers or operators at lonely railroad posts with time on their hands and extra money on their minds took on students with no thought for the aggregate effect on the craft. Even worse were the commercial plug factories and telegraph colleges that lured ingenuous boys and girls with promises of high salaries and respectable white-collar jobs and then pushed them, half-trained at best, into an already overstocked labor pool. One such Illinois enterprise, the artfully named Union Electric Telegraph Company, assured those contemplating its $40 course that "no other business in existence" had "so flattering a prospect of future expansion as Telegraphy"—a remarkable claim to make one year after the Great Strike. "The greatest evil which has assaulted us thus far is the large increase of late years in the number of telegraphic 'colleges' not to mention the vast number of private 'students' taught for a few dollars a head," declared the *Operator* in 1881. Again and again, craft journals condemned the uncontrolled manufacture of plugs, reserving a special vehemence for the profit-making colleges, which were routinely called dishonest. The shabby practices of many of the colleges even disgusted one Western Union official. "By no means send her to a so-called telegraph school," Norvin Green's private secretary advised a woman desiring to place her daughter at a key. "To do so would be a waste of time and money."[77]

Teaching students in ones and twos was especially prevalent on the rail lines—"inexhaustable quarries," one operator called them in 1879—which attracted the youth of the surrounding countryside.

Why, a Saint Louis Knight of the Key asked his fellows in 1883, was the average railroad operator's salary so low? "Because 'there's plenty of operators.' Why so plentiful? Because the very men who are grumbling at the reductions are furnishing the surplus. Brothers!" he pleaded, "pause a moment and think if you are not contributing to the cause of your downfall." But moral suasion was not enough to deal with the student problem. More forcefully, craft journals set out to expose and shame those who taught. "Agent J. H. Caffrey, of the C.R.I. & P., Auburn, Ills., keeps a student," the *Electric Age* broadcast in 1886. "Caffrey will regret this some day."[78]

Corporate practices compounded the problem. Some railroads, like the Reading, permitted teaching on their lines so long as the students received official permission.[79] The Western Union ran its school of telegraphy jointly with the Cooper Union Institute in New York, graduating young women who, the *Electric Age* remarked in 1887, got "the munificent salary of $18 per month—$3 more per month than the little check girls receive." Yet the sixty-odd graduates that the school turned out annually in the early 1880s were less a cause than a symbol of operator distress, since the Western Union's own policies on recruitment and apprenticeship were largely informal, decentralized, and haphazard.[80]

The way in which telegraphers were made was as much irrational as promiscuous. Like many railroads, the Western Union was something of a paradox: a corporate giant that monitored test offices and kept minute account of everything from messages handled to pencils consumed, but that left its dealing with employees to the vagaries of local practice and personality. The brotherhood, as the national operators' union, sought to do what the national telegraph company never had: build a uniform and predictable scheme of apprenticeship and promotion.[81]

To begin to do so, the brotherhood demanded the "suppression of fraudulent telegraph colleges, and the supplying of operators from the ranks of deserving clerks and office boys—the only students who are qualified to succeed us." The piecemeal teaching that had cheapened "our profession" would have to go, too. Instead, operators would pass the craft on as some artisans did, refusing to reveal the secrets of Morse to any save "a brother, sister, son or daughter." The exact criteria for graduating from apprentice to journeyman operator were less explicit (or kept secret), but a period of two or three years spent learning the ways of the wires seems to have been commonly expected. Determination to enforce these strictures evidently cost at least one Reading Railroad operator, J. H. Yohey, his job. The company placed a student with him, and Yohey, who objected, gave the novice "a tough time of it" before resigning rather than betray union principles.[82]

In a sense, the brotherhood was less creating a new kind of apprenticeship than trying to regularize and control what had generally evolved as the legitimate, though unenforceable, norm. Honorable and legitimate apprentices, John McClelland explained to a Senate committee, "rise from being check-boys and messengers. These boys in course of time, from their familiarity with the office and with the business, learn the rudiments, and, by seizing their opportunities, gain a knowledge of operating and in time become regular operators." No doubt it was all less earnest and tidy than McClelland implied. Under the best of circumstances adolescents can be difficult, and telegraph offices seldom presented the best of circumstances. "Do not forget to talk to the operators all the time," the sarcastic "Valuable Suggestions for Students, Messengers, and Others" advised aspiring telegraphers in 1871:

> Ask questions about everything you don't understand, and insist on answers in full. During [press] report hour entertain the receiver with pleasant conversations on the national debt, with statistics. . . . Problems in the Rule of Three are easy to demonstrate while he is receiving the stock market. Lean closely over him all the time, especially if you have had onions for dinner. . . . Read every message to be sent before it is hung on the hook, you will thus learn many important matters pertaining to other people's business, of which you would otherwise be ignorant. . . . If all the operators are busy get into conversation with some other student on the line. Call one of the operators to read what he says. *They like to read students' writing above all things.* . . .
>
> The stove should never be filled or shaken except at *report hour*, and no other time should be chosen for carpenter work, cracking nuts, gymnastics, wrestling, boxing, and chair balancing. Wear heavy boots while on duty, and walk *heavily* on the floor and upstairs—it shows a firmness of character highly appreciated by operators.[83]

Disciplining pesky check-boys was still easier than disciplining the labor market. The brotherhood's concept of a rationalized apprenticeship system always rested on the assumption that thorough organization would force the Western Union to either formally agree to a brotherhood monopoly of training or abide a fait accompli. The union evidently never thought of asking the state to tighten the spigot by licensing operators. After the brotherhood's collapse, though, some telegraphers, especially those on the railways, did. Like the contemporary stationary engineers, railroad operators sought government regulation as a way to enhance their economic power, raise their standing, and reassure a traveling public that associated incompetent operators with horrible train wrecks—wrecks such as the one that the *Boston Globe* reported during the Great Strike as

THE WORK OF A "PLUG"
The careless conduct of an
amateur operator
wrecks and burns two freight trains on
the Troy and Boston road,
wedging in and burning to cinders
five human beings.

The call for licensing neatly combined the operators' private interests with those of public service: young, inexperienced, and overworked telegraphers equaled low salaries and high death tolls on the rails. Not all demands for licensing were restricted to the operators who worked the roads, nor did they always stress the matter of safety; poor service, too, was a reason to clean up the craft through examinations. But license demands were an admission that the trade union tactic of direct pressure to restrict apprenticeship had failed.[84]

Brotherhood claims on apprenticeship were very much in the craft union tradition, but its welcome to telegraph employees of all kinds was innovative. District Assembly 45 was one of the first industrial unions in the nation, inviting linemen, clerks, and others on the Western Union payroll to enter its ranks.[85] Unlike earlier operator movements, its stance on the "woman question" was unequivocal: the brotherhood was also to be a sisterhood, and its aims included forcing the companies to pay the Ladies of the Key according to their skill and capacity, not their gender. This drive to weld a catholic alliance of telegraph wage earners embodied the Knights of Labor's ideal of a united producing class. Potentially, it was a combination to rival the power of the Western Union—and all that the Western Union stood for.

Industrial unionism in telegraphy turned out to be deceptively broad and fatally shallow. The common plight of brotherhood members as employees pulled them together, but the subcultures that uniquely set off operators from linemen, linemen from clerks, clerks from operators, and even operators from other operators tugged at them in a contrary and divisive way. Frustrated by the second brotherhood's stillbirth in 1887, the *Electric Age* soberly inquired, "Is thorough organization possible in this profession of ours?" It was a good question.[86]

For one thing, there was no such indivisible entity as a telegrapher. Some operators were fast, some slow. Some worked in large offices, some alone. Some were men, some women. Some were worldly, some hopelessly provincial. And all this mattered as much as their shared knowledge of Morse and their often shared employer. Generally—and I oversimplify—operators fell into two rough categories: the urban, higher-skilled press and commercial telegraphers who worked alongside others like them; and the rural, lesser-skilled operators, usually ensconced in signal towers or small-town depots along rail lines. Most Knights and Ladies of the Key belonged to the second group, but their prestige within the craft was low. The typical rural operator's indifferent talent and frequent need to break created bottlenecks in long-distance circuits that infuriated the big-city man whose status and salary depended upon his ability to keep up a rapid and uninterrupted stream of dots and dashes. A commercial operator, under great pressure, "with important messages accumulating, and specials and press reports expiring on his hands," would have to wait while a railway operator, working at his own pace and with his own priorities in mind, held up high-speed urban traffic. Stymied by such telegraphic rural idiocy, an exasperated first-class operator might hurl a caustic "Scat!" or "Swim out!" to try to clear his line. As Nattie Rogers, protagonist of the novel *Wired Love*, heard the call of a "little, out-of-the-way, country office" on her sounder, "she was conscious of holding in some slight contempt the possible abilities of the human portion of its machinery." Nattie was fictitious; her sentiments toward small-town operators were not.[87]

The stops and starts on rural circuits that so frustrated the urban telegrapher were not solely due to mediocre skill. Work routines in a small railroad office were quite unlike those in the industrial setting of 195 Broadway and its kin. Railroad operators frequently performed a great number of duties in addition to sending and receiving. While this made for variety, it could also make for harrying every bit as intense as that experienced by the specialized urban operators when the village telegrapher had to juggle his or her several responsibilities at the same time. "It is a great pity," lamented a country operator in 1886,

> that the "small fry" of the city offices cannot be placed temporarily in a position as manager, chief, receiving and delivery clerk, as well as day and night operator, all positions to be filled by one man that they might better appreciate the arduous duties involved. The duty is not a pleasant one at best, but is quite irritating when our city cousin becomes angry at the constant opening of the key to wait on a customer, to correct an error, to start out the messenger with an important C.N.D. and to answer the questions of an irate customer.

Or of a stupid one. "Thousands of so-called intelligent people," wrote W. B. Swindell, a rural North Carolina operator, "will ask if a train is coming while they hear it blowing." Silly questions, insults, freight rates, ticket prices, train schedules, signal lamps, switches, and, no doubt, mischievous children and dogs, all competed with the key and sounder for the station agent-operator's attention. To make matters worse, the salaries were notoriously low and the hours notoriously long.[88]

Rural posts were not always so hellish, and some operators did well in them. Most were of rural origin to begin with. Many did fit the stereotype of the country operator as gawky ploughboy or red-cheeked milkmaid who spoke a halting Morse. But others achieved a higher status locally, reinforcing what the *Electric Age* called "their close relations with rural life." Although he died fairly young, Norman Rugg, manager of the Western Union's Saratoga, New York, office, had become a fixture of the village community by 1871: paterfamilias, secretary and librarian of the Baptist Sunday school, YMCA director, member of the Saratoga Musical Association, and volunteer fire company officer. Alfred B. Connor's knowledge of poverty came not from a low telegrapher's salary but his experience as overseer of the poor in Manchester, Vermont. The town operator since 1874, Connor had also served as a selectman, and by 1897 was the Western Union manager, a freight and railroad agent, and president of the local agricultural association. Shortly before the Great Strike, another railroad operator told the *Telegraphers' Advocate* of his satisfaction with country life. Married and receiving $55 a month plus commissions, his house rent was cheap, his family ate well from their kitchen garden, and they were accumulating savings. But his contentment was not simply a matter of economy. "Above all, the town folks look upon me as a person of more than ordinary intelligence," he wrote, "and I have been chosen to fill many places of trust." Nor was he alone in his happy circumstances since, he added, "there are many others on this road who are similarly situated." Few could have been quite so well favored among the craft as a whole, but there is a plausibility about the notion of village telegrapher as important person. He or she was usually a "manager," and while they often managed only themselves, they were, within limits, their own bosses. They did perform a variety of duties and require a palette of knowledge that ranged from electricity to railway operations to commerce, and they did possess an understandable pride in their awesome responsibilities for the safety of hundreds of lives and millions of dollars of property. For small-town America, the local depot-cum-telegraph office was part of a "metropolitan corridor" through which rushed the urban, industrial forces reshaping the nation: a world of fast mails and fast freights, of Montgomery Ward and Standard Oil and standard time and—as the ubiquitous blue-and-white signs that so many country stations wore announced—of the Western Union.[89]

Minding the gate to the metropolitan corridor did not make a railroad operator a metropolitan. He or she was still a telegraphic bumpkin. John Lenhart, seventeen in 1852, trekked twenty-five miles from the hamlet called Beaver, where he ran the telegraph office, up to Pittsburgh "after clothing made by a tailor" because, as he later explained, there were "no artists sufficiently stylish in Beaver to suit me."[90] If country folk viewed the city and its metropolitan corridor with mixed envy, fascination, and suspicion, city people (excepting a minority of middle- and upper-class romanticizers disgusted by urban blight and crowding) saw rural districts as comic and backward places that anyone with sense left as soon as possible. Perhaps many who disdained country life were themselves not that far removed from it, and so wished to mark the distance between city and farm all the more clearly. In any case, along with the varied and growing catalogue of ethnic stereotypes, the dumb hick became a stock character in the sort of middling American popular culture that *Puck, Judge,* and *Life* typified. Because the butts of the hick jokes were Protestant whites, and because the caricatures were less viciously drawn than those depicting blacks, Jews, or the Irish, it is easy to forget that the jokes must have still been painful to their subjects. Telegraph journals were not free of such humor.

In sum, the contrast in working conditions and the cultural friction between city and country told in the brotherhood's failure to embrace all operators, and in the reluctance of the railroad operators to aid their striking commercial counterparts. In early July 1883, superintendent of telegraph Oscar W. Stager told Reading Railroad general manager J. E. Wootten that he feared little trouble from their men in the event of a walkout. "The Assembly at Pottsville I am creditably informed, has colapsed [*sic*]," he wrote, "and the Assembly at Reading has often times, not enough to complete a quorum." The bare mechanics of organizing posed a problem, of course. Two months before the Great Strike, John Campbell noted how hard it was to canvass and organize the many isolated trackside telegraphers. When the test came, some railroad men did stand by the brotherhood. On July 26, Stager relayed Western Union complaints to Wootten that two Reading offices "were annoying them very much by finding fault with the way in which their company were handling the business, and today refused to accept a message because the name of a well known firm to whom a message was addressed was not spelled correctly." The same road fired another of its men, F. McGuire, for refusing to transmit Western Union traffic the next month.[91]

But solidarity and militance during the walkout were largely urban phenomena. "Very few country operators in this vicinity have struck," reported the *Springfield Republican* from western Massachusetts. "It is only in the large cities that the telegraphic strikers enjoy the company and support of a crowd of their fellows," the *Nation* shrewdly observed. "The majority of them probably have to strike alone, or in twos or threes, and solitary strikers are not apt to have much heart or hope." Nor much desire to forfeit the bonds that many railroad operators had to work under as freight or ticket agents. When the railroaders whom John Campbell desperately called out in August 1883 stuck to their keys, they were affirming, rather than creating, a serious schism within the craft.[92] After the brotherhood's defeat, some tried to close the gap. "Now there is talk of organizing again," a man from Michigan wrote, addressing his colleagues in 1884:

> Well, what are you going to do with the railroaders? . . . What about the lonely plug out on the prairie, a hundred miles from nowhere[?] Now, city brother, "stow" that contemptuous smile for a few minutes, and let us talk about it. What is going to be done with the thousands of railroad operators in obscure places? Of course, their copy is not copper-plate, but in the event of any unpleasantness the Western Union finds them dangerously handy.
> United we stand, boys. Let one trial of "going it alone" suffice.

The revived brotherhood of 1886 did try to attract rail operators, but the latter found a more congenial home in their own union, the Order of Railway Telegraphers, which they began that same year. A distinctly conservative body, the ORT had the advantage of dealing with an industry less uniformly intransigent toward craft organization than the Western Union, and its slow and steady growth through the 1890s was in unflattering contrast to the decay of the rump brotherhood in the same period. The ORT did offer a refuge to commercial operators seeking to recover their organizational strength, but always with the understanding that the two branches of telegraphy had separate interests. And separate, and weakened, the branches remained.[93]

Generations also separated operators and limited the brotherhood's potential. In the first few minutes of the Great Strike at 195 Broadway, the *New York Times* recorded this exchange between two friends:

> "Come on, Ned," cried the tall man earnestly; "are you not going with us?"
> "No; I have had enough of strikes," said the other somewhat sadly. "I remember 1870."
> "So do I," replied the other bitterly, "and that memory is what rankles now."[94]

Some of the managers who fought the brotherhood that summer had themselves once been active in the National Telegraphic Union or even the Telegraphers' Protective League, having since made their peace with the Western Union and settled into a comfortable middle age.[95] The strikers of 1883, on the other hand, were presumably young bloods itching for action and unrestrained by family obligations or career commitments. Perhaps; but it appears less clear-cut than that. Telegraphy *was* a young person's occupation. One reporter found the dearth of "elderly or even middle-aged men" at a brotherhood meeting noteworthy, but that would hardly have surprised someone who knew the craft. Yet how old was "young"? There is no way to know the exact age distribution of brotherhood members, but it must have approximated that of the occupation overall, with the heaviest concentration in the late teens and early twenties. And the leadership? The data are meager, but based on a sample of eleven brotherhood activists whose ages in 1883 I could find, the firebrands seem to have been older than the typical operator, averaging 29.7 years.[96]

Peculiar generational ties very likely bound such men as Eugene O'Connor and John Campbell and John McClelland in their attraction to activism, and perceptions of career would have had a good deal to do with this. Unlike an eighteen- or twenty-year-old, an operator at thirty or thirty-four had a real stake in remaining in the craft, was more likely to have family responsibilities, and also more likely to feel frustrated at approaching middle age committed to an occupation that had denied him mobility and recognition. In that case, unionizing to wrest a commensurate salary and prestige made more sense to an older operator than to a younger one who had less reason to stay with a dead-end trade and more time to a better one. Time, in fact, pressed especially on a middle-aged operator because the physical prowess needed for first-class work usually began to decline at midlife. "This comparatively early impairment of skill is noticeable more often in the telegraph operator than is the case in almost any other vocation," John Taltavall explained. "At thirty, or at most thirty-five, years of age the ambitious telegraph operator should be prepared to graduate from his key to accept promotion either in the direct line of his employment, or otherwise." Some of the brotherhood leaders certainly were ambitious. After the Great Strike John Campbell went on to become a senior manager in the Postal Telegraph Company, and then went into business for himself as a dealer in telegraph poles and railroad ties. Thomas Hughes likewise gained a managerial desk with the Postal, Mortimer Shaw became a manager for the United Press, and John McClelland an agent for the Associated Press and then a newspaper editor. These men were also highly skilled operators, as was the brotherhood's most prominent woman, Minnie Swan. There is reason to believe, in short, that telegrapher unionism appealed most strongly to a segment of the craft elite.[97]

At the local level, it is impossible to know whom the brotherhood attracted. There is a scrap of evidence from Harrisburg, where three of the four men who struck were among the best paid in the office, but they returned to work within four days and their striking was more dutiful than militant. The maturity and skill that bound brotherhood stalwarts could also weaken their rapport with younger and less skilled telegraphers, whose commitment to the union, as to the key, was superficial and ephemeral. Five years after the defeat of 1883, the *Electric Age* blamed the organizational lassitude among operators on the unwillingness of the small aristocracy of high-salaried men to make common cause with the bulk of telegraphers whom they saw as a potential corporate wedge against their own favored position. True or not, the charges were a reminder that age differences, leavened by those of skill, undoubtedly influenced the rise and fall of the brotherhood.[98]

Tensions between white collars and blue ones also flawed the brotherhood and strained its relations with the labor movement. The adventurous plan of an industrial union combining manual and "brain" workers had a patchwork quality and a vague uneasiness about it. Different work experiences and cultural patinas kept any number of blue-collar workers from merging into an indistinguishable wage-earning mass. The distance between workbench and desk could not have made this any less so in the case of the brotherhood.[99]

Not that the labor movement sat with folded arms during the Great Strike. If ultimately inadequate, unions and the Knights of Labor did offer the operators support. The challenge to Jay Gould and the Western Union had a symbolic value for an emerging working-class movement that was obvious—"a test case," as one newspaper described the labor view of the episode.[100]

Expressions of worker support were frequent in the daily accounts of the walkout. "We are all in the same boat, and we are going to stand by the telegraph boys to our last dollar," vowed a Cleveland

Knight at a picnic held to raise funds for the strike. Baltimore glass-blowers pledged $500. In nearby Washington, $300 came from the bookbinders. Boston plasterers augmented their $100 contribution with promises of a ten-cent weekly per capita assessment, and Philadelphia shoemakers tendered $300 to the brotherhood.[101] The most consistent help came from the nation's printers, and "typographical" seemed interchangeable with "solidarity" during the Great Strike.[102] "The telegraphers are fighting Labor's fight," declared the *Irish World*, "and should have not only the moral aid, but also the material assistance of their brother soldiers in the great Army of Industry." Individual unions, central labor bodies, and Knights assemblies appeared to respond to the plea.[103]

This veneer of labor in common cause quickly cracked once the telegraphers gave up the fight. The acrimony that followed the defeat was not simply between brotherhood and Knights officers, and went beyond a squabble over tactics. The mutual bitterness involved the nature of the operators themselves.

Telegraphers of the brotherhood occupied a singular and paradoxical niche in 1883. They were wage earners and union members at the same time that they were middle class and "genteel." The Knights' idealism, which DA 45 embodied as an industrial union, never overcame an abiding sense of superiority toward the more usual kind of working man or woman—including those within the brotherhood. Condescension by telegraphers toward blue-collar folk was not new. As early as 1878, an Ohio operator told the state Bureau of Labor Statistics that reducing the workday to eight hours was unwise because "two-thirds of the laboring class of men would only spend two hours more of their time at saloons." The brotherhood's failure invigorated this snobbery. In his autopsy of the Great Strike, *Operator* editor W. J. Johnston's findings included an "unfortunate connection with a labor organization, the members of which were foreign to telegraphers in tastes, modes of living and in ideas."[104]

And none more foreign than the linemen. A wire chief at 195 Broadway is supposed to have inscribed the flyleaf of his logbook with these verses in 1873:

> When men are sent out on the wires,
> Armed with a coil, and spurs, and pliers;
> With care, the chiefs will in this tome,
> Note when they start, and when come home.

If e'er they should o'erstay their time,
And make the claim, they had to climb
The largest pole within the town,
The chiefs will also note this down.

But if the fragrance of the cup,
Should spoil their tale of climbing up,
The same will on the record go,
That Captain MacIntosh may know.

Tough, earthy, clad in jumpers and stout boots, the linemen made colorful copy during the strike. "We are coming here to the meeting to-morrow morning with a band, if they'll let us have one in the streets," declared James Smith, leader of New York's linemen, at the first strike rally, "and we'll carry our climbing-spurs over our shoulders for guns, and let the world know that we are not ashamed of ourselves." Nor need they have been ashamed, if loyalty to the brotherhood was the criterion of pride. But it was precisely their militance that troubled and embarrassed telegraphers. As befit a middle-class calling, the operators were determined to fight the Western Union in a gentlemanly way—that, after all, was what so impressed arbiters of respectable opinion such as the *New York Times* and *Harper's*. But the linemen, though brothers, were not gentlemen. "While it is possible that some of the linemen might indulge in violence to the property of the companies," the *Times* noted, "the brotherhood can and ought to restrain them, and there is every reason to be confident that it would do so." Some telegraphers were not so sure. "Our only fear," one confessed as the Great Strike began, "is lest the linemen kick over the traces and cut the wires."[105]

As it turned out, linemen did kick and cut. Early in the strike, rumors and cryptic incidents suggested that some of them had decided that sabotage of the monopoly's wires was a fair tactic. James Smith and other brotherhood officers denied that wire cutting was sanctioned, condemned it, and promised to help catch and prosecute any telegraphic francs-tireurs. As the brotherhood's fortunes declined, reports of wire cutting increased, always linked to the "less conservative" linemen.[106]

An aura of physical violence hung about the linemen, too, further mocking the union claim of a gentlemanly struggle. On August 6, a renegade lineman provoked a fight with striking ex-workmates in which a knife had flashed and drawn blood. Although brotherhood men were not the aggressors in the fray, they evidently had been drinking. When John Mitchell indignantly denied charges of having used the strike for personal gain, one lineman at the meeting commented, "The man who makes money out of this strike will stand a good chance of being treated like Carey"—referring to James Carey, an Irish informer for the British whom an avenging Fenian had recently cornered on board a steamer and shot dead.[107]

But the linemen found wire cutters more effective than revolvers in what they plainly saw as class war. "The brotherhood are too quiet here," a New York lineman complained to the *Irish World*. "They'll never get a settlement with Gould by crying down wire cutting and shouting up law and order. When a monopolist finds the law interferes with him he doesn't stick to principle, but he cuts its wires with golden instruments. We poor men have no capital. We have only our strong hands to help us." After Gould had prevailed, the *World* rebuked the operators for not having fought the Western Union, as had the linemen, on its own terms. Their gentlemanly balking had let a "golden opportunity" to smash the monopoly slip by.[108] Not only that: the telegraphers had been all too keen on pleasing the "capitalistic press," and now had defeat as a reward. But that was in character for them. "You, defeated telegraph operator, who have always been so anxious to keep 'communistic ideas' out of the meetings," jeered an *Irish World* correspondent, "—I ask you how under Heaven you ever expect to get a fair day's wages for a fair day's work out of Jay Gould so long as you refuse to discuss in your brotherhood his right to a monopoly?"[109]

Others shared his sentiments. As humbled operators charged the Knights with a sellout and and vowed to swear off unions and radicalism, labor activists simultaneously spoke of the brotherhood's conservatism, aloofness, opportunism, and soft backbone. When John Campbell's order to call off the strike came, New York linemen blamed "kid glove operators." A Wilkes-Barre, Pennsylvania, Knight named Terence Lynch wrote grand master workman Powderly in much the same spirit: "There has been a great deal of *gush* in the newspapers about the conduct of the telegraphers during the strike but to me their conduct brings a feeling of humiliation. When I consider the encouragement they received from labor organizations all over the country to whom *they* had never rendered any assistance and then think of the weakness displayed by them as a body I am disgusted with them."[110] Many working people in New York were disgusted, too, their feelings compounded of the operators' lukewarm commitment to other wage earners and the cultural pretension of their lower-middle-class rank. A local Knight, sympathetic to the telegraphers but equanimous, explained the reluctance of so many workers to wholeheartedly support the brotherhood:

They attended the meetings of the strikers, and found them to be a party of well-dressed young men and women, wearing clothes such, as a rule, neither they nor their families wore either on Sundays or holidays. They were characterized as "dudes," and the operators are, so to speak, the dudes of the laboring classes. The young men smoked cigars or cigarettes instead of pipes, and looked much more like clerks in dry goods stores, or like bookkeepers, than they did like what some of our people thought should be the outward and visible signs of laborers. Then, too, the leaders constantly counseled moderation, hissed at speakers who argued for the adoption of more violent measures, and altogether were different from the class of people they were accustomed to meet in the assemblies of laboring men. They had no confidence in what a member of my own assembly called them, the "kid-gloved laborers," and thought that donations to them would be thrown away, because they wouldn't hold out. They refused absolutely to believe that these men and women of an entirely different social scale would make so brave a fight as they did. The linemen were all right because they wore jumpers and overalls and appeared in their shirt sleeves occasionally. But the forty-five dollar suits, white neckties, "boiled" shirts, and stove-pipe hats were too much for many of the laboring men here, who didn't think such things consistent with people who called themselves laborers. That was the real cause of the apathy among laboring men here who are consistent members of the Knights of Labor, and who have never before refused to contribute liberally in aid of a strike.[111]

The perceptive Knight might have added that the fact that telegrams were a rarity in working-class neighborhoods could not have helped the operators' cause. Businessmen and the affluent sent and received wires in the Gilded Age, but the masses seldom did. It was one thing for workers to support striking brewers, whose product they knew and loved, or, as in Toronto in 1885, to support striking streetcar men, since many ordinary people regarded the horse cars as a necessity. A quasi-luxury item like a telegram was something else again.[112]

The Great Strike, mused the *Telegraphers' Advocate* after the collapse, had been "a representative movement" in which all workers, and not just the operators, had had a stake. By their weak support for the telegraphers, they had "put off the day of final reckoning between capital and labor."[113] The *Advocate* was partly right, though strangely silent on the brotherhood's own shortcomings in thought, word, and deed. The sheer power of the Western Union had much to do with the defeat, too, but in the end, white collars and blue collars had been more important to their wearers than a common yoke that, seen from above, obscured all color.

If the Brotherhood of Telegraphers was in the Knights of Labor, to what extent was the Knights of Labor in the brotherhood?

The Great Strike had been the first nationwide uprising of labor in the 1880s. The struggle with that most notorious of big businesses, the Western Union, had focused the amorphous antimonopolism that had been growing in the 1870s, but more important, it had underlined the parallel sentiments for a universal producers' revolt against the new realities of corporate capitalism. The brotherhood had given a material, if imperfect, demonstration of those sentiments by affiliating with the still young and obscure Knights of Labor. Telegraphers forming local assemblies were important in propagating the new Knights' gospel of wage-worker fraternalism. In places as distant and different as Canada and the American South, the first Knights of Labor in town were often Knights of the Key.[114]

Yet charters, by-laws, mottoes, and passwords do not necessarily make Cooperative Commonwealthmen and women. Did operators join the brotherhood to destroy the "wages system" and replace it with a producers' republic, or did they simply—or pure and simply—want Samuel Gompers's "more"?

The two ends need not have been mutually exclusive. Recent studies of the Knights and Gilded Age labor refute the earlier claims of Gerald Grob and others that "reformist" and "pragmatic" (or even, amazingly, "middle-class") unionists vied with each other in the period and represented distinct and antagonistic points of view. On closer examination, Grob's ideological contenders turn out to be cardboard cutouts rather than the complex humans who actually peopled the labor movement of the 1880s.[115] What's more, ideology can exist on different levels within the same organization. Leaders and members may have varying perceptions of such fundamentals as class. Still, there must be consensus enough for men and women to band together in common cause. What was the operator's cause?

At the least, it was protection from the Western Union and the promise of material improvement of some kind. The very size of the industry's principal employer made even the "genteel" telegraphers willing to form a union in a day when most ordinary workers remained unorganized.[116] Brotherhood recruiting circulars stressed that a strong union would mean countervailing power to the great monopoly, fair remuneration, and a stabilized labor market through controlled apprenticeship. By joining DA 45, John Costello told a Senate committee, he and his fellows had sought "something for our services besides a bare subsistence . . . mutual assistance and protection in obtaining reasonable compensation for our services" from their employers. Thomas H. Winsor, of the Buffalo brotherhood, said essentially the same thing when he began a letter to Terence Powderly explaining, "Local Assembly No 1926 (Telegraphers) desiring to better their financial condition," and then went on to ask the Knights leader to "favor them and others by delivering a good rousing lecture upon Labor" in the coming month. The safety that organization offered was very much on John Campbell's mind when he wrote the general manager of the Reading Railroad during the Great Strike to take the part of an operator fired for refusing to handle Western Union business: "When the Brotherhood orders any of its members to do any act which causes loss to the members, such members must be protected even should the whole power of the Brotherhood be exerted. We dislike the idea of making threats," Campbell threatened, "but our men *must* be protected." Protection could extend to other kinds of dangers. In the laissez-faire world of the 1880s, workers turned to unions for sick and death benefits, and though the brotherhood did not stress friendly society functions, it did perform them.[117]

Less tangible but no less important, operators found warmth and camaraderie in the union and its ritual. It is easy enough to snicker along with W. J. Johnston as he pronounced good riddance to the brotherhood's "whisperings, its mummery of grips, badges and passwords," but this misses the powerful appeal that such forms had for contemporary workers. The secrecy even makes sense given the fragility of the labor movement and the power of capital. But ritual was not merely defensive. If affirmed solidarity and dignity. It served, as Richard Oestreicher notes, as "social glue," and not only for working-class Americans. Where social welfare was a private and voluntary concern, the ritual of organizations providing it had much emotional content for members. Being unionists engaged in common struggle could only have enhanced such feelings. "The initiations," a reporter wrote of the Boston brotherhood during the Great Strike, "are even more impressive than the other ceremonies, and are so conducted that every member is a party to the performance of them. The exercises are conducted amidst a silence that of itself makes them possessed of a peculiarly deep solemnity." When the same assembly formally expelled three deserters from the cause, the 200 members present then rose in unison, left hands over hearts and right hands raised oathlike, and reaffirmed their dedication to the brotherhood. It was, the *Globe* recorded, an "imposing sight." And for the participants, an imposing experience as well.[118]

By any reckoning, material gain, social security, and fellowship were important attractions for operators who joined the brotherhood. They were also limited goals. John Costello pronounced DA 45 "the most conservative organization that could be possibly got together," and perhaps it was. Nor was Costello the only one in the movement to make the claim.[119] Yet others saw the brotherhood and the Knights of Labor as more than an improved kind of trade union and evinced an interest in questioning and changing the shape of economy and society. The Knights' talk of "cooperation" between producers had truly radical implications. Which was the authentic voice of the brotherhood—and of the Knights?

It is difficult to know. At best the Knights were eclectic, at worst ambiguous. They represented the political and cultural coming of age of the first generation faced with full-blooded industrial capitalism. They were young enough to ask exciting and embarrassing questions about the "wages system," but old enough to still be puzzled and troubled about property rights and the boundaries of class. When John Campbell called the Great Strike "a mild sort of revolution" before the Senate hearings, he was being both politic and utterly illogical—but not necessarily disingenuous. If we think of this generation of labor activists as transitional—not in the sense of stumbling along a path that inevitably leads in the "correct" direction of pragmatic trade unionism, but in being open to musing, exploration, and experiment—then the elusive and occasionally contradictory things that the Knights said and did make more sense. To twentieth-century radical eyes, the Knights sometimes look like ideological Gumbys, stretching this way over a class line, bending that way over coopera- tion, or tying themselves in knots around the money question. But perhaps their movements were less loose than ours rigid.[120]

The Gilded Age labor movement had a refreshing open-endedness that the Knights mirrored. Look through the pages of *John Swinton's Paper* in the mid-1880s and find Greenbackers, German socialists, Single Taxers, pure-and-simple men, Irish Land Leaguers, and Knights as peaceable neighbors in the journal's columns. What this lacked in uniformity it made up for in variety and wholesome debate. Currents of reform and activism overlapped and interacted, and probably nowhere so much as in the Knights of Labor.[121]

This richness and fecundity was also a drawback. It was one thing to condemn the depredations of a bloated capitalist, but quite another to agree on exactly what a capitalist was. Definitions of class, Leon Fink points out, were often elastic. The factory was ascendent but not yet universal in the late nineteenth century. The world of the small workshop, with its owner-craftsman who, like his employees, was also a "producer," was not yet an archaism. And so the practice of ex- cluding the manufacturer from the nonproductive, parasitical "capi- talist" class still had plausibility. Trade unionists of the 1870s spoke favorably of "cooperation between capital and labor." Bankers, bro- kers, lawyers, speculators, and the like were drones, and the Knights barred them. But former Knights grand secretary Charles H. Litch- man could address a rally during the Great Strike and distinguish be- tween "legitimate" and "illegitimate" capital.[122]

The same kind of thinking existed within the brotherhood. Even with the Western Union as adversary, some strove to prove them- selves reasonable and responsible employees, asking only fair pay and decent treatment in return. Organization, wrote Robert De Akers in 1882, was necessary in the new corporate age because a strong op- erators' union would thus be able to "arbitrate" (that is, collectively bargain) with an equally strong Western Union. But such an arrange- ment betokened an ultimate harmony of interests, not class war, since it would guarantee, he argued, "safety to capital and justice to labor." Shortly before the Great Strike, the brotherhood's quasi- official organ spoke warmly of 195 Broadway manager William Dealy's attitude toward the fledgling union, and hoped that other company officials around the nation would follow his example. This "thorough understanding" between employer and employee dissolved within a month. Yet even during the walkout, declarations of cross-class harmony continued, especially when so many antimonopolists outside the labor movement smiled on the brotherhood in its fight with the Western Union. Reformers were eager enough to reciprocate the operators' friendly professions toward "legitimate" capitalists. One Bostonian spoke eloquently of the "moral mortgage" that operators held on the telegraph companies and, hastily banishing "the grisly phantom of the Commune," called instead for "the rich and well-to-do" to help right the wrongs of the present system in such a way as to assure fair and equal protection for labor as well as capital.[123]

After the defeat, John Mitchell blamed the loss on the brotherhood's affiliation with an organization that openly encouraged class antagonism. Capitalists who would have otherwise supported the telegraphers held back, he claimed, "because they foresaw in its success a general struggle between employers and employes backed by the Knights of Labor." The wistful search for harmony persisted after 1883. "The strongest organizations cause the least trouble," declared the *Telegraphers' Advocate* two years later, speaking in praise of "arbitration" that would "amicably" settle differences between labor and capital. Foolish and arrogant company officials, the *Electric Age* warned, by refusing to recognize the second brotherhood, were only "further widening the breach that now separates and antagonizes the interest" of employers and operators. One day soon, prophesied the head of the New York brotherhood in 1887, the telegraph corporations would wake up and accept the union as a responsible partner; then, "as is now the case with the Brotherhood of Locomotive Engineers," a grateful Brotherhood of Telegraphers would "invite the attendance at the opening of the annual conventions of the presidents and general superintendents" of the industry. That same year, James P. Kohler, a New York telegrapher and Single Taxer, spoke sincerely and unblushingly of "the wages that should come to us as laborers and the dividends that should go to our employers," and then, untroubled by any sense of self-contradiction, went on to damn "corruption, wage-slavery and landlordism."[124]

Personal ties with superiors (and the feeling that they too, ultimately, were telegraphers) deepened ambiguity about the battle lines between labor and capital. The growing estrangement between managers and operators in the period was clear and continual, but it was not invariable. The *Electric Age* could scornfully refer to Western Union general superintendent R. C. Clowry as "Reduction Contraction Clowry," but it was not always so easy to hate lesser officials. On the eve of the Great Strike, an Albany man praised local manager F. W. Sabold for "not find[ing] it incompatible with a strict sense of official duty to do a good turn for the men under his charge whenever an opportunity offers." The size of the office was important here, too. In 1881, a Chicagoan contrasted the city's main Western Union complex unfavorably with "the smaller interior" offices "where honors are easy, and where official dignity may, if it chooses, get down off its pedestal and 'swap lies' with the boys." That probably described affairs at Harrisburg, whose men admitted just before the 1883 walk-out that they had no local grievances to speak of and in fact enjoyed "privileges that the operators in large cities have been deprived of." The force at Louisville was about twice as large as Harrisburg's, but there, too, operators could retain a sense of identity and place within the work setting. In the office record book for April 1882, routine entries about branch office wire troubles and a change from duplex to simplex on the New Orleans circuit sandwich the decidedly nontelegraphic information that "B. Hicks got married today."[125] Even in larger offices, some managers and strikers had good-naturedly shaken hands to disclaim any personal animosity when the 1883 struggle began. More than one manager expressed sympathy for the union's cause, and brotherhood spokesmen in turn argued that many junior managers were as much victims of the Western Union as ordinary operators.[126]

Telegraphers occasionally gave their bosses gifts and testimonial dinners, although how heartfelt and popular such tributes were is hard to gauge. Company policy frowned on gifts unless meant as retirement or farewell gestures, and they may at times have paralleled the practice on some railroads of serving as semibribes to superiors. But even when aboveboard, there was an implicit social pressure in the gift subscriptions that made them far from spontaneous. Reading Railroad vice-president Theodore Voorhees in fact forbade a memorial collection under way in 1895 because such testimonials were "frequently placed before persons who feel virtually obliged to contribute, when their own families may need the amount, no matter how little it may be." In any case, the tributes and gifts seem to have slackened off after the 1870s.[127]

Welfare capitalism would have made employer-employee harmony more palatable, but there was little of it in telegraphy. Managers bestowed kindnesses, but on an ad hoc and individual basis, as William Orton did in 1866 when he authorized a subordinate to "make privately—as if on your own volition—such moderate disbursements as will meet the wants of the most pressing cases" of U.S. Telegraph Company employees about to lose their jobs in that year's merger. Not surprisingly, a good deal of the Western Union's paternalism, such as it was, originated in response to independent organization among operators. The National Telegraphic Union's creation of a mutual insurance plan in 1867 prompted the company to form the Telegraphers' Mutual Benefit Association (which paid death benefits) very soon thereafter, and at about the same time, the forerunner of the Western Union's house organ appeared—ostensibly as an independent journal—to compete with the genuinely independent *Telegrapher*. And perhaps in response to the brotherhood's emergence, there were by the late 1880s also the semiofficial Telegraphers' Aid Society (to dispense limited sick payments) and a Serial Building Association (to finance home purchases), all of which, although receiving Western Union gifts, were still largely paid for by the operators themselves. The company was much more generous to its senior managers. In 1879, the same year in which Western Union directors ordered that what amounted to a de facto pension for one Michigan operator of $50 a month be ended "lest it be taken as a precedent for other claims of the same character," the board also gave an ailing vice-president, John Van Horne, a sixty-day vacation, with salary, on top of a $500 stipend to pay for a sea voyage to restore his health. Paid vacations for Western Union telegraphers, though, were still unknown in the 1890s. Operators were allowed to send free personal messages ("dead heads") and might also get passes on allied railroads, superintendents willing. That was how Miss E. B. Thornton, a Western Union operator at Portsmouth, New Hampshire, managed to visit friends in Vermont in 1876 without paying train fare. Too, there were the company lunchrooms, and the sponsoring of sports. But these were all more fragments than a system.[128] At least one company, the Bankers & Brokers, had briefly experimented with an employee profit-sharing plan in 1870, and after the failed strikes of 1870 and 1883, craft journals suggested that such schemes would replace class friction with "industrial conciliation." The Western Union thought otherwise and never adopted any such "cooperative" plan in the

Gilded Age. For those who sought it, whether sophisticated managers or conservative telegraphers, harmony remained elusive.[129]

However hazy or supple class lines might become for operators, they did not disappear. No telegrapher had the privilege of peering over Norvin Green's shoulder in 1882 as he wrote polite notes to large stockholders to accompany their equally large dividend checks— $10,500 to Zenas Crane, $11,337 to Sidney Shepard, and $16,294.50 to Amasa Stone—but those swearing allegiance to the new operators' union that year did not need to.[130]

The brotherhood's existence embodied some kind of consensus that the corporation and its workers did not have fundamentally shared interests. Not that operators were always bucking for a fight. On a practical level, the Western Union was a dangerous and resilient foe. On a theoretical level, some within the labor movement, including those holding radical views, were wary of strikes. The Knights officially frowned on them, and followed, rather than led, when constituent assemblies took to the picket line. But you could be both class conscious and leery of strikes for very good reasons. Capital, particularly corporate capital, was a formidable opponent. Additionally, the state, despite the pieties of laissez-faire, was apt to side with capital in any struggle. During the railroad strikes of 1877, still vivid and lurid reminders of the potential of class warfare, federal bluecoats had acted in the interests of the companies. Samuel Gompers, not one to shy away from a well-conceived strike, knew firsthand about capital's claim on the use of state power; had the young cigarmaker not ducked into a doorway during the Tompkins Square "riot" of 1874, a mounted policeman's club would have brained him. The telegraphers' walkout of 1883 left the Knights and the labor movement a mixed legacy. Despite the defeat, it certainly inspired some to continue to battle monopoly, and it forced the Knights to debate and amend their strike policy (although, as Norman Ware argued, the order's growth and success in the mid-1880s was more in spite of official doctrine than because of it). A national assessment for locked-out window glass workers in October 1883 invoked "the disastrous blow caused by the defeat and annihilation of the telegraphers' Brotherhood" to remind Knights that "no sacrifice should be too great to avert the repetition of such a calamity." But the Great Strike also disheartened some and reinforced the belief that strikes were the wrong way to abolish the wages system.[131] Strikes, John McClelland told Senator Henry Blair in 1883, "as a rule are failures as remedial measures." But they were not a blind, meaningless lashing out by labor. On the contrary, McClelland asserted, strikes were "the direct outcome of education. The working classes as they became educated have a clearer idea of their rights."[132]

"Rights" had distinctly republican overtones. The Jeffersonian ideal of a free and equal citizenry—of "manly," independent Americans who supported, defended, and governed themselves—was often fused with the nineteenth-century labor movement's demands for an end to the iniquity and inequity of industrial capitalism. If political serfdom or slavery was unjust and "unmanly," so, too, was economic subservience. The claim that all citizens were persons equal before the law was ludicrous when some of the "persons" were corporations employing hundreds or thousands of real human beings. This invocation of republicanism and equal rights was a powerful device for two reasons: it drew upon a common fund of American civic culture, and it took a nominally political concept and raised it to a social and economic plane. Equality in the polling place began in the workplace. This had been the credo of a young nation of yeomen and craftsmen. The coming of corporate capitalism had perverted and destroyed this social equipoise. The redress had to be economic.[133]

Telegraph unionists and their supporters made pointed use of the republican appeal. "The natural inheritance of every man is his own labor," Boston's master workman Charles Chute told a reporter during the Great Strike. "The patrimony of the poor workingman lies in the strength and dexterity of his hands, and it is the sacred duty of the government within the jurisdiction of which he lives to protect him in his natural rights." Under a just settlement with the Western Union, a speaker told Chute's local assembly, the "faithful employe shall have secured to him that birthright of all Americans, 'manly independence.'" By the same token, the ironclad oath forced on the defeated telegraphers, John Swinton sadly observed, meant that "they had to surrender their birthright as American citizens by deserting the Telegraphic Brotherhood to which they were bound and the Knights of Labor to which they were pledged." Republican themes continued to color operator activism after the walkout. An 1887 mass meeting of New York telegraphers in support of Henry George's United Labor Party fashioned resolutions that spoke of the deplorable dependence of the worker on his employer "as if he were not an equal, free born and independent American citizen," all of which made a mockery of "the spirit of independence which is guaranteed us by the Constitution of the United States." And a decade after the Great Strike, the feeble and struggling Order of Commercial Telegraphers, in a polite appeal to the Western Union for recognition that made the obligatory bow toward the "deep, mutual interest" linking capital and labor, nevertheless rebuked the firm for being "antagonistic to the exercise of certain rights belonging to employes as freemen."[134]

Melding the old claims of civic equality with the newer ones of economic justice had radical implications. Dissastisfaction with the status quo meant countering the commonplace of 1883 with a vision of something better, and equally important, acting on that vision. Revolutions need not go forward, of course; they can be reactionary as well. Gerald Grob and those who share his interpretation of the Knights have argued that the order was in fact backward-looking and anachronistic.[135] That seems a flawed judgment. A "preindustrial" workplace may have shaped some Knights, but the varieties of alternative that the order propounded were more synthetic than atavistic. The republican-labor amalgam is a perfect example of this. So were the "sub-culture of opposition" and "alternative hegemony" that Knights scholars have identified as part of the movement. Both drew on the past and the present to declare cultural independence from the values of competition and selfish individualism.[136] They looked to the future as well, particularly in the matter of cooperation—the ownership and control of an enterprise by those creating its wealth. The cooperative idea was not, as Gerald Grob argued, simply aimed at "establishing the workers as small independent entrepreneurs" to reproduce an antique congeries of Jacksonian mills and workshops. Certainly a cooperative national telegraphic system was no such fossil.[137]

The idea was not new. Although the Telegraphers' Protective League activists of 1870 had resigned themselves to the inevitability of corporate ownership of the wires, a letter to the *Telegrapher* the next year urged operators to better their lot by forming their own company.[138] His suggestion attracted no following in the 1870s, but talk and excitement about cooperation accompanied the brotherhood's rise early in the next decade. At delegate Harry Orr's prompting, the union's first national convention in October 1882 appointed a committee to study the question of cooperative telegraphy. The inaugural issue of the brotherhood's mouthpiece, the *Telegraphers' Advocate*, discussed cooperation at length. The coming of a new, large-scale economy of corporations and "monopolies" had rendered the antebellum wage system obsolete, the paper explained. Workers of all kinds now found that "the fruit of their labor is in a great measure being lost to them" and gained by big employers. Yet the answer was not to disassemble the current industrial society but to democratize it. "Changing conditions on the one side demand changing systems on the other. If this sort of 'communism' [that is, large-scale enterprise] is to be admitted at all, it is reasonable that it should be exercised for the benefit of all concerned." Telegrapher trade unionism was important, but it was not enough. "While we are looking to present and temporary benefits," cautioned the *Advocate*, "let us not lose sight of the permanent. Together with union of men let us have union of purpose in the direction of that which to us should be of vital importance—Cooperation."[139]

Telegraphers (and Knights) no doubt found the idea of cooperative enterprise attractive for varying reasons. One man wrote the *Advocate* to laud the plan because "the whole thing would be a grand step forward for our profession, as well as to [*sic*] demonstrate the practicability of cooperation and the American idea of common sense and justice to all, as against the communistic and foreign idea of strikes." The author of "A Telegraphist's Dream" was less concerned with class conflict and more with the meshing of individual and group interests that a co-op firm would effect:

> Resting my head against the glass partition,
>   I fell asleep, and soon began to dream.
> I thought I had secured a good position
>   With a co-operative telegraphic scheme.
>
> I thought these words appeared before my vision,
>   Written in gold upon the office wall:
> "He will do most to better his condition
>   Who does most for the interest of all."
>
> The principle was carried out in practice;
>   Each man to business strictly did attend.
> The explanation's plain; indeed the fact is
>   Each had an interest in the dividend.[140]

Philadelphia's dentist-telegrapher Harry Orr likewise thought that, as their own bosses, operators could both eliminate the skimming of "middlemen or outsiders" and ply their craft cheerfully and industriously. "It was my hope that that would be the result of the organization of the Brotherhood," he told a Senate hearing. John McClelland defined cooperation even more broadly. Like Orr, he called for doing away with middlemen and restricting any co-op telegraph company to those who performed telegraphic labor. Provided sufficient capital, he testified, "the linemen now in the employ of the telegraph companies could construct the line, and the operators and the managers now in the employ of the telegraph companies could operate it."[141] But where, Senator Henry Blair asked, would the cooperators get the capital to set up their company? From the government, replied McClelland:

> If the Government should say to the telegraphers' organization as it is at present constituted, embracing all the talent and skill necessary to conduct a system of telegraphing from the highest to the lowest branches of it—if the Government should say . . . "We will take your labor and skill, which we know you possess, as sufficient security—as sufficient basis for credit, and we will advance you the necessary capital to carry on the business," it seems to me that would be entirely practicable. Because it is upon the labor of the employes of capital that the capitalist obtains his credit now, and why should not the same system be extended by the Government to such an organization of workingmen?

In fact, why not enable *all* producers to benefit from such a scheme of state credit? "These organizations of different industries," McClelland explained, "would be the recognized contractors for the performance of their several kinds of work. They would then carry on the different branches of trade only to the extent that was found necessary."

"And all the profits of each avocation," Blair inquired, "would be distributed, I suppose, among those engaged in it?"

"Certainly," said McClelland.[142]

Like many nineteenth-century labor radicals, McClelland embraced a "producerist" doctrine that rested on the labor theory of value. In one colloquy with Blair, McClelland repeatedly refused to accept the senator's premise that a return on invested capital was legitimate. If only workers derived the benefit from a machine that they ran, Blair argued, it would be just as unfair as the capitalist retaining all the profit, since "the capitalist constructs the machine, does he not?"

"Not at all," corrected McClelland, "it is invented and constructed by labor."

"But the capitalist furnishes the money which pays the wages which the laborer receives while he is constructing the machine."

"Yes, but he takes the money in the first place from the laborer."

Nor would McClelland let Senator James George's definition of "capital" go unchallenged at another point. "Modern political economy," he countered, " would call it the unpaid labor of the working people." McClelland's plan for the state furnishing credit to producer co-ops had a decided syndicalist cast to it. Comparing the contemporary order with the cooperative one that the Ontario-born telegrapher proposed should gradually replace it, Blair asked whether corruption might then sharply decline because "it would be more difficult to purchase [that is, bribe] an entire legislature" than under present conditions. Replied McClelland, "I do not see any necessity for legislatures as they are at present constituted." McClelland's radical vision also had limits. How democratized he intended the shop floor to be under employee ownership is open to question, since he evidently saw no need to dispense with either specialization or hierarchy. In any case, few Knights, and still fewer telegraphers, shared McClelland's commitment to cooperation. When Senator Wilkinson Call asked John Costello whether the brotherhood was based on the goal of cooperative telegraphy, the latter demurred. "No sir," he said, "I do not understand that that is our object." The brotherhood was simply a trade union and that, Costello asserted, was "the general sentiment." It evidently was. Both Harry Orr and McClelland, keen cooperators that they were, confessed that most brothers and sisters had little interest in the matter.[143]

Such interest as there was picked up during the Great Strike. On July 23, the *Boston Globe* reported that the operators' union was exploring the possibility of setting up a co-op firm, and during the following week the details of a proposed alternative to the Western Union emerged. But the plan envisioned cooperation of a markedly conservative kind: the Merchants' & Telegraphers' Association was to be a joint venture between operators and businessmen. The association was a blend of the original brotherhood idea for a worker-owned system and that of a New Jersey silk manufacturer, John Cutter, who, like many independent businessmen, resented the power of the Western Union. "Many rich merchants who have become anti-monopolists because of railroad and telegraph mismanagement and tyranny" were said to be joining Cutter in support of the venture, and one account had 200 enthusiastic letters flowing into his office asking to be put down as subscribers. "Capitalists have promised us that they will help make the enterprise a success," exulted John Campbell.[144]

The brotherhood would supply the labor and managerial skill of its members, while the merchants, bankers, and brokers who subscribed would furnish the bulk of the capital. If no model of worker collectivism, neither was the Merchants' & Telegraphists' Association an ordinary business. There would be no stock per se, but "initiation fees of life membership," at $200, limited one to a customer. "A member cannot increase his interest, nor diminish it, nor terminate it," a brotherhood circular explained. "Membership not being property is not marketable, so cannot fall into the hands of sheriff or surrogate." Nor could it be "bulled, beared, [or] consolidated." In essence, the association was a producer-consumer co-op.[145] Brotherhood leaders urged operators to subscribe—the $200 could be paid in installments—and to canvass hometown businessmen for memberships in the association. "I believe I can raise $200,000 or more among my antimonopoly friends in New York City," R. H. Ferguson, a Knights organizer in upstate New York, wrote Terence Powderly. "All I want is the authority to try and I will go there and then work here in this city and I suggest that the assemblies be Each asked to take a share or more at $200."[146]

But there were few takers, either among the Knights or the business community. The press had surely exaggerated the extent of support for the scheme. Wealthy merchants and bankers did often hate the Western Union, but their alliance with the striking telegraphers was tenuous and ephemeral. Beyond that, they were no fools when it came to what they did with their money. It was much cheaper to wish the brotherhood well than to throw $200 in the direction of a dubious venture. Such capitalists, the *Operator* concluded after the walkout, were "chary of investment in an enterprise the success of which, in the absence of precedent, must be extremely problematical." After the initial excitement at the prospect of throttling Jay Gould and his monopoly subsided, businessmen of probity had second thoughts about the association. And with good reason. Any new telegraph company, Western Union officials pointed out, would have to secure a great network of rural and urban rights-of-way. "No new company can be successful without the contracts between the railroads and Western Union," declared a corporate officer. He was right. And if substantial bankers and merchants were reluctant to fund the association, who would—$40-a-month branch office operators? By summer's end, the plan for a cooperative telegraph company, like the Great Strike, was dead.[147]

Telegraphers had sought to better their condition by forming unions. Unions, though, had had little effect on the craft's decline. Operators also tried the cooperation route to end the Western Union's "grinding," but that, too, had failed. They consequently turned to the one remaining source of redress: the state.

Some did so hesitantly. Gilded Age Americans, and no less so labor activists, still harbored ambivalence about the state and the citizen's relation to it. The same republican ethos that workers so tellingly used in combination with demands for economic justice also contained a classical liberal strain in which the state was a government by the people—not by professionals and placemen—whose legitimate functions were limited and largely negative. Strong and intrusive central governments and the legalized robbery of mercantilism were part of the tyranny and decadence of the Old World; civil liberties and laissez-faire were the bases of the enlightenment of the New. Nineteenth-century Americans of all classes, David Montgomery writes, shared an "incapacity to envision the state as an administrative agency, rather than simply as a lawgiver," and this surely applied to operators contemplating a government-run telegraph system as their last hope.[148]

Suspicion of the state was not just a matter of theory. Labor activists of the 1880s had evidence enough within their lifetime of the repressive potential of government in class strife. And so some operators shied away from statist solutions, offering instead something that partook of both antimonopolism and a kind of syndicalism. Pointing to the success of the Brotherhood of Locomotive Engineers, one man warned his craftmates in 1888 that only a strong union capable of "enforcing its righteous demands" would solve their problems, not "class legislation," which was "always dangerous to individual liberty." If you must pass laws, he wrote, pass ones that break up "monopolies, trusts and combinations of what-so-ever character." Fair play and an open field would take care of the rest.[149]

But the verities of classical political economy were a stale loaf by the 1880s, increasingly hard to swallow and no longer very nourishing. The corporate economy taking shape no more resembled that of the early Republic than the Western Union resembled the Boston Post Road. Massed capital and labor's attempt to mass in response were part of this transformation; an extension of governmental responsibilities would have to be as well. Besides, a government telegraph was more evolutionary than revolutionary—it was only moving along a logical continuum to go from carrying letters to sending telegrams. The state had built or subsidized canals, railroads, and the like because they were commercial arteries serving the public. Why not now the telegraph as well?[150]

Operators were not alone in asking that question. Accompanying the invigorated antimonopolism of the period was a renewed interest in public ownership of the nation's wires. Postal telegraphy was a staple of radical and reform platforms, but proponents of the various government telegraph schemes included those of otherwise quite conservative bent, among them several postmasters general, members of congress, and prominent editors. It also attracted a fair constituency of brokers, merchants, bankers, and other solid capitalists whose interests were more immediate in breaking the Western Union's hold on commercial communications. The plans ranged from an outright government monopoly similar to the European systems to semiprivate contracting arrangements under license, but all took a state role of some kind for granted.[151]

"Government," though, often seemed interchangeable with "corruption" in the age of the Tweed Ring, the Star Route Fraud, and the Credit Mobilier. In that case, replied postal telegraphy advocates, establish the system on a meritocratic, civil service basis. A state monopoly was at least accountable to the people; the Western Union had only to answer to its stockholders. Rational and impartial personnel policies were exactly what operators had been demanding from their private employers anyway, so embracing a state-run system was a happy marriage of self-interest and reform for the Knights and Ladies of the Key. "In behalf of the telegraphers," former manager Alfred Seymour addressed senators three days after the Great Strike ended, "as one of those who have appeared before this committee representing the telegraphers in part, I wish to state that they look to Congress and the Government for relief in the future. . . . before all, the telegraphers desire a Government system of telegraph, I believe." Concluded the *Electric Age* in 1886: "It may be that the corporation will never yield justice to the men. In such an event, the latter will find it to their advantage to hasten postal telegraphy."[152]

A good way to do so was to become politically active. To the extent that operators as a group supported any political faction in the 1880s, they chose Henry George's independent United Labor Party of 1886–88, a movement that appealed to a broad coalition of reform and labor activists, especially during his 1886 run for the New York City mayoralty. Henry George was an old friend of the telegraphers. He had warmly supported the brotherhood in 1883, and his Single Tax theory admitted a state role in owning and operating natural monopolies. Four years after the Great Strike, campaigning for state office in New York, he asked a gathering of operators who had turned out to hear him: "Couldn't you work as comfortably for the Government as for the Western Union? The north and south pole of our platform is the governmental control of all monopolies. Band together to disseminate our principles. Talk with your brother operators over the wire. Give them something to think about." His auditors were convinced. Calling themselves the Telegraphers' Association, they adopted a resolution supporting George and his ticket.[153]

It made good sense for them to rally to a man committed to setting up a public telegraph system, but some operators' devotion to George went deeper. For believers, the Single Tax was an epiphany: the operators' long-standing decline was but another manifestation of the "land question." It was foolish, declared James Kohler, the operator who stumped for George and the United Labor Party in 1886, to blame the paucity of telegraphic berths on the "student question" or the "lady operator question." No. "There is better game," he told his fellows, and that was the "land question."[154] Next year, like-minded operators formed a Telegraphers' Land and Labor Club to discuss and propagate the Single Tax idea among the craft. Renouncing "strikes, boycotts, and all other artificial means of alleviating our condition as wage-earners" (and that included the "folly to attempt to build a fence around our trade"), club members instead urged operators to turn to the ballot box and the state.[155]

Georgite doctrine did not charm everyone. Washington, D.C.,

telegrapher H. S. Larcombe dismissed the Single Tax as "communistic." L. H. Morgan, of Leavenworth, Kansas, maintained that operators would better their condition by swearing off drink and pool halls, not by engaging in politics and reform. The *Electric Age*'s "De" penned a tart piece in which he had an imaginary conversation with a spectral operator. "I was talked to death on the 'Private ownership of land,'" the ghost explained. "If you want to avoid a sure death, get on the day force where there are no Henry George men."[156]

For those who did turn to the United Labor Party, ethnicity, as well as immediate self-interest and economic theory, may have played a role. If, as the evidence strongly suggests, a large number of urban telegraphers were of Irish-American background, the Georgite emphasis on the "land question" dovetailed with an abiding Irish concern with matters of land and poverty. Eric Foner has demonstrated that agitation over an Ireland oppressed by landlords and British imperialism combined in the 1880s with domestic labor and reform activism in a dynamic way. Prominent among these companionate reform currents was the Single Tax. Nowhere was this unique mix more visible than in the *Irish World*, a journal that managed, in equal parts, to cover the labor movement, general reform efforts, and the fate of the Irish on both sides of the Atlantic—and even more important, to make explicit the connections between all three.[157] The *World* was no stranger to the telegraphers. It had supported the brotherhood enthusiastically in 1883, and after the defeat castigated it for its priggishness in general and its official aloofness from the land question in particular.[158] Perhaps some operators active in the poststrike brotherhood reconsidered the relevance of the Single Tax to their own plight and that of their cousins in Ireland. In any case, the Knights, Georgites, and transplanted Hibernians were often of a piece in the Gilded Age labor movement. It seems appropriate that an ardent United Labor Party man who urged his fellow telegraphers to follow his example in 1887 was named John J. Flanagan.[159]

Flanagan is symbolic in more ways than one. Very likely he was the same J. J. Flanagan whom we met at the National Telegraphic Union's 1865 convention arguing that accepting clerks as members would degrade the union. Flanagan and his colleagues had come a long way since then: from conservative benefit society to militant trade union to industrywide wage-earners' alliance to politicized occupational group. The last two incarnations covered more distance than they superficially imply. As Knights and Single Taxers, telegraphers had accepted a reading of their circumstances that went beyond immediate and narrow interest. However vague and contradictory the notions of the Knights and simplistic the land fetish of the Georgites, both pointed to social problems and offered social solutions. That the various operators' efforts failed, from the National Telegraphic Union through the brotherhood, is only part of the story. Their failures were a process of exploration and discovery, not steps in a teleological climb to the Cooperative Commonwealth. The political path that many craft activists adopted in the late 1880s was as much a product of frustration as insight, but it was also a significant break with the past. Turning to politics and the state had its dangers, of course. The radical republican ideology of equal rights that could question the justice of the economic order, Richard Oestreicher observes, could also have a profoundly reactionary content, longingly invoking a mythical past blessed by a "naturally harmonious relationship between classes." But envisioning a government-owned telegraph system was no more a throwback than the earlier cooperative plans of the brotherhood. Both, to paraphrase two students of the Knights, were dreams of what might be. And both were the result of what the Knights liked to call education.[160]

EPILOGUE

On August 3, 1981, the Professional Air Traffic Controllers Organization (PATCO), a union that had endorsed the right-wing presidential
candidacy of Ronald Reagan the year before, struck against its employer, the federal government, demanding improvements in pay
and working conditions in that notoriously high-stress occupation.
Now in office, Reagan—who had responded to PATCO's preelection
support with a pledge "to work very closely with you to bring about a
spirit of cooperation between the President and the air traffic controllers"—promptly set out to break the strike. Within a few months he
had done so, decertifying the union, firing 11,000 of its members, and
filling their places with scabs. The president had hewed to the letter
of the law, but his actions were meant as much to symbolize the new
administration's attitude toward the labor movement as to honor his
constitutional obligations. Workers took the lesson to heart. Postal
service employees accepted a contract that many of them would have
otherwise rejected had PATCO's fate not been fresh in their minds.
The Reagan administration, and the social forces that it represented,
had used the air controllers' strike to redeclare class war in the most
vigorous terms.[1]

This was no Great Strike redivivus. Air traffic controllers were not
telegraphers, nor the Federal Aviation Administration the Western
Union. The broad support that the operators had attracted was missing, too. Few Americans felt sorry for strikers earning $30,000 to
$40,000 a year whose walkout had put personal interest before the
safety of the flying public.[2]

Yet there were similarities between 1883 and 1981. Like some telegraphers, air traffic controllers worked under intense pressure. Medical and emotional problems often went with the job. Most controllers
quit in their forties, and only 11 percent reached formal retirement.
And like the Brotherhood of Telegraphers, PATCO drew criticism for
its handling of the strike. AFL-CIO leaders unofficially censured the
union for having "acted precipitously" and neglecting "a broad education program to convince Americans to support their views."[3]

Differences between the labor movement and PATCO in fact went
a good deal deeper than tactics. The controllers' relative affluence
dulled sympathy for their cause among other unionists. Privately,
AFL-CIO chiefs told one journalist that the strikers' high salaries,
"particularly compared to industrial workers earning $15,000 to
$20,000 a year," made it hard to take up PATCO's cause with any en-
thusiasm. All the more galling was the controllers' support of Reagan
in 1980. Although PATCO's endorsement had come as much from ex-
asperation at the policies of the FAA under the previous Carter administration as from political conservatism, their backing for the
California Republican had angered and disgusted the AFL-CIO hierarchy. The strike's illegality made labor bureaucrats tread cautiously,
but their "lukewarm" support for PATCO also betrayed the tension
and antipathy between the national labor movement and its air traffic
controllers' affiliate.[4]

One hundred years after the Great Strike, the new middle class
that the operators had presaged is no longer new, but the ambiguity
and instability of its peculiar social position remain. The telegraphers
of 1883 are long gone, yet later kindred occupations—air traffic controllers among them—continue to embody much the same mix of
class and culture: paid well above the average, possessing a white-
collar, technical specialty, but still subordinate and vulnerable employees who must form a union little different from those of carpenters or steelworkers to protect themselves. But what blue-collar union
would prefix its name with the word *professional*, as PATCO did? And
what occupational group normally reckoned a profession would have
to use that same word to establish its status? "American Professional
Medical Association" or "American Professional Bar Association"
sound both pointless and ludicrous. Air traffic controllers, though,
had no such cultural self-assurance. Or take another manifestation of
the lower middle class of the jet age: stewardesses and stewards organized themselves into the Association of Professional Flight Atten-

dants, a name that likewise reveals a vague social insecurity. And all of this resonates with the "genteel" telegraphers of the 1880s.[5]

Much has changed in the past century. We are undergoing a third industrial revolution. The old "smokestack" industries decline or move to more profitable, low-wage settings; a new "high-tech" service economy, with its small managerial and technocratic elite and its vast and growing white- and pink-collar proletariat, is proclaimed the wave of the future; and the misery of a huge urban black underclass mounts while both the work force and poverty become the new women's spheres. Technological innovation underlies these changes, but so do the dynamics and recurring crises of a world capitalist economy. Rather than the "permanent revolution" that corporate publicists so enthusiastically celebrated in the 1950s, the Affluent Society of post–World War II America was a fleeting truce in a shifting and inveterate conflict. When the informal economic and military empire of the United States faltered in the 1970s and 1980s, the social contract at home dissolved. A "middle-class" America stagnated and shrank.

Gilded Age telegraphers would probably recognize many aspects of the current crisis, for the 1880s, too, was a time when strong, swift, and erratic economic currents undermined or swept away established notions of the dignity and justice due workers and citizens. The Knights of Labor had set out to resist that degradation. They had tried to measure the new forces in the workplace and marketplace against a scale calibrated in self-respect and commonwealth rather than profit and loss.

In the short run, the Knights failed. Powerful adversaries defeated them, but they defeated themselves, too. They did so not out of stupidity or masochism, but out of misjudgment and force of habit. Most people are conservative in the true sense of the word. Oppression is painful, but breaking out of an accustomed mold is sometimes more painful—at least in the short run. Genuine conservatism is not necessarily a bad thing. Culture and convention can be formidable means of resistance to pernicious change. Such was the role that republicanism and domesticity played for nineteenth-century American men and women undergoing a capitalist industrial revolution. But culture and convention can also be immobilizing ruts. That was why laborers and kid-gloved laborers eyed each other with suspicion, if not outright dislike, in 1883. The Knights struggled with this problem as much as with those of the wages system, monopoly, and cooperation. Their failure was not for lack of sincere effort.

But in the long run, the Knights—including the Knights and Ladies of the Key—did not fail. They still speak to us. They caution us about the illusory quality of white collars and "professional" unions and "middle-class" workers. They teach us about the stultifying tenacity of culture, but also of its ambivalence and power: of its ability to retain what was best in our past, to reject what is worst in our present, and to create what will be noblest in our future.

NOTES

1 A MILD SORT OF REVOLUTION

1 *Telegraphers' Advocate*, Aug. 1, 1883 (hereafter cited as *TA*); *Journal of the Telegraph*, Feb. 15, 1875 (hereafter *JT*); David Homer Bates, *Lincoln in the Telegraph Office* (New York, 1907), 131, 408.

2 *TA*, Aug. 1, 1883; *Boston Herald*, July 16, 20, 23, 1883 (hereafter *BH*); John B. Taltavall, *Telegraphers of To-Day* (New York, 1893), 178–179; U.S. Senate, *Report of the Committee of the Senate upon the Relations between Labor and Capital* (Washington, D.C., 1885), 1:911. For a somewhat different account, see *New York Herald*, July 17, 1883 (hereafter *NYH*).

3 *Electric Age*, June 1, 1886 (hereafter *EA*); Senate, *Labor and Capital*, 1:50–51; George E. McNeill, ed., *The Labor Movement: The Problem of To-Day* (Boston, 1887), 391.

4 *Boston Globe*, July 11, 12, 1883 (hereafter *BG*); *BH*, July 12, 1883; *Reading* (Pennsylvania) *Times*, July 5, 1883; *New York Tribune*, July 12, 1883 (hereafter *NYTr*).

5 *NYTr*, July 13, 14, 15, 1883; *BG*, July 14, 1883.

6 For a full list of the firms presented with the bill of grievances, see *TA*, Aug. 1, 1883.

7 *NYTr*, July 16, 1883; *Baltimore Sun*, July 18, 1883 (hereafter *BS*); *BG*, July 19, 1883.

8 *Cleveland Plain Dealer*, July 17, 1883 (hereafter *CPD*); *BG*, July 18, 19, 1883; see also *BS*, July 18, 1883.

9 *BH*, July 17, 19, 1883; *BG*, July 19, 1883; *NYTr*, July 19, 1883; *New York Times*, July 19, 1883 (hereafter *NYT*).

10 *NYTr*, July 20, 1883; *CPD*, July 19, 1883; *Harrisburg Daily Telegraph*, July 19, 1883 (hereafter *HDT*).

11 *NYT*, July 20, 1883; *BH*, July 23, 1883; *BG*, July 19, 1883; *NYTr*, July 20, 1883. On Dealy's reaction, cf. *TA*, Sept. 1, 1883.

12 *NYT*, July 20, 1883; *BH*, July 20, 1883; *CPD*, July 19, 1883; *Atlanta Constitution*, July 20, 1883 (hereafter *AC*); see also *HDT*, July 19, 1883; *BS*, July 20, 1883; *New Orleans Picayune*, July 20, 1883 (hereafter *NOP*).

13 *NYTr*, July 20, 1883; *BG*, July 19, 20, 1883; Senate, *Labor and Capital*, 2:56; *Boston Evening Transcript*, July 21, 1883 (hereafter *BET*); *TA*, Aug. 1, 1883. For a local Western Union office holding its own, see *HDT*, July 20, 1883;

14 *NYT*, July 20, 1883; Senate, *Labor and Capital*, 2:56, 59; *NOP*, July 20, 1883; *NYTr*, July 20, 1883. See also *BG*, July 20, 1883.

15 *BET*, July 25, 1883.

16 *NYT*, July 21, 1883. See also *BG*, July 24, 1883.

17 *BG*, July 21, 23, 24, 1883; *AC*, July 24, 1883; for the close ties between Gould and Eckert, see Matthew Josephson, *The Robber Barons* (New York, 1934), 205–206; and Maury Klein, *The Life and Legend of Jay Gould* (Baltimore, 1986), 197, 199, 281, 389.

18 *NYT*, July 22, 1883; *NYTr*, July 22, 1883; *BG*, July 24, 1883; Record Book, Louisville Western Union office, in box 16, Western Union Collection, National Museum of American History Archives, Smithsonian Institution (hereafter WUCS). See also *BG*, July 23, 1883.

19 *BG*, July 23, 24, 1883; *CPD*, July 21, 23, 24, 25, 27, 1883; *NOP*, July 23, 1883; *BH*, July 22, 1883; *AC*, July 25, 1883; *NYTr*, Aug. 7, 1883; *NYT*, July 21, 22, 1883.

20 *Springfield Republican*, July 22, 1883 (hereafter *SR*); *BH*, July 22, 1883; *NYH*, July 21, 22, 1883. See also *CPD*, July 28, 1883; *BH*, July 28, 1883.

21 *BH*, July 25, 1883; *AC*, July 22, 1883; *CPD*, July 25, 1883. The division of labor among the brotherhood strike committees was fourfold: Finance and Relief, Intelligence, Law and Order, and Skirmishing. *NOP*, July 21, 1883.

22 *CPD*, July 21, 1883; *NYTr*, July 23, 1883; *BET*, July 24, 1883. See also *NYT*, July 20, 24, 1883; *BET*, July 25, 1883.

23 *NYT*, July 20, 21, 23, 1883; *NYTr*, July 20, 23, 1883; *CPD*, July 27, 1883; *St. Louis Post Dispatch*, July 25, 1883 (hereafter *SLPD*); *BS*, July 23, 1883. See also *NYT*, July 18, 22, 25, 28, 1883; *NYTr*, July 29, 1883; *AC*, July 20, 1883; *BG*, July 16, 1883;

24 *BG*, July 23, 1883; *BH*, July 23, 1883; *NYT*, July 21, 1883; *Harper's Weekly*, Aug. 18, 1883; *TA*, Aug. 1, 1883; *NOP*, Aug. 8, 1883. See also *TA*, Aug. 16, Sept. 1, 1883; *BS*, July 21, 1883; *NYTr*, July 28, Aug. 10, 1883; *BG*, July 18–22, Aug. 3, 5, 1883; *SR*, July 22, Aug. 6, 19, 1883; *BET*, July 20, 21, 24, Aug. 4, 18, 1883; *NOP*, July 18, Aug. 18, 1883; *NYT*, July 23, 26, 30, 1883; *Frank Leslie's Illustrated Newspaper*, July 28, Aug. 4, 1883; *BH*, July 23, 25, 31, 1883; *CPD*, July 25, 1883.

25   *BG*, July 19, 27, 29, 1883; *NYT*, July 31, Aug. 9, 1883. See also *BS*, Aug. 15, 1883.

26   *NOP*, Aug. 1, 1883; *NYTr*, July 20, 1883; *Hampshire Gazette and Northampton Courier*, July 24, 1883; *AC*, Aug. 4, 1883; *BET*, July 25, Aug. 1, 1883; *NYTr*, July 28, 1883; *BG*, Aug. 14, 1883. See also *BS*, July 20, 1883; *BG*, July 20, 1883; *TA*, Aug. 1, 1883; *BH*, July 25, 26, Aug. 14, 1883; *AC*, Aug. 18, 1883; *NYTr*, July 21, 29, 30, 1883; *NYT*, Aug. 1, 6, 1883; *NOP*, July 27, 29, 1883; *BET*, July 19, 20, 23, Aug. 18, 1883.

27   *BG*, July 22, 29, 1883; *NYT*, Aug. 3, 1883; *NOP*, July 28, Aug. 2, 1883; *NYT*, July 24, 27, Aug. 9, 1883. See also *NYT*, July 28, Aug. 4, 1883; *NOP*, July 28, 1883; *CPD*, July 20, 1883; *TA*, Aug. 16, 1883; *BH*, July 25, 1883.

28   *BG*, July 23, 27, 28, 31, Aug. 4, 8, 10, 1883; *NYTr*, July 23, 1883; *NYT*, July 26, 31, Aug. 9, 1883; *BH*, July 26, 29, 1883. See also *BG*, July 19, 23, 27, 28, Aug. 4, 5, 17, 1883; *BET*, July 27, 28, 1883; *NOP*, July 22, 31, Aug. 2, 1883; *NYT*, July 23, Aug. 8, 9, 18, 1883; *CPD*, Aug. 9, 1883; *AC*, July 29, Aug. 2, 1883.

29   *NYT*, July 24, Aug. 4, 15, 1883; *TA*, Aug. 16, 1883.

30   *NYT*, Aug. 4, 1883; *BH*, Aug. 3, 1883. See also *NYT*, July 28, 29, 1883; *NYTr*, July 18, 19, 1883; *BG*, July 14, 1883.

31   *NOP*, July 25, Aug. 2, 1883; *CPD*, Aug. 3, 1883; *BG*, Aug. 5, 13, 1883; *NYT*, Aug. 3, 6, 16, 1883. See also *BH*, Aug. 13, 16, 1883; *BG*, July 19, 29, 1883; *NYT*, July 31, Aug. 6, 9, 14, 1883.

32   *CPD*, July 27, 1883. See also *NYT*, July 22, 30, Aug. 6, 12, 1883; *BH*, July 26, Aug. 1, 1883; *NOP*, July 30, 31, 1883; *NYTr*, July 27, 1883; *AC*, Aug. 1, 1883.

33   *BG*, July 24, 25, Aug. 3, 1883; *Life*, Aug. 16, 1883; *Puck*, Aug. 1, 8, 1883; *AC*, July 22, 1883.

34   *BET*, July 27, 1883; *EA*, Oct. 1, 1886.

35   *Life*, Aug. 16, 1883; *Puck*, Aug. 8, 1883; *BG*, July 28, 1883; *BET*, July 28, Aug. 27, 1883; *NYT*, July 28, Aug. 2, 15, 1883; *EA*, June 1, 16, 1886.

36   *BET*, July 20, 1883; *CPD*, July 26, 1883; *NYT*, July 24, 1883; *NOP*, July 31, 1883; Daniel J. Czitrom, *Media and the American Mind* (Chapel Hill, N.C., 1982), 23–27.

37   *BG*, Aug. 1, 1883.

38   *BG*, July 26, 31, 1883; *NYT*, July 26, 1883. For details of the settlement, see *CPD*, Aug. 11, 1883; *NYT*, Aug. 10, 1883.

39   *EA*, July 1, 1886; Josiah C. Reiff to Robert Garrett, Aug. 15, 1883, in box 1, Garrett Family Papers (Ms. no. 979), Manuscripts Division, Maryland Historical Society, Baltimore; *BG*, July 31, 1883. See also *BS*, July 18, 1883.

40   *BG*, July 21, 31, 1883.

41   *BH*, July 30, Aug. 1, 1883; *BET*, Aug. 1, 1883; *BG*, Aug. 1, 1883.

42 *NYT*, Aug. 1, 2, 1883. See also *BG*, Aug. 2, 1883.
43 *BG*, July 22, Aug. 1, 2, 12, 1883; *BH*, July 31, Aug. 5, 1883. See also *NYTr*, July 18, 19, 1883; *CPD*, July 25, 1883; *BH*, Aug. 3, 1883; *NOP*, July 26, 1883.
44 *NYT*, Aug. 4, 1883; Terence V. Powderly (hereafter TVP) to Layton, Aug. 6, 8, 1883, in Powderly Papers (microfilm of original collection at Catholic University).
45 *BG*, Aug. 2, 1883. Cf. Aug. 3, 1883.
46 *BG*, Aug. 6, 7, 1883; *BET*, Aug. 6, 1883; *NYTr*, Aug. 7, 1883; *NYT*, Aug. 6, 7, 1883.
47 *BG*, Aug. 9, 10, 15, 1883; *NOP*, Aug. 8, 12, 1883.
48 *BG*, Aug. 7, 8, 1883; *NYTr*, Aug. 1, 11, 12, 1883.
49 *BH*, July 22, 1883; *BG*, July 30, 1883. See also *BH*, Aug. 11, 1883.
50 *NYTr*, Aug. 7, 1883.
51 *NYT*, Aug. 8, 1883; *NYTr*, Aug. 8, 1883; *BET*, Aug. 8, 1883; *NOP*, Aug. 16, 17, 1883. See also *NYT*, Aug. 17, 1883; *BH*, Aug. 20, 1883; *NYTr*, Aug. 10, 1883.
52 *BG*, Aug. 15, 17, 1883; Senate, *Labor and Capital*, 1:1080. See also ibid., 1:891; *BG*, Aug. 3, 5, 7, 17, 1883; *NYT*, Aug. 3, 4, 9, 14, 15, 18, 1883; *NOP*, Aug. 18, 1883; *CPD*, Aug. 9, 1883.
53 *BG*, Aug. 10, 1883; *HDT*, Aug. 9, 1883; *TA*, Sept. 1, 1883.
54 *BH*, Aug. 3, 1883; *NYT*, Aug. 11, 12, 1883; *BG*, Aug. 17, 1883; *HDT*, Aug. 9, 1883. See also *BG*, Aug. 4, 1883; *NOP*, Aug. 5, 12, 1883; *AC*, Aug. 11, 17, 1883. For denials of a brotherhood decline, see *BG*, Aug. 4, 9, 11, 1883; *BET*, Aug. 11, 1883; *CPD*, Aug. 15, 1883; *BH*, Aug. 13, 1883.
55 *TA*, Aug. 16, 1883; *NYT*, Aug. 16, 1883; *BG*, Aug. 16, 1883; *NYTr*, Aug. 16, 1883.
56 J. C. Reiff to Robert Garrett, Aug. 15, 1883, box 1, Garrett Papers.
57 *BG*, Aug. 18, 1883.
58 *NOP*, Aug. 18, 1883; *BG*, Aug. 19, 1883. See also *TA*, Sept. 1. 1883.
59 *NYT*, Aug. 15, 1883; *BG*, July 19, 1883; *AC*, July 24, 1883; *BET*, July 23, Aug. 18, 1883. See also *BH*, July 12, 1883.
60 Criticism of the brotherhood's strategy predated the collapse by almost a week. *NYT*, Aug. 11, 1883; *BH*, Aug. 11, 1883. See also *BG*, July 24, 1883, for an outline of the strike callout sequence.
61 *TA*, Sept. 1, 1883; *BG*, Aug. 21, 1883. See also *BG*, Aug. 16, 1883.
62 *NYTr*, Aug. 21, 1883; *BH*, July 23, 1883; *NYT*, Aug. 18, 1883; *BG*, Aug. 18, 19, 1883. See also *NOP*, Aug. 18, 1883.
63 *NYT*, Aug. 17, 1883; *BG*, Aug. 18, 1883; *NOP*, Aug. 19, 1883; *BH*, Aug. 19, 1883. See also *TA*, Aug. 16, 1883; *NYT*, Aug. 19, 1883; *AC*, Aug. 23, 1883; *BET*, Aug. 18, 1883; *BG*, Aug. 18, 19, 1883; and for earlier intimations of this sentiment, *BH*, Aug. 12, 1883.

64 *TA*, Sept. 1, 1883.

65 *CPD*, Aug. 22, 1883; *NYT*, Aug. 20, 1883; *EA*, July 1, 1886. See also *TA*. Sept. 1, 1883; *BG*, Aug. 22, 1883; *NYTr*, July 24, 1883.

66 McNeill, *Labor Movement*, 392; *BG*, Aug. 21, 1883.

67 Vidkunn Ulriksson, *The Telegraphers: Their Craft and Their Unions* (Washington, D.C., 1953), 50; *EA*, Aug. 16, 1886; *BG*, Aug. 19, 21, 1883; *NYTr*, Aug. 23, 1883. See also Norvin Green to Senator Wilkinson Call, Jan. 24, 1884, Western Union Telegraph Company presidents' letter books, Secretary's office, Western Union Corporation, Upper Saddle River, N.J. (hereafter WULB).

68 *TA*, Sept. 1, 1883; *NYTr*, Aug. 23, 1883.

69 *Puck*, Aug. 29, 1883; Senate, *Labor and Capital*, 1:891.

2   ANATOMY OF AN INDUSTRY

1 Alfred D. Chandler, Jr., *The Visible Hand* (Cambridge, Mass., 1977), 79, 89, 207, 240–244. On the antebellum phase of this change, the classic study remains George Rogers Taylor, *The Transportation Revolution* (New York, 1951).

2 On the size and complexity of telegraph and railroad corporations, see Chandler, *Visible Hand*, 89, 189, 288–289.

3 Elisha P. Douglass, *The Coming of Age of American Business* (Chapel Hill, N.C., 1971), 480–483.

4 Robert Luther Thompson, *Wiring a Continent* (Princeton, N.J., 1947), chap. 20 passim, and 334; Douglass, *Coming of Age*, 484–485; William Orton to George F. Davis, Jan. 17, 1866, WULB; Thomas C. Cochran and William Miller, *The Age of Enterprise* (New York, 1942), 115–116.

5 Douglass, *Coming of Age*, 484; Alvin F. Harlow, *Old Wires and New Waves* (New York, 1936), 331–332.

6 James D. Reid, *The Telegraph in America* (New York, 1879), 813–815.

7 *BH*, July 26, 1883; Senate, *Labor and Capital*, 1:868, 1070. See also ibid., 1:881, 901, 921; *NYTr*, July 20, 1883; Thompson, *Wiring a Continent*, 443–444.

8 *BH*, July 26, 1883; Thompson, *Wiring a Continent*, 444; Czitrom, *Media and the American Mind*, 23–27.

9 U.S. Department of Commerce, *Historical Statistics of the United States* (Washington, D.C., 1975), pt. 1, p. 201, pt. 2, p. 788. The adjusted figures are in constant 1910–14 dollars. For somewhat different and even more impressive profit figures, see Department of Commerce and Labor, *Statistical Abstract of the United States* (Washington, D.C., 1911), 257.

10 *Statistical Abstract*, 257.

11   Meetings of June 3, Dec. 9, 1874, in Western Union Telegraph Company, "Records, Directors and Stockholders" (minute books), book A, Secretary's Office, Western Union Corporation, Upper Saddle River, N.J. (hereafter WUMB); *Historical Statistics*, pt. 2, pp. 787–788. Profit rate is expressed as percent return (in net income) on total book capitalization, excluding the years 1870–72, for which book value figures are missing. I have reckoned the dividend rates as a percentage of the year's total book capitalization.

12   *Telegrapher*, Jan. 7, 1871; Klein, *Jay Gould*, 197, 199, 201–205, 279–281; Josephson, *Robber Barons*, 205–206.

13   Klein, *Jay Gould*, 272–273, 310, 314, 334–335, 381–382, 384–386, 474; Jay Gould to Robert Garrett, July 12, 1881, box 1, Garrett Papers; Douglass, *Coming of Age*, 485–486; Julius Grodinsky, *Jay Gould* (Philadelphia, 1957), 462. See also Chandler, *Visible Hand*, 197–200.

14   David H. Bates to Robert Garrett (copy), July 27, 1885, box 19, Garrett Papers; Klein, *Jay Gould*, 196; Douglass, *Coming of Age*, 480, 484–487; Josephson, *Robber Barons*, 206–207; Grodinsky, *Jay Gould*, 282, 462; *BG*, July 19, 1883; *NYTr*, July 28, 1883; meeting of Sept. 30, 1882, minute book B, WUMB; E. B. Grant, *The Western Union Telegraph Company: Its Past, Present and Future* (New York, 1883), 30.

15   Douglass, *Coming of Age*, 486–487; *NYH*, Jan. 6, 1870; *Telegrapher*, Sept. 3, 1870, July 24, 1875; *Operator*, May 15, Dec. 15, 1875, June 1, 1883; *BG*, July 19, 1883; Senate, *Labor and Capital*, 1:893.

16   For a claim that competition meant increased salaries for first-class Western Union operators, see Norvin Green to James F. Demarest, April (n.d.) 1884, WULB. On the effects of competition on receipts and expenses, see Meetings of June 1, 1870 (Treasurer's Report) and Dec. 9, 1874, minute book A, WUMB.

17   Meeting of June 15, 1866, minute book A, WUMB; *Operator*, Jan. 15, Sept. 1, 1881; Senate, *Labor and Capital*, 1:228–229; U.S. Senate, 48th Cong., 1st sess., 1884, S. Rept. 577, p. 194; Thompson, *Wiring a Continent*, 422; Harlow, *Old Wires*, 413; *EA*, Sept. 1, Dec. 16, 1887, Jan. 16, Mar. 1, 1888; *Telegrapher*, Jan. 9, 1875.

18   *JT*, Mar. 16, 1881.

19   Grant, *The Western Union*, 33, 49; Norvin Green to Sen. James B. Beck, Mar. 15, 1884, WULB; "Statistics of the Western Union Telegraph Company for the Years Ended 30th June 1867–1875," Manuscript Division, New York Public Library; Senate, *Labor and Capital*, 1:901, 907–908, 964–965, 2:56. See also James D. Reid, *The Telegraph in America* (New York, 1886), 742.

   A table submitted by the Western Union to the Senate Education and Labor Committee hearings in 1883 gives a much smaller number of main and branch offices (1,286) run solely by the company than

Grant's total of 2,516, although the table excludes operators earning under $30 a month, which probably explains the difference.

20 Grant, *The Western Union*, 54; Klein, *Jay Gould*, 384–386; Grodinsky, *Jay Gould*, 22–23; Senate, *Labor and Capital*, 1:953–954.

21 Bates, *Lincoln in the Telegraph Office*, 124–125, 137, 403–404, 408; *Electrical World*, Mar. 18, 1893 (hereafter *EW*); *Operator*, Jan. 15, 1875; *BH*, July 15, Aug. 9, 1883; Harlow, *Old Wires*, 325; Josephson, *Robber Barons*, 203–204; Klein, *Jay Gould*, 197, 199, 281, 289. See also *Telegrapher*, Feb. 4, 1871; Frank Lewis Dyer and Thomas Commerford Martin, *Edison: His Life and Inventions* (New York, 1929), 1:165.

22 *Operator*, Sept. 15, 1879; Bates, *Lincoln in the Telegraph Office*, 27, 30, 360, 408; *EA*, Nov. 1, 1886.

23 Harold C. Livesay, *Andrew Carnegie and the Rise of Big Business* (Boston, 1975), 33; Western Union Telegraph Company, *Rules, Regulations, and Instructions* (Cleveland, 1866); idem., *Rules and Instructions* (New York, 1870), box 16, WUCS; idem., *Rules* (n.p., 1884), box 41, WUCS; William Orton to A. R. Brewer, Nov. 14, 1867, WULB; Norvin Green to Albert C. Stebbins, May 5, 1880, WULB. For telegraph company rules in the 1850s, see *Shaffner's Telegraph Companion*, Oct. 1855, 396–399.

24 *NYT*, July 20, 1883; *NYTr*, July 20, 1883; *Telegrapher*, Sept. 3, 1870; *CPD*, July 30, 1883; *JT*, May 15, 1869; *EA*, Mar. 1, 1887; Senate, *Labor and Capital*, 1:286.

25 Chandler argues in *The Visible Hand* (pp. 95, 205) that the military influence on the shape of the new corporate bureaucracies was minimal, but curiously enough, in discussing the Western Union (p. 198), he notes that the telegraph giant "relied on the same line and staff distinctions as those used for the railroads." The terms *line* and *staff* are of unmistakably military provenance.

26 Senate, *Labor and Capital*, 1:963.

27 S. Rep. 577 (1884), 258–259; *JT*, May 15, 1869, Feb. 15, 1875; Charles L. Buckingham, "The Telegraph of To-Day," *Scribner's*, July 1889; *Scientific American*, Mar. 26, 1892; *EA*, Oct. 1, 1886, July 1, 1887; R. R. Bowker, ed., "Great American Industries. Electricity," *Harper's*, Oct. 1896, p. 734; *EW*, Jan. 30, 1892. On hours, see Senate, *Labor and Capital*, 1:119, 154–156, 168; *Operator*, Dec. 1, 1884; Reid, *Telegraph in America* (1879), 572.

28 *JT*, May 15, 1869; *Telegraph Age*, Jan. 16, 1893, Apr. 16, 1894; Senate, *Labor and Capital*, 1:155; *Operator*, Feb. 15, 1875, Jan. 1, 1876, May 15, 1884; *Telegrapher*, July 31, 1875. See also ibid., Sept. 4, 1875; *TA*, July 1, 1883; *CPD*, July 30, 1883; *EA*, Apr. 16, 1887.

29 Dyer and Martin, *Edison*, 1:105; *Telegraph Age*, Apr. 16, Aug. 1, 1893; William Orton to Anson Stager, Apr. 27, 1870, WULB. See also *Review of the Telegraph and Telephone*, Aug. 15, 1882 (hereafter *RTT*).

30   *Telegrapher*, May 7, 1870; *EA*, June 16, 1886; *Operator*, Nov. 15, 1883; *JT*, Nov. 15, 1876. See also *RTT*, Apr. 15, 1882.

31   "The Telegraph," *Harper's New Monthly Magazine*, Aug. 1873, p. 347; Ella Cheever Thayer, *Wired Love: A Romance in Dots and Dashes* (New York, 1879), 18–19; *Operator*, Mar. 1, 1881; *NYTr*, July 22, 1883; U.S. Senate, 43d Cong. 1st sess., 1874, S. Rept. 242, p. 48; *EA*, June 1, Sept. 1, 1886.

32   William Orton to J. W. Phelps, Feb. 12, 1869, WULB; Norvin Green to Murat Halstead, Nov. 8, 1883, WULB. See also meeting of Oct. 8, 1884 (president's annual report), minute book B, WUMB; H. W. Spang to F. B. Gowen, Mar. 26, 1879, box 218, Reading Railroad Papers (Ms. no. 1520), Hagley Museum and Library, Wilmington, Del.

33   Senate, *Labor and Capital*, 1:933–934; Hugh Coyle to John W. Garrett, Feb. 27, 1873, box 87, B & O Railroad Papers (Ms. no. 2003), Manuscripts Division, Maryland Historical Society, Baltimore; Norvin Green to Albert C. Stebbins, May 5, 1880, WULB; Green to Murat Halstead. Nov. 8, 1883, WULB; *Telegrapher*, Oct. 31, 1875. See also Lewis N. Jacobs to George Senf, July 9, 1863, in "Old Correspondence and Forms," box 48, WUCS; *Electrical Review*, July 26, 1883; J. H. Bunnell and Co., *Students' Manual for the Practical Instruction of Learners of Telegraphy* (New York, 1882), 4; *TA*, June 1, 1883; W. C. Quincy to John W. Garrett, Apr. 25, 1878, box 45, B & O Papers.

34   Frank Parsons, "The Telegraph Monopoly," pt. 5, *Arena*, May 1896, p. 953; Senate, *Labor and Capital*, 1:119, 156, 881, 901, 921, 933–934; *Operator*, Sept. 15, 1874; *EA*, July 1, 1886; *AC*, July 22, 1883; *NYTr*, July 20, 1883; W. C. Quincy to J. W. Garrett, Apr. 25, 1878, box 45, B & O Papers; *Electrical Review*, May 31, 1883.

35   *JT*, May 15, 1869; S. Rept. 242 (1874), 15; *Operator*, May 15, 1875; Senate, *Labor and Capital*, 1:132, 765–766, 769; *NYTr*, July 17, 1883.

36   *Operator*, May 15, 1875, Dec. 1, 1884; *CPD*, July 30, 1883; *Telegraph Age*, Mar. 16, 1897; record books, Western Union office, Harrisburg, Pa., box 65, WUCS; *NOP*, July 19, 1883.

37   *NYT*, July 30, 1883; Senate, *Labor and Capital*, 1:172; Dyer and Martin, *Edison*, 1:51.

38   *CPD*, Aug. 4, 1883; *BG*, July 24, 1883; *EA*, Sept. 16, 1887; S. Rept. 577 (1884), 259.

39   *Operator*, May 15, 1875; *CPD*, July 30, 1883. See also Parsons, "Telegraphy Monopoly," pt. 5, p. 953; Senate, *Labor and Capital*, 1:156; *EA*, July 1, 1886; *Operator*, Sept. 15, 1874.

40   Senate, *Labor and Capital*, 2:1272–1273; *JT*, Nov. 1, 1869. See also *Telegrapher*, Jan. 2, 1875; Charles Barnard, "The Telegraph of To-Day," *Harper's New Monthly*, Oct. 1881, pp. 714–716; *TA*, June 1, 1883; *NYTr*, July 17, 23, 1883; R. Riordan, "Recent Advances in Telegraphy," *Popu-*

lar Science Monthly, May 1876, pp. 72–73; *John Swinton's Paper*, Jan. 24, 1886 (hereafter *JSP*); George Harrington to A. J. Creswell, Feb. 8, 1874 (reprinted in circular), box 1, Garrett Papers.

41 Paul B. Israel, "Invention and Corporate Strategies: Western Union and Competition," paper delivered before the Society for the History of Technology conference, Oct. 1986, pp. 6, 22; C. H. Summers to R. C. Clowry, Sept. 4, 1888, in "Old Correspondence and Forms," box 48, WUCS; Norvin Green to H. Graf, June 17, 1892, WULB; Elizabeth Faulkner Baker, *Technology and Women's Work* (New York, 1964), 244–245; *Monthly Labor Review*, Mar. 1932, pp. 501ff.; *JT*, Jan. 1, 1870; *EA*, June 1, 1886, Feb. 1, 1887; *BH*, July 19, 1883; Senate, *Labor and Capital*, 1:159–160; *BET*, July 20, 1883; *BG*, July 21, 1883; *TA*, July 1, 1883; Walter P. Phillips, *Sketches Old and New* (New York, 1897), ix, 208.

42 *JT*, Mar. 1, 1870; *BH*, July 26, 1883; Barnard, "Telegraph of To-Day," 708–711.

43 Barnard, "Telegraph of To-Day," 711; Dyer and Martin, *Edison*, 1:155.

44 *Statistical Abstract of the United States*, 257; *Historical Statistics of the United States*, pt. 1, pp. 200–201. For pressure on operators to increase output, see also the *Magnet*, Feb. 4, 1880; *Operator*, Feb. 15, 1880, Nov. 18, 1882.

45 *BG*, July 19, 1883. For the scale of volume that dictated the use of varying kinds of circuits, see *TA*, Aug. 1, 1883.

46 Senate, *Labor and Capital*, 1:131. See also Chandler, *Visible Hand*, 200.

47 Bowker, "Great American Industries," 734; *JT*, May 15, 1869; "The Telegraph," *Harper's New Monthly*, Aug. 1873, p. 349; William Orton to William Hunter, Dec. 4, 1875, WULB; Josephson, *Robber Barons*, 271; Norvin Green to editor of the *Tribune*, Apr. 24, 1884, WULB; Meeting of Feb. 21, 1867, minute book A, WUMB. See also Meetings of Dec. 11, 1878, Mar. 12, 1879, minute book A, WUMB; Orton to James Gamble, Dec. 28, 1875, WULB; Orton to Anson Stager, Jan. 4, 1876, WULB.

48 *EA*, Mar. 1, July 1, 1887; S. Rept. 577, pp. 258–259; *EW*, Jan. 20, 1892; Reid, *Telegraph in America* (1879), 572; *Operator*, Feb. 15, 1875. On later lunchroom welfare capitalism, cf. Margery W. Davies, *Woman's Place Is at the Typewriter* (Philadelphia, 1982), 124.

49 *Operator*, May 15, 1876.

3   THE KNIGHTS OF THE KEY

1   U.S. Census Manuscript Population Schedules, 1880, Baltimore City, Md.; idem., Dauphin County, Pa. (Harrisburg, Londonderry, Lower Swatara, Middletown, Middle Paxton, Borough of Dauphin, South Hanover, Rockville, Susquehanna, Lenkerville, Millersburg, Steelton,

Lykens, Williams). In the Baltimore sample, all but two were men, and the ages of three unknown; all but two of the Harrisburg group were men.

2   Twelfth U.S. Census (1900), *Special Reports, Pt. 2: Occupations* (Washington, D.C., 1904), ccxv, ccxviii, 20–21.

A sample of seventy-five operators from Harrisburg (and one nearby township) for 1900 has even higher, though probably atypically so, figures: 50 percent married, average age (all but three men) of 30.3 years. U.S. Census Manuscript Population Schedules, 1900, Dauphin County, Pa. See also Department of the Interior, Ninth Census (1870), *Statistics of the Population of the United States* (Washington, D.C., 1872) 1:676, 688, 707; idem, Tenth Census (1880), *Statistics of the Population of the United States* (Washington, D.C., 1883), 1:757, 778, 794; idem, Eleventh Census (1890), *Report of the Population of the United States, Pt. 2* (Washington, D.C., 1897), 304, 374–375; Twelfth Census, *Occupations*, 506.

3   Ninth Census, 1:706–707; Tenth Census, 1:757; Eleventh Census, pt. 2, pp. 356–357.

4   Quoted in *Operator*, Mar. 1, 1874.

5   *JT*, Feb. 15, 1871; *EA*, Oct. 1, Nov. 1, 1886; Census Manuscript Schedules, 1880, Dauphin County, Pa.

6   Census Manuscript Schedules, 1880, Baltimore City; idem, 1880, Dauphin Co., Pa. For the Baltimore sample, the remaining household heads were petty white collar (11 percent), entrepreneurial (13 percent), professional or managerial (7 percent), farmer (1 percent); for Harrisburg, petty white collar (9.5 percent), entrepreneurial (14 percent), farmers (11.9 percent). For the working-class backgrounds of aspiring operators, see also *TA*, Oct. 16, 1885.

7   *NYT*, July 21, 1883; *EA*, Jan. 1, 1887; Phillips, *Sketches*, 91–101.

8   *JSP*, Mar. 13, 1887; Census Manuscript Schedules, 1880, Baltimore City; Tenth Census, 1:513; Twelfth Census, *Occupations*, 68–69; *EA*, Nov. 1, 1886; *Telegrapher*, Sept. 11, 1875. On Irish-Americans, see also Daniel J. Walkowitz, *Worker City, Company Town* (Urbana, Ill., 1978), chap. 1 and passim.

9   Senate, *Labor and Capital*, 1:895; *Operator*, July 1, 1879; *EA*, Nov. 1, 1886, Oct. 1, 1887, Feb. 1, 1888; Bates, *Lincoln in the Telegraph Office*, 360. See also Taltavall, *Telegraphers of To-Day*; Reid, *Telegraph in America* (1886), chap. 46; *EA*, Sept. 1, Oct. 1, Nov. 16, 1886; *Operator*, Feb. 15, 1879.

10   *JT*, Feb. 1, 1868, Apr. 11, 1869. See also July 15, 1870.

11   Dyer and Martin, *Edison*, 1:60 and passim; Livesay, *Andrew Carnegie*, chaps. 2–3; Albert Bigelow Paine, *Theodore N. Vail: A Biography* (New York, 1929), 14–23, 36–41; Harrisburg Western Union record books,

box 65, WUCS; Harrisburg City Directory, 1880; *RTT*, Nov. 1, 1882; *Electrical Review*, Nov. 8, 1883; *HDT*, Sept. 4, 1883; Luther Reily Kelker, *History of Dauphin County, Pennsylvania* (New York, 1907), 3:593–594; Harlow, *Old Wires*, 421–422. See also *EA*, June 1, Nov. 1, 1886.

12 B. B. French to Charles Frederick Wood, Nov. 1, 1848, box 2 ("Communicatons: Telegraphy"), Archives, Division of Electricity and Modern Physics, National Museum of American History, Smithsonian Institution (hereafter DEA); William P. Westervelt to Charles F. Wood, Oct. 26, 1851, box 2, DEA; S. L. Sadler to Wood, Aug. 5, 1853, box 2, DEA; Dyer and Martin, *Edison*, 1:73–74; McNeill, *The Labor Movement*, 390; Phillips, *Sketches*, 64; Bates, *Lincoln in the Telegraph Office*, 408.

13 *Operator*, Sept. 15, 1880. On the Old Timers, see also *EA*, June 16, 1886, Sept. 1, 1887; *Electrical Review*, Oct. 4, 1883.

14 *Telegrapher*, Feb. 18, 1871; *JT*, June 1, 1872, Jan. 15, 1875.

15 *Operator*, Nov. 15, 1883, Jan. 1, 1884; J. H. Bunnell & Co., *Students' Manual*, 4: Senate, *Labor and Capital*, 1:937. Cf. ibid., 1:938–940.

16 *Telegraph Age*, Aug. 16, 1893; Syracuse Western Union record book, box 53, WUCS; *EA*, Dec. 16, 1886, Jan. 1, 1888.

17 U.S. House of Representatives, *Postmaster General's Report*, House Exec. Doc. 1, pt. 4, 51st Cong., 2d sess. 1890, p. 122; Richard T. Ely, "Should the Government Control the Telegraph?" *Arena*, Dec. 1895, p. 51; *EA*, May 16, 1888. See also *EW*, Dec. 3, 1887; *Telegraph Age*, Nov. 1, 1893, Jan. 16, Nov. 16, 1898, Feb. 16, 1904; Dyer and Martin, *Edison*, 1:58–59; *EA*, Mar. 1, 1887.

18 *Postmaster General's Report*, p. 122, *Telegrapher*, July 31, Sept. 25, 1875; *RTT*, Sept. 1, 1882; *BH*, July 23, 1883; *Operator*, Apr. 1, 1882, Nov. 15, 1883, Apr. 4, May 30, 1885; Phillips, *Sketches*, 246; Senate, *Labor and Capital*, 1:227. See also S. Rept. 577, p. 256; Dyer and Martin, *Edison*, 1:104.

19 *Telegrapher*, Oct. 29, 1870, June 24, 1871. "Lefferts" refers to Marshall Lefferts, an early Western Union technician and manager. See also ibid., Nov. 2, 1867; *JT*, May 1, 1872. By 1886 a few telegraph companies were granting paid vacations, but not the Western Union. *EA*, Aug. 16, Oct. 1, 1886.

Such corporate parsimony was not restricted to the Western Union. For denials of vacations to Reading Railroad operators, see E. R. Adams to Theodore Voorhees, June 7, 10, 1893, and Voorhees to Adams, June 13, 1893, box 124, Reading Papers; C. M. Lewis to Voorhees, Aug. 28, 1901, Voorhees to W. G. Besler, Aug. 30, 1901, Voorhees to Lewis, Sept. 4, 1901, box 432, Reading Papers.

20 *Shaffner's Telegraph Companion*, May 1854; W. W. Shoch to J. W. Garrett,

Dec. 2, 1864, Garrett to Superintendent of Telegraph, Dec. 6, 1864, box 87, B & O Papers.

21   *JT*, June 15, 1870, Mar. 15, 1873; *Operator*, Feb. 15, 1881, Nov. 11, 1882. See also ibid., May 1, 1881.

22   *BG*, July 17, 20, 1883; *BH*, July 16, 1883; *NYT*, July 18, 1883.

23   *BG*, July 20, 1883; *TA*, Oct. 16, 1885; *EA*, Apr. 1, 1887; *JT*, Sept. 15, 1871; *Telegrapher*, Dec. 26, 1864, Jan. 7, 1871, June 12, Oct. 9, 1875; *Operator*, Feb. 1, 1887.

24   Taliaferro P. Shaffner, *The Telegraph Manual* (New York, 1859), 707–708. See also *Telegrapher*, Oct. 9, 1875.

25   *JT*, Dec. 15, 1876; *Operator*, June 13, 1885. See also *Telegrapher*, Jan. 7, 1871, Oct. 9, 1875; *Telegraph Age*, Jan. 1, Mar. 1, 1898.

26   *Telegrapher*, Oct. 9, 1875; A. Michael McMahon, *The Making of a Profession: A Century of Electrical Engineering in America* (New York, 1984), 4, 8–9, 29, 36–40.

27   *Inquirer* quoted in *Operator*, May 15, 1877; Senate, *Labor and Capital*, 1:894.

28   *EA*, Apr. 16, 1887; *BG*, July 17, 1883; *Operator*, May 15, 1877; *NYTr*, July 17, 1883; *NYT*, July 17, 1883; *TA*, July 16, 1883; *RTT*, Aug. 15, 1882; *Electrical Review*, May 31, 1883; *Telegraph Age*, Mar. 16, 1893, Feb. 16, 1897, Apr. 1, 1898; Senate, *Labor and Capital*, 1:112, 126, 231.

29   Walter Licht, *Working for the Railroad* (Princeton, N.J., 1983), 269; Western Union Telegraph Company (hereafter WUTC), *Rules*, editions of 1866, 1870, and 1884; William Orton to A. Stager, Dec. 18, 1875, WULB; Iowa Bureau of Labor Statistics (BLS), *Eleventh Biennial Report* (Des Moines, 1905), 385–386; Syracuse Western Union record book, box 53, WUCS; *Telegraph Age*, June 1, 1898. For the contrasting personnel politics of the privately owned Anglo-American Telegraph Company, see E. Weedon to H. Weaver, May 24, 1870, Weedon to General Manager, Dec. 6, 1879, Feb. 24, 1880, in Heart's Content Cable Station letter books, Anglo-American Telegraph Co., microfilms of originals at Heart's Content (Newfoundland) Cable Museum, in DEA; and *RTT*, Oct. 16, 1882.

30   Meetings of Dec. 11, 1878, Mar. 12, 1879, minute book A, WUMB; William Orton to A. Stager, Oct. 2, 1875, WULB.

31   William Orton to George W. Gray, April 21, 1869, WULB. See also Orton to Mary E. McConkey, Oct. 1, 1867, Orton to George W. Lee, Feb. 18, 1870, WULB; Norvin Green to O. L. Woodward, Oct. 27, 1880, WULB; Dyer and Martin, *Edison*, 1:99; D. H. Bates to H. C. Keyes, Nov. 27, 1872, box 48, WUCS. For local managerial regulation of hours, see *AC*, July 20, 1883.

32   William Orton to A. Stager, Mar. 4, 1868, WULB; Norvin Green to

R. B. Vance, Jan. 9, 1880, WULB. See also Green to Philip Judge, May 3, 1884, WULB. For similar practices in the Reading Railroad, see F. B. Gowen to J. E. Wootten, Feb. 26, 1883, box 250, Reading Papers.

33   Norvin Green to Wilkinson Call, Jan. 24, 1884, WULB. For two instances of pesonnel decisions in which skill and ability seem to have been the sole determinants, see Green to J. H. Rugg, Oct. 4, 1882, and Green to James L. Norris, Oct. 6, 1882, WULB. For examples of personnel decisions affecting operators on a contemporary railroad, see H. W. Spang to J. E. Wootten, Feb. 2, 1878, box 211, Reading Papers; O. W. Stager to Wootten, July 18, 1883, box 250, Reading Papers; E. R. Adams to Theodore Voorhees, Nov. 11, 1893, Box 124, Reading Papers; L. Horton, Jr., to M. Landis, May 4, 1896, box 158, Reading Papers.

34   Green to H. Graf, June 17, 1892, WULB.

35   *BH*, July 16, 1883; Senate, *Final Report and Testimony Submitted to Congress by the Commission on Industrial Relations* (Washington, D.C., 1916), 10:9493; Senate, *Labor and Capital*, 1:134; Dyer and Martin, *Edison*, 1:66, 68, 72–73; Thompson, *Wiring a Continent*, 388; W. W. Shoch to J. W. Garrett, Dec. 2, 1864, William D. Gentry to Garrett, Dec. 6, 1864, box 87, B & O Papers; *JT*, Oct. 15, 1868. On wide variations in pay and conditions in the 1850s, see Thompson, *Wiring a Continent*, 245–246.

36   Senate, *Labor and Capital*, 1:134, 893; Meetings of June 9, Dec. 8, 1875, minute book A, WUMB. On Western Union profits and dividends, see also *Historical Statistics*, pt. 2, 787–788.

37   William Orton to A. Stager, Oct. 2, Dec. 18, 1875, WULB.

38   W. B. Hibbard to "All Employes of WU Tel Co.," Dec. 22, 1875, "Old Correspondence and Forms," box 48, WUCS; Senate, *Industrial Relations*, 10:9493; *Operator*, Dec. 15, 1875. For earlier cuts, see *Telegrapher*, July 24, Aug. 21, 1875.

39   *Telegrapher*, Sept. 3, 1870; Senate, *Labor and Capital*, 1:226; Harrisburg Western Union record books, box 65, WUCS. For detailed examples of pressure on lower managers to cut expenses, see William Orton to A. Stager, Jan. 4, 1876, WULB. See also *NYH*, Jan. 6, 1870; *BG*, July 12, 16, 1883; Senate, *Labor and Capital*, 1:125, 193; *Operator*, May 15, Oct. 15, 1875, June 1, 1883; Edwin Gabler, "Kid-Gloved Laborers: Gilded Age Telegraphers and the Great Strike of 1883" (Ph.D. diss., University of Massachusetts at Amherst, 1986), p. 158. For temporary salary increases, see *Operator*, Jan. 1, Oct. 15, 1881.

40   *Operator*, Jan. 15, 1880. For examples of similar drives for economies on a contemporary railroad, see W. C. Quincy to J. W. Garrett, April 25, 1878, box 45, B & O Papers.

41   S. Rept. 577, p. 194; *Operator*, Jan. 15, 1881. On mergers and job market

constriction, see *Operator*, Apr. 1, 1879, Sept. 1, 1881; Thompson, *Wiring a Continent*, 422; Harlow, *Old Wires*. 413; *EA*, Sept. 1, 1887. For the apparent exception of the Western Union–B & O merger of 1887–88, see *EA*, Dec. 16, 1887, Jan. 16, Mar. 1, 1888. On mergers and salary cuts, see Senate, *Labor and Capital*, 1:228–229.

42   Senate, *Labor and Capital*, 1:103; McNeill, *Labor Movement*, 390–391. On the demand for good operators during the Civil War, see J. J. G. Riley to J. W. Garrett, Sept. 14, 1864, box 87, B & O Papers.

43   *Telegrapher*, June 4, 1870, Feb. 1, 1875; *Operator*, Feb. 15, 1881. See also *Telegrapher*, Jan. 9, May 8, 1875.

44   Senate, *Labor and Capital*, 1:117; William Orton to E. B. Wesley, Sept. 30, 1875, WULB. See also *Operator*, Oct. 15, 1884; *AC*, July 21, 1883; *NYT*, July 15, 1883; *NYTr*, July 31, 1883.

45   Senate, *Labor and Capital*, 1:116; *Telegraph Age*, Aug. 1, Dec. 1, 1907. See also Dyer and Martin, *Edison*, 1:59; Senate, *Labor and Capital*, 1:118; 149–150; *Operator*, Mar. 1, 1874; *Irish World and American Industrial Liberator*, Aug. 4, 1883 (hereafter *IW*); *BH*, Aug. 15, 19, 1883; *EA*, May 2, 1887; *NYT*, July 16, 1883; *NYTr*, July 17, 18, 1883.

46   Dyer and Martin, *Edison*, 1:73–74; *Operator*, July 15, 1875; *EA*, June 16, 1886, Mar. 16, Apr. 1, 1887; *JT*, Apr. 1, 1868; *BG*, July 12, 1883; Senate, *Labor and Capital*, 1:151, 266. See also Minnie Swan Mitchell, "Lingo of Telegraph Operators," *American Speech*, Apr. 1937, p. 155.

47   *JT*, Oct. 15, 1868; *Telegrapher*, Oct. 15, 1870; *EA*, Jan. 16, 1887; *Telegraph Age*, Aug. 16, 1893. Telegraph managers, too, moved about, though in a different and usually much more favorable context. See, e.g., A. B. Chandler to Robert Garrett, May 6, Nov. 17, 1882, box 1, Garrett Papers; J. C. Reiff to Robert Garrett, Mar. 5, 1883, box 1, Garrett Papers; Louisville Western Union record book, entries for Dec. 31, 1884, Nov. 16, 1890, box 16, WUCS; E. R. Adams to J. E. Wootten, May 6, 1880, box 225, Reading Papers; Taltavall, *Telegraphers of To-Day*, passim.

48   *EA*, June 1, 1886, Apr. 1, 1887, Jan. 1, 1888; *NYT*, July 14, 1883; *Telegraph Age*, May 16, June 16, 1893, May 16, July 16, 1897, Apr. 1, 1898. See also *EA*, May 2, 16, July 1, 1887; *Telegrapher*, Feb. 4, 1871; *Operator*, Apr. 1, 1882, May 15, 1883; *Telegraph Age*, Mar. 16, 1897.

49   Syracuse Western Union record book, box 53, WUCS.

50   Harrisburg Western Union record books, box 65, WUCS. My method for these sources involved sampling operators on the payroll for October of each year and reckoning turnover by changes in personnel (managers, operators, clerks, and messengers) from October to October. The year 1880 was missing, as was the page for Oct. 1879; for the latter I substituted June 1879, and for the former I considered some-

one present in 1879 and 1881 likely to have been present in 1880 as well.

51   Harrisburg record books, box 65, WUCS; *BG*, Aug. 16, 1883; *NYT*, Aug. 16, 1883; Taltavall, *Telegraphers of To-Day*, 199-200.

52   Harrisburg record books, box 65, WUCS; Taltavall, *Telegraphers of To-Day*, 143; Census Manuscript Schedules, 1880, Dauphin County, Pa.

53   Harrisburg record books, box 65, WUCS; Census Manuscript Schedules, 1880, Dauphin County, Pa.; idem., 1900, Dauphin County, Pa.; Harrisburg City Directory, 1882, 1890, 1900. On Spahr, cf. Theodore Voorhees to C. G. Hancock, July 3, 1893, box 124, Reading Papers. For examples of long tenure elsewhere, see Syracuse record book, box 53, WUCS; Louisville record book, box 16, WUCS; *Telegraph Age*, Aug. 16, 1893; Taltavall, *Telegraphers of To-Day*, passim.

54   W. J. Johnston, *Telegraphic Tales and Telegraphic History* (New York, 1880), 58–59; *Operator*, Dec. 15, 1875; WUTC, *Rules* (1884), 12. See also *Operator*, Jan. 1, Apr. 15, 1876.

55   Dyer and Martin, *Edison*, 1:127; WUTC, *Rules* (1866), 30, and (1870), 20; *Telegraph Age*, July 1, 1898. See also WUTC, *Rules* (1884), 12; Norvin Green to Clara Brown, Oct. 15, 1880, WULB.

56   Phillips, *Sketches*, 224–225; *Telegraph Age*, Apr. 16, 1897; Dyer and Martin, *Edison*, 1:84–85; *EA*, Mar. 1, 1888. See also *EA*, Aug. 1, 1887.

57   Mitchell, "Lingo of Telegraph Operators," 154–155; Thayer, *Wired Love*.

58.   *NYT*, July 12, 1883; *Telegrapher*, Jan. 30, 1865; *Operator*, Apr. 15, 1876, June 1, 1881, June 15, 1883; WUTC, *Rules* (1870), 15, and (1884), 15; Norvin Green to Clara Brown, Oct. 15, 1880, WULB. See also Thayer, *Wired Love*, 48.

59   *Operator*, June 15, 1883; WUTC, *Rules* (1884), 12; *NYT*, July 12, 1883. See also WUTC, *Rules* (1870), 18. A note inserted in the 1884 *Rules* in the Smithsonian Archives, referring to the rule in question, quips, "There were more violations than of the Volstead law."

60   "Souvenir, the American Telegraphers' Tournament Association, Philadelphia, October 30–31, 1903," box 39, WUCS; *Operator*, Oct. 1, 1875, Nov, 1, 1877, Aug. 15, 1884; *EW*, May 24, 1890, Apr. 1, 1893.

61   *NYT*, July 22, 1883; *TA*, June 16, 1883.

62   *Telegrapher*, Dec. 26, 1864; *Operator*, May 15, 1876. See also *Telegrapher*, Jan. 21, 1871.

63   Dyer and Martin, *Edison*, 1:99–100; *EA*, Sept. 16, 1887; *Operator*, Jan. 1, 1879, Sept. 15, 1883.

64   Phillips, *Sketches*, 224; *Operator*, June 15, 1879; *EA*, Oct. 15, 1887; Mitchell, "Lingo of Telegraph Operators," 155; interview with Carl H. Scheele, Oct. 14, 1986.

65   *JT*, Apr. 1, 1868, Apr. 15, 1870; Senate, *Labor and Capital*, 1:941; *Operator*, Dec. 1, 1874; Senate, *Industrial Relations*, 10:9429; *EA*, Oct. 15, 1887, May 1, 1888. See also *EW*, Apr. 14, May 12, 1888; *Telegraph Age*, Feb. 1, 1897, July 1, 1898; *EA*, Jan. 1, 16, Feb. 1, Mar. 1, 1888.

66   *JT*, July 15, 1868; *Telegrapher*, Sept. 11, 1875. On operator sports, see also *Operator*, Mar. 1, 1881, Oct. 21, 1882; *HDT*, July 21, 23, 1874; *Telegraph Age*, Jan. 1, 1897. For a chess club at 195 Broadway, see *RTT*, Sept. 1, 1882.

67   *Operator*, Nov. 15, 1874; *TA*, June 1, 1883. See also *EA*, Feb. 1, Oct. 15, 1887, Mar. 1, Apr. 1, 16, 1888; *JT*, Nov. 1, 1873; *Operator*, May 1, Aug. 1, 1874, Feb. 15, 1875, Feb. 1, Apr. 1, July 15, 1876, May 15, Sept. 1, 1877, Mar. 1, 1880, Dec. 1, 1881; *NYTr*, July 23, 1883; *Telegraph Age*, Feb. 16, Mar. 16, Dec. 1, 1897, Feb. 16, Mar. 1, 1898.

68   *EA*, Feb. 1, Apr. 1, 16, May 2, 1887; *Telegraph Age*, Aug. 1, 1897; *Telegrapher*, May 8, June 1, 1875. On telegraphers' terms, see Mitchell, "Lingo of Telegraph Operators"; and Hervey Brackbill, "Some Telegraphers' Terms," *American Speech*, Apr. 1929.

69   C. Wright Mills, *White Collar* (New York, 1951), chap. 4; Alan Stanley Horlick, *Country Boys and Merchant Princes* (Lewisburg, Pa., 1975), 12, 168–169, 170–171, 178; Stuart M. Blumin, "The Hypothesis of Middle-Class Formation in Nineteenth-Century America: A Critique and Some Proposals," *American Historical Review*, Apr. 1985.

70   E. P. Thompson, *The Making of the English Working Class* (New York, 1964), 9–11, is a brilliant and seminal discussion of the dynamics of class and culture.

71   *BH*, July 23, 1883.

72   *Telegrapher*, Jan. 30, 1865. See also Sept. 26, 1864.

73   *Telegrapher*, Jan. 30, 1865, July 24, 1875; WUTC, *Rules* (1866), 31, and (1870), 21; Louisville, New Albany and Chicago Railway, *Rules of the Transportation Department* (Chicago, n.d., ca. 1892), 45, in box 105, WUCS; Dyer and Martin, *Edison*, 1:84–85; *JT*, Apr. 1, 1869, Jan. 15, 1872. See also Licht, *Working for the Railroad*, 84.

74   *JT*, Aug. 2, Sept. 1, 1869; *Operator*, Jan. 15, Dec. 15, 1876; *TA*, June 16, 1883; *EA*, Aug. 16, 1886, Feb. 1, Apr. 1, 1888; Phillips, *Sketches*, 39–46, 61–72, 139–149; *NYT*, July 20, 1883; *CPD*, Aug. 7, 1883. On operator temperance, see *IW*, Aug. 4, 1883.

75   O. W. Stager to J. E. Wootten, May 13, 1881, box 233, Reading Papers; *Operator*, Mar. 1, 1880; Paine, *Vail*, 22. On operator dissipation, see also *Telegraph Age*, July 1, 1893; Licht, *Working for the Railroad*, 236; Dyer and Martin, *Edison*, 1:86; Paine, *Vail*, 19.

76   J. J. G. Riley to J. W. Garrett, Sept. 14, 1864, box 87, B & O Papers; Dyer and Martin, *Edison*, 1:61. See also William D. Gentry to J. W. Garrett, Oct. 18, 1864, box 12, B & O Papers.

77   *Operator*, Aug. 1, 1874, June 1, 1875.

78   Senate, *Labor and Capital*, 1:820; *Operator*, June 1, 1879. See also *HDT*, July 14, 1883; *Telegraph Age*, July 1, 1893; *Operator*, May 15, 1876, Mar. 15, 1879; *JT*, Feb. 1, July 15, 1868.

79   *TA*, July 16, 1883; Senate, *Labor and Capital*, 1:117, 149–150, 231. See also *BG*, July 17, 1883; and for operators as "artisans," Norvin Green to H. Graf, June 17, 1892, WULB.

80   *BG*, July 17, 1883; Brotherhood of Telegraphers of the United States and Canada (hereafter BTUSC), *Proceedings of the Executive Board* (Pittsburgh, 1882), 10, in Powderly Papers; *NYT*, July 15, 1883.

81   *EA*, Nov. 16, 1886; *NYTr*, July 16, 1883; Senate, *Labor and Capital*, 1: 116–117, 220; *BG*, July 20, 1883. See also *Operator*, June 16, 1883. For similarly favorable (and invidious) middle-class editorial views of the operators, see *NYT*, July 21, 1883; *Harper's Weekly*, Aug. 18, 1883. On the spurious dichotomy between hand and brain work, see Harry Braverman, *Labor and Monopoly Capital* (New York, 1974), chap. 1 and passim.

82   North Carolina BLS, *Eighth Annual Report* (Raleigh, 1894), 274; *Chicago Tribune*, July 29, 1883, quoted in *NYTr*, July 31, 1883; Senate, *Labor and Capital*, 1:117; Phillips, *Sketches*, 95.

83   Andrew Carnegie, *Autobiography of Andrew Carnegie* (Boston, 1920), 37–38.

84   *Operator*, June 15, 1883; Senate, *Labor and Capital*, 1:117, 149–150; Phillips, *Sketches*, xv. For complaints about the skimpy education of many early operators, see Shaffner, *Telegraph Manual*, 761.

85   *HDT*, Dec. 22, 1874, Apr. 30, May 18, Sept. 7, 1875, Mar. 30, 1876, Oct. 20, 29, Dec. 7, 26, 29, 31, 1883, June 8, 16, 30, Nov. 13, 1885; Census Manuscript Schedules, 1880, Dauphin County, Pa. For examples of managers or operators locally prominent in civic, social, or political activities, see Obituary Scrapbook no. 3, p. 51, Dauphin County Historical Society, Harrisburg, Pa.; *HDT*, Sept. 7, Nov. 2, 1883, Jan. 27, Apr. 8, May 5, June 22, 1885; *Telegraph Age*, Apr. 1, 1894, Feb. 1, July 1, 1897, Mar. 16, 1908; D. Vetter to H. W. Spang, July 20, 1878, box 211, Reading Papers.

86   Senate, *Labor and Capital*, 1:231. See also *BH*, Aug. 15, 1883; *Operator*, May 15, 1876; *Telegraph Age*, July 1, 1893.

87   *JSP*, Apr. 6, 1884; *BET*, Aug. 20, 1883; Senate, *Labor and Capital*, 1:937. On single operators' living standards, see, e.g., *Operator*, June 1, 1875, Jan. 1, 1880; Senate, *Labor and Capital*, 1:118.

88   *Telegrapher*, Feb. 4, 1871; Senate, *Labor and Capital*, 1:150, 177–178, 250; *BS*, July 17, 1883; Harrisburg record books, box 65, WUCS; Census Manuscript Schedules, 1900, Dauphin County, Pa.; O. W. Stager to J. E. Wootten, June 13, 1881, box 233, Reading Papers; *TA*, June 1,

1883. See also *JSP*, Apr. 6, Aug. 24, 1883; *Operator*, Aug. 15, 1874, July 15, 1879.

89   For the "starvation wages" complaint, *NYT*, July 18, 1883.

90   Senate, *Labor and Capital*, 1:120, 236. For Harry Orr's domestic situation and expenses, see ibid., 1:177–178.

91   Senate, *Labor and Capital*, 1:132, 765–766; *NYTr*, July 17, 1883; Illinois BLS, *Third Biennial Report* (Springfield, 1884), 388–389.

92   My profile of operator salaries draws on the following: Senate, *Labor and Capital*, 1:103, 118, 134, 151, 177–178, 908, 965; *Telegrapher*, Mar. 18, Aug. 5, 1871; S. Rept. 242, p. 50; S. Rept. 577, pp. 257–258; Thompson, *Wiring a Continent*, 338; Harlow, *Old Wires*, 419; Norvin Green to Murat Halstead, Nov. 8, 1883, WULB; *Electrical Review*, May 31, 1883; *BS*, July 17, 1883; *BH*, July 16, 1883; *NYTr*, July 16, 17, 1883; Dyer and Martin, *Edison*, 1:66, 68, 72–73; Parsons, "Telegraph Monopoly," pt. 4, *Arena*, Apr. 1896, pp. 805, 807–808; *EA*, May 2, 16, Oct. 15, Nov. 16, 1887, Apr. 16, May 1, 1888; *Operator*, Mar. 1, 1874, May 15, 1877, July 15, Dec. 1, 1879, Jan. 1, 1880; Syracuse record book, box 53, WUCS; *RTT*, Oct. 2, 1882; *SLPD*, July 25, 1883; Kansas Bureau of Labor and Industrial Statistics (BLIS), *Third Annual Report* (Topeka, 1888), 289–290; Michigan BLS, *Second Annual Report* (Lansing, 1885), 241; E. R. Adams to Theodore Voorhees, June 10, July 1, 1893, box 124, Reading Papers. See also Iowa BLS, *Eleventh Biennial Report* (Des Moines, 1905), 387; idem, *Twelfth Biennial Report* (Des Moines, 1907), 184–185; idem, *Thirteenth Biennial Report* (Des Moines, 1908), 234–235; Senate, *Industrial Relations*, 10:9303–9304, 9307.

93   Senate, *Industrial Relations*, 10:9493; *Historical Statistics*, pt. 1, 200–201.

94   Harrisburg record books, box 65, WUCS; *Historical Statistics*, pt. 1, 200–201.

95   Senate, *Labor and Capital*, 1:177–178; Harrisburg record books, box 65, WUCS; Kelker, *History of Dauphin County*, 3:593–594; *Historical Statistics*, pt. 1, 200–201.

96   For the secular trend of operators' wages for 1875–97, see U.S. Commissoner of Labor, *Fifteenth Annual Report* (Washington, D.C., 1900), 2:1478–1480; on steady work patterns, see *Operator*, May 15, 1877; Senate, *Labor and Capital*, 1:155–156.

97   BTUSC, *Proceedings*, 10; *NYT*, July 21, 1883; Senate, *Labor and Capital*, 1:966; Senate, *Wholesale Prices, Wages and Transportation*, 52d Cong., 2d sess., 1893, S. Rept. 1394, pt. 4, pp. 1277–1360; Stanley Lebergott, *Manpower in Economic Growth* (New York, 1964), 290–295, chap. 6; Massachusetts BLS, *Sixth Annual Report* (Boston, 1875), 261, 306; Illinois BLS, *Third Biennial Report*, 389; Michigan BLS, *Second Annual Report*, 236–241; Kansas BLIS, *Third Annual Report*, 289–290; Lloyd G.

Reynolds, *Labor Economics and Labor Relations*, 8th ed. (Englewood Cliffs, N.J., 1982), 232; David M. Gordon, Richard Edwards, and Michael Reich, *Segmented Work, Divided Workers* (Cambridge, England, 1982), 119–120, 149–150. See also Licht, *Working for the Railroad*, 126.

98   Senate, *Labor and Capital*, 1:231; Senate, *Wholesale Prices*, pt. 4, 1573–1581; Michigan BLS, *Second Annual Report*, 236–241; Kansas BLIS, *Third Annual Report*, 206–209, 289. See also Michigan BLS, *Tenth Annual Report* (Lansing, 1893), 1046–1048, 1050–1051, 1061–1063, 1090–1091; David B. Tyack, *The One Best System* (Cambridge, Mass., 1974), 62.

99   Massachusetts BLS, *Sixth Annual Report*, 221ff.; Lizabeth A. Cohen, "Embellishing a Life of Labor: An Interpretation of the Material Culture of American Working-Class Homes, 1885–1915," in *Material Culture Studies in America*, ed. Thomas J. Schlereth (Nashville, Tenn., 1982), 292–293; *Operator*, June 1, 1875.

100   *NYT*, July 18, 25, 1883; *Operator*, Oct. 15, 1883; *Telegraph Age*, Feb. 15, 1904. See also *Telegraph Age*, Mar. 16, 1908.

101   Senate, *Labor and Capital*, 1:1084; Reid, *Telegraph in America* (1886), 696; *Nation*, July 19, 1883; Leon Fink, *Workingmen's Democracy* (Urbana, Ill., 1983), 94.

102   *Telegraph Age*, Apr. 16, May 16, 1893, Dec. 1, 1897. See also Feb. 16, 1897.

103   For the proliferation of etiquette books in the postbellum years, see Arthur M. Schlesinger, *Learning How to Behave: A Historical Study of American Etiquette Books* (New York, 1947), 33–34.

104   *Operator*, Sept. 1, 1874; *Telegraph Age*, Sept. 1, 16, Oct. 16, Dec. 12, 1897.

105   [Jonathan Baxter Harrison], "Study of a New England Factory Town," *Atlantic Monthly*, June 1879, 699–700. On lower-middle-class disdain for workers, see also Upton Sinclair, *The Jungle* (reprint; New York, 1960), 105; Gordon K. Lewis, *Puerto Rico: Freedom and Power in the Caribbean* (New York, 1963), 447. On the pretentiousness and exclusionary cultural boundaries of the lower middle class in Britain, see Gareth Stedman Jones, "Working-Class Culture and Working-Class Politics in London, 1870–1900," *Journal of Social History*, Summer 1974, p. 507; E. J. Hobsbawm, *Labouring Men* (New York, 1964), 273; David Lockwood, *The Blackcoated Worker* (London, 1958), 32.

106   Census Manuscript Schedules, 1880, Dauphin County, Pa.; idem, 1880, Baltimore City, Md.

107   On class and cultural overlap, see Fink, *Workingmen's Democracy*, 12–13. For evidence of converging residential patterns of lower-middle and upper-working-class persons in postbellum Boston,

see Mark Peel, "On the Margins: Lodgers and Boarders in Boston, 1860–1900," *Journal of American History*, March 1986, 813ff. For notions of respectability and self-education among Scottish urban skilled craftsmen, see Robert Q. Gray, *The Labour Aristocracy in Victorian Edinburgh* (Oxford, England, 1976), 130.

4   DEAR BROTHERS AND SISTERS

1   *BG*, July 19, 1883. Cf. *NYH*, July 20, 1883.

2   Reid, *Telegraph in America* (1879), 170–171; *Telegrapher*, Oct. 31, 1864, July 3, 1875; Virginia Penny, *The Employments of Women* (Boston, 1863), 101–102; Harlow, *Old Wires*, 420; Albert Rhodes, "Women's Occupations pations," *Galaxy*, Jan. 1876, p. 52; "The Telegraph," *Harper's New Monthly*, Aug. 1873, p. 347; Frances E. Willard, *Occupations for Women* (New York, 1897), 132.

3   U.S. Census Manuscript Population Schedules, 1880, New York City. See also population reports of the Ninth Census (1870), 1:706–707; Tenth Census (1880), 1:757; Eleventh Census (1890), pt. 2, pp. 356–357, 374–375; Twelfth Census (1900), *Occupations*, 20–21; Massachusetts BLS, *Sixth Annual Report*, 96; idem, *Fifteenth Annual Report* (Boston, 1884), 8, 39, 42.

   As to the representativeness of my sample of 102 women, there were perhaps 200 female operators in New York City in 1883, so at a conservative estimate, the sample covers about half the city's women telegraphers in the early 1880s. See *NYT*, July 14, 1883.

4   Ninth Census, 1:676, 688; Tenth Census, 1:778, 794; Eleventh Census, pt. 2, p. 304; Twelfth Census, pt. 2, p. 506; Reid, *Telegraph in America* (1879), 575, and (1886), 636, 653, 666. See also Senate, *Labor and Capital*, 1:116. On the growing feminization of telegraphy in the twentieth century, see Elizabeth Faulkner Baker, *Technology and Woman's Work* (New York, 1964), 244.

5   *JT*, Nov. 2, 1868, July 15, 1876; *TA*, June 1, 1883; Senate, *Labor and Capital*, 1:886; *EA*, Oct. 1, 1886. For women running branch and depot offices, see also *TA*, July 16, 1883; *EA*, June 1, Sept. 1, 16, Oct. 1, 16, 1886, Oct. 1, 1887; *BH*, July 15, 1883; Penny, *Employments of Women*, 101; *Operator*, Mar. 1, 1881. For later conditions and problems of women branch office operators, see *Charities and the Commons*, Oct. 5, 1907, p. 864.

6   *TA*, Aug. 1, 1883; Massachusetts BLS, *Sixth Annual Report*, 94; *Telegrapher*, Jan. 21, 1871; Maine Bureau of Industrial and Labor Statistics, *Second Annual Report* (Augusta, 1889), 78–79; *JT*, Sept. 15, 1871; *EA*, May 16, 1887.

7   Elizabeth Beardsley Butler, *Women and the Trades* (New York, 1911), 294.

8   Martha Louise Rayne, *What Can a Woman Do?* (Detroit, 1885), 140. Cf. Buckingham, "Telegraph of To-Day," 6.

9   *BG*, July 28, 1883; Massachusetts BLS, *Sixth Annual Report*, 96. See also ibid., 95.

10   *JT*, May 15, 1869, Feb. 15, 1875. See also *NYT*, July 20, 1883; *NYTr*, July 20, 1883; *EA*, Apr. 16, 1887; and cf. Buckingham, "Telegraph of To-Day," 5.

11   *TA*, June 16, 1883. See also *Operator*, May 15, 1876.

12   *JT*, May 15, 1869, Feb. 15, 1875; *Operator*, May 15, 1875; Reid, *Telegraph in America* (1879), 572; Rayne, *What Can a Woman Do?*, 136; *NYT*, July 20, 1883; *EA*, Apr. 16, 1887. The proportion of women in the metropolitan main offices varied between 25 and 31 percent. See also Butler, *Women and the Trades*, 292.

13   *Telegrapher*, Oct. 15, 1870, Mar. 6, 1875; Rayne, *What Can a Woman Do?*, 139.

14   Rayne, *What Can a Woman Do?*, 142–143; George J. Manson, *Work for Women* (New York, 1883), 25–26.

15   Thayer, *Wired Love*, 28–29; Norvin Green to H. Graf, June 17, 1892, WULB; Rayne, *What Can a Woman Do?*, 136–137; Willard, *Occupations for Women*, 133; *Operator*, Sept. 15, 1880, May 16, 1885; *Telegraph Age*, Sept. 16, 1897. For the persistence of check-girl apprenticeships into the World War I era, see Helen Christene Hoerle and Florence B. Saltzberg, *The Girl and the Job* (New York, 1919), 70.

16   Rayne, *What Can a Woman Do?*, 141; Hoerle and Saltzberg, *Girl and the Job*, 71–72; Butler, *Women and the Trades*, 369; *EA*, Oct. 16, 1886; Senate, *Labor and Capital*, 1:895. See also *BH*, July 24, 1883.

17   *EA*, June 1, 1886; *TA*, June 1, 1883; *Operator*, July 2, 1883, May 2, 1885; *Telegraph Age*, June 1, 1898, Sept. 1, 1900. For highly skilled female operators, see also *JT*, May 2, 1870; *Telegrapher*, Jan. 2, 1875; *Operator*, June 15, 1884; *EA*, Dec. 1, 1886; Massachusetts BLS, *Sixth Annual Report*, 95; *Telegraph Age*, Aug. 16, 1897.

18   Census Manuscript Schedules, 1880, New York City; *EA*, June 1, 1886, Feb. 1, May 16, 1887; *Operator*, May 15, 1875, June 15, 1884; Reid, *Telegraph in America* (1879), 572, and (1886), 732–733. See also *Operator*, Feb. 1, 1880; *Telegrapher*, Jan. 2, 1875; Syracuse record book, box 53, WUCS; *Telegraph Age*, Aug. 16, 1893, June 1, 1898; Gabler, "Kid-Gloved Laborers," 242–243.

19   Census Manuscript Schedules, 1880, New York City; Reid, *Telegraph in America* (1886), 732–733.

20   *JT*, Dec. 15, 1870; Senate, *Labor and Capital*, 1:895; *CPD*, July 21, 1883;

NYT, June 17, 1877; Charles H. Garland, "Women as Telegraphists," *Economic Journal*, June 1901, p. 259. See also C. H. Summers to R. C. Clowry, "Report of Wheatstone Circuits West of Chicago," Sept. 4, 1888, in "Old Correspondence and Forms," box 48, WUCS; Willard, *Occupations for Women*, 134.

21 *EA*, Oct. 16, 1886. On telegraphy as a dead-end career for women, see Willard, *Occupations for Women*, 134; Manson, *Work for Women*, 26; Thayer, *Wired Love*, 29; Lida A. Churchill, *My Girls* (Boston, 1882), 10; Hoerle and Saltzberg, *Girl and the Job*, 71–72.

22 Davies, *Woman's Place Is at the Typewriter*, 94. See also p. 172.

23 *Telegrapher*, Feb. 27, 1865; *Operator*, Aug. 1, 1883. See also *Telegraph Age*, Sept. 1, 1897.

24 See, e.g., Norvin Green to H. Graf, June 17, 1892, WULB.

25 *EA*, Oct. 1, 1886, May 2, 1887; *BG*, July 28, 1883; *NYT*, July 23, 1883; *NYH*, July 23, 1883; Senate, *Labor and Capital*, 1:384; Linda M. Girard to F. B. Gowen, Jan. 11, 24, Feb. 12, 1883, box 250, Reading Papers; Census Manuscript Schedules, 1880, New York City. See also *NYH*, Aug. 21, 1883.

26 Census Manuscript Schedules, 1880, New York City; on food consumption, see Massachusetts BLS, *Sixth Annual Report*, 221ff.; and Illinois BLS, *Third Biennial Report*, 388–389. On young women operators in Britain as support for parents, see *NYT*, June 17, 1877.

27 *Telegrapher*, Apr. 10, 1875; Churchill, *My Girls*, 19–22; Census Manuscript Population Schedules, 1870, 1880, Hyde Park (Norfolk County), Mass.; *JT*, July 15, Aug. 1, 1876.

28 Census Manuscript Schedules, 1880, New York City. The servant was a fifty-five-year-od Irishwoman; both Molly, nineteen, and her parents were native born.

29 Cindy S. Aron, "'To Barter Their Souls for Gold': Female Clerks in Federal Government Offices, 1862–1890," *Journal of American History*, Mar. 1981.

30 *EW*, Nov. 29, 1890; Churchill, *My Girls*, 16–17; Thayer, *Wired Love*, 28. See also Davies, *Woman's Place Is at the Typewriter*, 63. Churchill had herself been a telegrapher. *Telegraph Age*, Feb. 1, 1897.

31 *NYT*, Mar. 17, 1869; Census Manuscript Schedules, 1880, New York City.

32 Hasia R. Diner, *Erin's Daughters in America* (Baltimore, Md., 1983), 46, 71, 94; Twelfth Census, *Occupations*, 72–73; Census Manuscript Schedules, 1880, New York City.

33 Thomas Dublin, *Women at Work* (New York, 1979), 35, 40; Diner, *Erin's Daughters*, 46. See also Kathy Peiss, *Cheap Amusements* (Philadelphia, 1986), 69.

34   *IW*, Aug. 4, 1883; *Telegrapher*, Feb. 6, Apr. 10, 1875; Thayer, *Wired Love*, 28. See also Churchill, *My Girls*, 16–17, 28–29; *EA*, Oct. 1, 1886, May 2, 1887.

35   Massachusetts BLS, *Third Annual Report* (Boston, 1872), 112. See also Mary P. Ryan, *Womanhood in America* (New York, 1975), 199.

36   Phillips, *Sketches*, 105–114; Thayer, *Wired Love*, 28–29. See also Churchill, *My Girls*. Dorothy Richardson was not an operator, though her background (a village in Pennsylvania, a Protestant, Scotch-Irish family) and proclivities (she taught in the village school) made her similar to the operators I am discussing here. Richardson's parents died suddenly when she was eighteen (ca. 1900), which prompted her to leave for New York seeking "lady-like" work. After a number of temporary and marginal factory jobs, she finally did get a white-collar position. Richardson, *The Long Day*, in *Women at Work*, ed. William L. O'Neil (Chicago, 1972), 17 and passim.

37   *JT*, May 15, 1869, May 2, 1870, Aug. 1, 1876; Census Manuscript Schedules, 1880, Hyde Park, Mass.; *Telegrapher*, Jan. 2, 1875.

38   See also Thayer, *Wired Love*, 28–29. For the "metropolitan corridor," see John R. Stilgoe, *Metropolitan Corridor* (New Haven, Conn., 1983).

39   Census Manuscript Schedules, 1880, New York City; Aron, "'To Barter Their Souls for Gold.'"

40   *NYT*, Mar. 17, 1869; *EA*, Dec. 16, 1886, July 1, 1887.

41   Diner, *Erin's Daughters*, 46. See also David M. Katzman, *Seven Days a Week* (New York, 1978), 231, 241; Ileen A. De Vault, "Work and Honor: The Daughters of Pittsburgh's Skilled Workers" (unpublished paper).

42   Census Manuscript Schedules, 1880, New York City.

43   *Telegrapher*, Apr. 10, 1875; Massachusetts BLS, *Sixth Annual Report*, 96. On the general desirability of white-collar work for Gilded Age women, see Davies, *Woman's Place Is at the Typewriter*, 64–65; Susan Porter Benson, "'The Customer Ain't God': The Work Culture of Department Store Saleswomen, 1890–1940," in *Working-Class America*, ed. Michael H. Frisch and Daniel J. Walkowitz (Urbana, Ill., 1983), 188.

44   *NYT*, Mar. 17, 1869; Massachusetts BLS, *Fifteenth Annual Report*, 76–81. See also Rayne, *What Can a Woman Do?*, 19–21; Massachusetts BLS, *Third Annual Report*, 101; and for the early 1900s, Butler, *Women and the Trades*, 338.

45   On education and white-collar work for women, see Davies, *Woman's Place Is at the Typewriter*, Table 2; Janice Weiss, "Educating for Clerical Work: The Nineteenth-Century Private Commercial School," *Journal of Social History*, Spring 1981, p. 413.

46   *Godey's Lady's Book*, July 1853, p. 84; *JT*, July 1, 1868, Dec. 15, 1870;

Rayne, *What Can a Woman Do?*, 139–140. See also Senate, *Labor and Capital*, 1:935; Butler, *Women and the Trades*, 26.

47 Diner, *Erin's Daughters*, 140. See also p. 71.

48 De Vault, "Work and Honor," 13ff.; Fink, *Workingmen's Democracy*, 94.

49 Census Manuscript Schedules, 1880, New York City; DeVault, "Work and Honor," 17.

50 *NYT*, July 14, 23, 1883; Senate, *Labor and Capital*, 1:384–385. See also *Telegraph Age*, Jan. 1, Apr. 1, 1897; Linda M. Girard to F. B. Gowen, Jan. 24, 1883, box 250, Reading Papers; U.S. Commissioner of Labor, *Fourth Annual Report* (Washington, D.C., 1888), 46–47.

51 Rayne, *What Can a Woman Do?*, 141; *EA*, Aug. 16, 1886. See also Richardson, *The Long Day*, 194.

52 *BG*, July 28, 1883.

53 Thayer, *Wired Love*, 25–26. See also ibid., 29; and Peel, "On the Margins."

54 Reid, *Telegraph in America* (1886), 739; *Operator*, Dec. 15, 1883; *BH*, July 20, 1883; Churchill, *My Girls*, 58; Richardson, *The Long Day*, 19–20.

55 *BG*, July 28, 1883. On tension between white- and blue-collar working women, see Peiss, *Cheap Amusements*, 173.

56 *EA*, Aug. 1, 1887.

57 *Operator*, Sept. 1, 1879. See also *EA*, Feb. 1, 1887; Peiss, *Cheap Amusements*, 170; Richardson, *The Long Day*, 184–185. On marriage and operators' social origins, see Gabler, "Kid-Gloved Laborers," 250–251.

58 *BH*, July 15, 1883.

59 Davies, *Woman's Place Is at the Typewriter*, 52, 55, 91. For arguments that telegraphy was really suited to be women's work, see *BH*, Aug. 19, 1883; *Nation*, Aug. 23, 1883.

60 *Telegrapher*, Dec. 26, 1864, Nov. 6, 1865. But the NTU constitution evidently did not actually bar women either. Ibid., Nov. 1, 1865.

61 *TA*, Oct. 16, 1885; *EA*, Sept. 16, 1886, Apr. 16, 1887. See also *Telegrapher*, July 3, 1875; *Operator*, June 1, 1883; *NYT*, Aug. 10, 1883; New York State BLS, *Sixth Annual Report* (Albany, 1889), 1039; Davies, *Woman's Place Is at the Typewriter*, 91.

62 Penny, *Employments of Women*, 101–102; *BH*, July 15, 1883; Rayne, *What Can a Woman Do?*, 138–139, 143; Garland, "Women as Telegraphists," 260–261; *Operator*, June 1, 1885. See also *NYT*, Aug. 10, 1883. For the reluctance of railroad superintendents to hire women operators, see O. W. Stager to J. E. Wootten, Mar. 17, 1882, box 241, Reading Papers.

63 William Orton to T. T. Eckert, Nov. 20, 1868, WULB; Orton to J. W. Phelps, Feb. 12, 1869, WULB; *JT*, Apr. 15, May 1, 1868, May 1, Nov. 1, 1869, Dec. 15, 1870, Oct. 16, 1871; *NYT*, Mar. 17, 1869; Senate, *Labor and Capital*, 1:886; *Operator*, June 15, 1884; Rayne, *What Can a Woman*

Do?, 136, 141; *EA*, Nov. 1, 1886, May 16, June 16, 1887; Norvin Green to H. Graf, June 17, 1892, WULB. On telegraph schools and corporate training of operators in the late nineteenth and early twentieth centuries, see also Thomas Woody, *A History of Women's Education in the United States* (New York, 1929), 2:68–69; Hoerle and Saltzberg, *Girl and the Job*, 70; Senate, *Industrial Relations*, 10:9320–9321.

64   *JT*, Nov. 1, 1869, Jan. 1, 1870; *Telegrapher*, Jan. 2, 1875; Barnard, "Telegraph of To-Day," 714–716; *BG*, July 21, 1883; *BH*, July 19, 1883; *BET*, July 20, 1883; *BS*, July 17, 1883; Senate, *Labor and Capital*, 1:159–160, 2:1272–1273; *JSP*, Jan. 24, 1886; *EA*, Feb. 1, 1887; Senate, *Industrial Relations*, 10:9398–9399, 9408–9409, 9415–9416, 9423; C. H. Summers to R. C. Clowry, Sept. 4, 1888, box 48, WUCS; Baker, *Technology and Women's Work*, 244–245; Helen Hoerle, *The Girl and Her Future* (New York, 1932), 47–48.

65   *JT*, June 1, 1868; *Telegrapher*, Oct. 31, Nov. 28, 1864, Nov. 1, 1865, Sept. 11, 1875; *TA*, Oct. 16, 1885; *EA*, May 2, 1887.

66   *TA*, Aug. 1, 1883; BTUSC, *Proceedings*, 11; *NYT*, July 14, 28, 1883; *BH*, July 15, 1883; *BG*, July 14, 1883; *SR*, July 22, 1883. Cf. *NYT*, July 11, 1883. For earlier arguments for equal pay, see *Telegrapher*, Feb. 27, Apr. 3, 1875.

67   *BG*, July 19, 1883. See also *NOP*, July 24, 1883; Senate, *Labor and Capital*, 1:813.

68   BTUSC, *Proceedings*, 24; *NYTr*, July 16, 1883. See also *CPD*, July 13, 1883; *NYTr*, July 13, 1883; *BS*, July 18, 1883. The Knights of Labor's equal pay demand followed much the same logic. See Gregory S. Kealey and Bryan D. Palmer, *Dreaming of What Might Be* (Cambridge, England, 1982), 320–321.

69   *NYT*, July 18, 1883; *NYH*, July 18, 1883.

70   Manson, *Work for Women*, 25–26; Rayne, *What Can a Woman Do?*, 137, 143; Senate, *Labor and Capital*, 1:886; Maine BLIS, *Second Annual Report*, 78–79, 104. See also Penny, *Employments of Women*, 101–102; O. W. Stager to J. E. Wootten, Sept. 16, 1881, box 233, Reading Papers.

71   *IW*, Aug. 4, 1883; Senate, *Labor and Capital*, 1:103, 116, 188; *BG*, July 19, 28, 1883; *NYT*, July 14, 18, 1883; *NOP*, July 24, 1883; *NYTr*, July 13, 17, 1883; *NYH*, July 17, 1883; Syracuse record book, box 53, WUCS. For later charges of both a structural salary bias against women operators (of as much as 100 percent) and a consistent use of them to replace male operators at lower pay, see Butler, *Women and the Trades*, 293–294, 343; *Charities and the Commons*, Oct. 5, 1907.

72   Senate, *Labor and Capital*, 1:191, 895; *NYT*, July 23, 1883; *JSP*, June 1, 1884; *IW*, Aug. 4, 1883; Norvin Green to H. Graf, June 17, 1892; New York State BLS, *Third Annual Report* (Albany, 1886), 153; Garland, "Women as Telegraphists," 260; *NYH*, July 21, 1883. See also *Telegra-*

pher, Jan. 30, 1865; Phillips, *Sketches*, 49–57, 105–114; Butler, *Women and the Trades*, 293; Rayne, *What Can a Woman Do?*, 137–138; Davies, *Woman's Place Is at the Typewriter*, 91; Hoerle and Saltzberg, *Girl and the Job*, 69.

73   *Operator*, May 15, 1876; *Telegrapher*, Nov. 28, Dec. 26, 1864, Jan. 21, 1871.

74   *Telegrapher*, Feb. 27, 1865; *Operator*, Aug. 1, 1883; *CPD*, July 21, 1883; S. Rept. 242, p. 50. See also Butler, *Women and the Trades*, 293–294.

75   Massachusetts BLS, *Sixth Annual Report*, 96; *BH*, July 19, 1883; Linda M. Girard to F. B. Gowen, Jan. 24, 1883, box 250, Reading Papers; *BG*, July 28, 1883. See also *Telegrapher*, Dec. 26, 1864; *Telegraph Age*, Sept. 1, 1897.

76   *SR*, July 22, 1883; *NYTr*, July 21, 29, 1883; *NYT*, July 20, 21, 29, 1883; *BH*, Aug. 7, 1883; *BET*, July 19, Aug. 7, 1883; *CPD*, July 17, 1883; *NOP*, July 18, 1883. See also *BG*, July 29, 1883.

77   *NYT*, Aug. 5, 1883. See also *BG*, Aug. 15, 1883; *CPD*, July 23, 1883; *NYTr*, July 25, 1883; *TA*, Aug. 16, 1883.

78   *NYT*, July 20, 1883; *BH*, July 20, 1883; Senate, *Labor and Capital*, 1:190; *Telegraph Age*, July 16, 1893. See also *NYT*, July 16, 21, 1883; *NOP*, July 20, 1883.

79   Kealey and Palmer, *Dreaming of What Might Be*, 144; *IW*, Aug. 4, 1883; *BG*, July 29, 1883; *NYT*, July 24, 1883; *BH*, July 24, 1883.

80   *BG*, July 20, Aug. 11, 1883; *NYT*, July 20, 21, 28, Aug. 12, 1883; *BH*, July 20, 1883; *NOP*, July 20, 1883; *SR*, July 23, 1883; *NYTr*, July 18, 1883. For women scabs in the 1870 and 1907 strikes, see Reid, *Telegraph in America* (1879), 548; *JT*, Jan. 15, 1870; Butler, *Women and the Trades*, 294.

81   *CPD*, July 23, Aug. 16, 18, 1883; *TA*, Aug. 16, 1883.

82   *BG*, July 20, 21, Aug. 11, 1883; *NYT*, July 26, 1883; *NYTr*, July 23, 1883; *NYH*, July 21, 22, 1883.

83   *NYT*, July 31, 1883; *NYH*, Aug. 19, 1883.

84   *NYTr*, July 20, 31, 1883; *NYT*, July 28, 1883; *NYH*, July 21, 1883.

85   *CPD*, July 30, Aug. 18, 1883; *AC*, July 24, 1883; *BG*, July 23, 1883. See also ibid., July 16, 20, 1883; *TA*, Aug. 16, 1883; Senate, *Labor and Capital*, 1:190; *NYT*, July 14, 21, 31, 1883; *IW*, Aug. 4, 1883; *NYH*, July 25, 28, 1883; *EA*, Oct. 1, 1886. For charges that the brotherhood had "bulldozed" women into joining the strike, see *BG*, July 27, 1883; *NYH*, Aug. 19, 1883; *NYTr*, Aug. 5, 1883.

86   *NYT*, July 25, 1883; *Operator*, Mar. 1, 1882; *TA*, June 1, 1883.

87   *NYT*, July 27, 1883; *NYTr*, July 28, 1883. See also *NYT*, July 23, 28, 1883; *NYH*, July 28, 1883.

88   *BG*, Aug. 13, 18, 1883; *CPD*, Aug. 1, 1883; *IW*, Aug. 4, 1883; *BH*, Aug.

20, 1883; *NYT*, Aug. 18, 1883. See also *Telegraph Age*, July 16, 1893; *CPD*, July 27, 1883; *NYT*, Aug. 19, 24, 25, 1883; *IW*, Aug. 11, 1883; *Operator*, Aug. 1, 1883. For the participation and loyalty of women in the 1870 and 1907 strikes, see *NYTr*, Jan. 7, 12, 1870; *NYT*, Jan. 6, 1870; *Charities and the Commons*, Oct. 5, 1907; Butler, *Women and the Trades*, 292–294; U.S. Senate, *Report on Conditions of Women and Child Wage-Earners in the United States*, 61st Cong., 1st sess., 1911, S. Doc. 645, 10:195.

89   Senate, *Labor and Capital*, 1:384–385, 907; *NYH*, Aug. 21, 1883; *NYT*, Aug. 18, 1883; *BG*, Aug. 18, 19, 1883; Norvin Green to Gen. Daniel McClure, Jan. 16, 1884, WULB; Green to Helene Dietrichson, Apr. 3, 1884, WULB; William Orton to A. L. Hatch, June 7, 1869, WULB; Orton to E. B. Wesley, Sept. 30, 1875, WULB; Orton to Hiland R. Hulburt, Jan. 11, 1876, WULB; Taltavall, *Telegraphers of To-Day*, 178–179, 199. See also Norvin Green to Wilkinson Call, Jan. 29, 1884, WULB; *BG*, Aug. 20, 1883; *NYTr*, Aug. 18, 19, 21, 1883; *NOP*, Aug. 19, 1883; *TA*, Sept. 1, 1883; *NYH*, Aug. 19, 1883; *NYT*, Aug. 22, 24, Sept. 7, 1883. On later rehires, see *IW*, Oct. 6, 1883; *EA*, Oct. 1, 1886.

90   *NYTr*, July 20, 1883; *NYH*, July 28, 1883; Walkowitz, *Worker City, Company Town*, 119, 174; Census Manuscript Schedules, 1880, New York City (60 percent of the 102 women in my sample from this census came from fatherless households).

91   Diner, *Erin's Daughters*, 66, 99–100. For the militancy of young Irish women carpet mill workers in 1885, see Susan Levine, *Labor's True Woman* (Philadelphia, 1984), 92. For the noteworthy militancy of British female weavers in the 1840s, see Dorothy Thompson, *The Chartists* (New York, 1984), 219.

92   *NYH*, July 20, 1883; *NYT*, July 23, 28, Aug. 24, 1883; *Telegrapher*, Apr. 24, 1875; *Operator*, Oct. 1, 1874. See also *Telegrapher*, Jan. 30, 1865, Jan. 23, 1875; Reid, *Telegraph in America* (1879), 170–171; *EA*, May 16, 1887; *Operator*, Sept. 15, 1874, Apr. 15, 1876; *JT*, Dec. 15, 1870, Jan. 15, 1872. Cf. *BG*, Aug. 5, 1883.

93   On women's sphere, see Nancy F. Cott, *The Bonds of Womanhood* (New Haven, Conn., 1977). On domesticity, including the working-class variant, see Levine, *Labor's True Woman*, 121, 132–135, 141; Kealey and Palmer, *Dreaming of What Might Be*, 317; Jones, "Working-Class Culture," 486, 487; Gray, *Labour Aristocracy*, 99; Diner, *Erin's Daughters*, chap. 7. On cooperative values as typical of female upbringing, see Ryan, *Womanhood in America*, 149.

94   Both Susan Levine and Kealey and Palmer note that the working-class domesticity that the Knights of Labor celebrated, while itself conservative, was also used as a basis for attacking industrial capitalism (which

had begun eroding that domestic ideal). My argument about the women operators' noteworthy loyalty during the strike, which I arrived at independently of these scholars, nevertheless parallels and confirms their insights. See *Labor's True Woman*, 121, 132–135, 141; and *Dreaming of What Might Be*, 317. On the internal contradictions of domesticity, see also Cott, *Bonds of Womanhood*, 197–206.

95   *NYT*, July 20, 1883; *NYTr*, July 20, 1883; *BG*, July 24, Aug. 15, 1883.

5   KID-GLOVED LABORERS

1   The older and generally hostile view of the Knights held that the order was reactionary and utopian, a curious relic of Jacksonian reformism that could not realistically deal with a modern industrial economy —in contrast to the pragmatic and effective "pure and simple" business unionists of the American Federation of Labor stripe, personified by Samuel Gompers, who represented an authentic (and nonideological) working-class response to American conditions. This interpretation drew heavily on the so-called Wisconsin School of labor history represented by pioneer scholars John Commons and Selig Perlman, and its last and most polished version was Gerald N. Grob's *Workers and Utopia* (1961; reprint, New York, 1969). Grob's monograph reflected both the Commons-Perlman tradition and the generally conservative tone of post–World War II American academe. The "Consensus School" historians writing in the 1940s and 1950s argued against the existence of a significant strain of American radicalism in the past, stressing instead a nonideological, pragmatic, and cross-class agreement on liberal capitalist values. Grob (p. 189) went so far as to assert that Gilded Age workers "had adopted a middle-class value system and psychology." The only study of telegraph unionism to date, Vidkunn Ulriksson's *The Telegraphers*, shares the Consensus School view—not surprisingly, since Ulriksson (himself a former telegrapher) was a student of Selig Perlman.

The recent scholarship that has influenced my own reading of the Knights reflects the tempering of the "new" social history of the past twenty or so years and is generally sympathetic, though not uncritical, toward the order. Three prominent examples of this Knights revisionism are Fink, *Workingmen's Democracy*; Kealey and Palmer, *Dreaming of What Might Be*; and Richard Oestreicher, "Solidarity and Fragmentation: Working People and Class Consciousness in Detroit, 1875–1900" (unpublished manuscript). Finally, in reviewing Knights historiography, I am compelled to mention an older study, Norman J. Ware's *The Labor Movement in the United States 1860–1895* (New York,

1929). Ware was skeptical, perhaps even cynical, and certainly disillusioned, but his rambling and idiosyncratic book on the order remains informative and stimulating.

2　Ulriksson, *The Telegraphers*, 16; Thompson, *Wiring a Continent*, 389–390; David Montgomery, *Beyond Equality* (New York, 1967), 458–459.

3　Ulriksson, *The Telegraphers*, 16; Thompson, *Wiring a Continent*, 389–390; *Telegrapher*, Nov. 1, 6, 1865.

4　Montgomery, *Beyond Equality*, 458–459; Ulriksson, *The Telegraphers*, 16–17. Neither did the NTU's militant successor, the TPL, attend the national labor congresses.

5　McNeill, *Labor Movement*, 390; Ulriksson, *The Telegraphers*, 18–20.

6　Ulriksson, *The Telegraphers*, 18–20; *Cincinnati Inquirer*, Jan. 4, 1870, quoted in *NYH*, Jan. 6, 1870. For charges of the consecutive reduction scheme persisting as late as 1907, see Butler, *Women and the Trades*, 294.

7　Ulriksson, *The Telegraphers*, 20–21.

8　Telegraphers' Protective League, "Confidential Circular," box 26, WUCS; Ulriksson, *The Telegraphers*, 17. On "pure and simple" unions, see Ware, *Labor Movement*, 168–169; and John Laslett, "Reflections on the Failure of Socialism in the American Federation of Labor," *Mississippi Valley Historical Review*, Mar. 1964.

9　Ulriksson, *The Telegraphers*, 23–24.

10　See chapter 3, above.

11　"Confidential Circular," box 26, WUCS.

12　*NYH*, Jan. 6, 1870; *Historical Statistics*, pt. 1, pp. 200–201, pt. 2, pp. 787–788; *Statistical Abstract*, 257; *EA*, Dec. 16, 1886.

13　*BH*, July 15, 1883; "Confidential Circular," box 26, WUCS; Ulriksson, *The Telegraphers*, 28; Meeting of June 1, 1870 (Treasurer's Report), minute book A, WUMB.

14　Ulriksson, *The Telegraphers*, 24–29; *JT*, Feb. 1, 1870. See also *BG*, July 25, 1883.

15　*Telegrapher*, Nov. 19, 1870, Jan. 28, Apr. 15, 1871; Ulriksson, *The Telegraphers*, 29; William Orton to A. Stager, Feb. 9, 1870, WULB; Orton to George W. Lee, Feb. 18, 1870, WULB. See also Orton to J. N. Ashley, Mar. 2, 1870, WULB.

16　*Historical Statistics*, pt. 2, p. 788.

17　*Operator*, Jan. 1, 1876, Aug. 15, 1879, June 1, 1883; *Telegrapher*, Oct. 9, 1875; *Telegraph Age*, May 16, 1907. On Western Union blacklisting and harassment, see *Operator*, Apr. 1, 1879; *BG*, July 17, 1883; *NYT*, July 17, Aug. 3, 1883; *CPD*, July 30, 1883; L. Horton to Theodore Voorhees, Aug. 12, 1895, box 146, Reading Papers.

18　*Operator*, Nov. 1, 1878, Jan. 15, 1880, Aug. 1, 1882; *NYT*, July 17, 1883.

19　*Operator*, Jan. 15, 1875, Nov. 1, 1878, Sept. 1, 1879. On Eckert, Gould, and the Western Union, see Klein, *Jay Gould*, 197, 199; Harlow, *Old Wires*, 235; Josephson, *Robber Barons*, 205; Dyer and Martin, *Edison*, 1:165; *Telegrapher*, Feb. 4, 1871.

20 *Telegrapher*, Jan. 14, 28, 1871. See also Feb. 4, 1871. For arguments to use telegraphic journals as a means of redress for operators, see *Telegrapher*, Aug. 27, Sept. 24, Dec. 24, 1870; *Operator*, Dec. 9, 1882.

21 *Telegrapher*, July 29, 1871.

22 *JT*, May 15, Sept. 16, Oct. 1, 1872.

23 *Telegrapher*, Dec. 15, 18, 25, 1875; William Orton to A. Stager, Dec. 18, 1875, WULB. See also Orton to J. W. Simonton, Dec. 13, 1875, WULB. For mention of a Telegraphers' Protective Union that was supposed to have lasted from 1875 to 1877, see Ulriksson, *The Telegraphers*, 32.

24 *Telegrapher*, Aug. 12, 1871; *Operator*, Jan. 1, July 15, Dec. 15, 1875, Jan. 15, 1876. See also ibid., Jan. 15, 1881.

25 *Operator*, Sept. 1, 1877, Nov. 1, 1878. See also Jan. 1, Oct. 15, 1881.

26 David Montgomery, *Workers' Control in America* (Cambridge, England, 1979), 11–15; Braverman, *Labor and Monopoly Capital*, 96.

27 Jonathan Prude, "The Social System of Early New England Textile Mills: A Case Study, 1812–1840," in *Working-Class America*, ed. Frisch and Walkowitz, 22; James R. Green, *The World of the Worker* (New York, 1980), 103.

28 *BG*, Aug. 21, 1883; *Telegraph Age*, Mar. 1, 1897, Feb. 1, 1898, Mar. 16, 1908.

29 WUTC, *Rules* (1866), 31, and (1870), 20; *Telegraph Age*, July 1, 1898. See also Dyer and Martin, *Edison*, 1:84–85; Norvin Green to Clara Brown, Oct. 15, 1880. WULB.

30 *JT*, June 15, 1874; *Telegraph Age*, Sept. 1, 1907; *NYT*, July 12, 1883; *TA*, July 1, 1883. On deteriorating service, mistakes, high pressure, and craft pride, see, e.g., *JT*, Jan. 15, 1875; *Operator*, Aug. 1, Sept. 15, 1881.

31 *Telegrapher*, Oct. 15, 1870. On high turnover as a kind of informal resistance by semi- and unskilled factory workers in the early twentieth century, see Gordon, Edwards, and Reich, *Segmented Work, Divided Workers*, 148–149.

32 *Operator*, July 15, Aug. 1, 1879, Apr. 15, 1880.

33 Ibid., June 1, July 15, Nov. 15, 1881, Feb. 1, 1882. See also July 1, 1881.

34 Ibid., Aug. 15, Sept. 1, 15, 1882. For a defense of Bates, see *RTT*, Oct. 2, 1882.

35 *Operator*, Jan. 1, Aug. 15, 1882. See also Aug. 1, 1882.

36 Ware, *Labor Movement*, xviii, chaps. 2–4.

37 Ibid., chap. 4.

38 *BH*, July 23, 1883; *EA*, June 1, 1886; *Operator*, Feb. 1, 1882.

39 *Operator*, Feb. 1, 15, Apr. 1, 1882.

40 Ware, *Labor Movement*, 128; *Journal of United Labor*, May 1882 (hereafter *JUL*); Terence V. Powderly, *Thirty Years of Labor* (Philadelphia, 1890), 330. I am obliged to Miriam Chrisman and Dean Ware for help in translating the Latin motto.

41 BTUSC, *Proceedings*, 19, 24; idem, Circulars, Dec. 27, 1882, May 20, 1883, in Powderly Papers. Membership totals broke down this way: 3,883 railroad operators, 3,429 commercial operators, 742 nonoperators, and 139 "out of service". Of the total membership, 501 were listed as being in "Bad Standing."

42 *TA*, June 1, 1883. See also *NYT*, July 12, 1883.

43 BTUSC, Circular, May 20, 1883; *JUL*, June, 1883.

44 BTUSC, Circular, June 25, 1883, Powderly Papers.

45 BTUSC, *Proceedings*, 13–17; McNeill, *Labor Movement*, 391; *AC*, July 20, 1883.

46 *Bradstreet's*, July 28, 1883, quoted in *Operator*, Aug. 1, 1883; J. C. Reiff to Robert Garrett, Aug. 15, 1883, box 1, Garrett Papers; Senate, *Labor and Capital*, 1:911. See also *BH*, July 16, 28, 1883; *BG*, July 31, 1883; *HDT*, July 19, 1883.

47 *BH*, July 16, 1883; BTUSC, Circular, June 25, 1883.

48 *BG*, July 16, 1883. The brotherhood used such a device as early as December 1882, but not all local assemblies did, and John Campbell recommended it only as a last resort. Circular, Dec. 27, 1882.

49 *NOP*, July 19, 1883; *HDT*, July 18, 1883; Senate, *Labor and Capital*, 1:184; *Telegraph Age*, July 16, 1893. Cf. Ulriksson, *The Telegraphers*, 32.

50 *Telegraph Age*, July 16, 1893; *EA*, July 1, 1886.

51 *Telegraph Age*, July 16, 1893; J. C. Reiff to Robert Garrett, Aug. 15, 1883, box 1, Garrett Papers.

52 New York State BLS, *Third Annual Report*, 587, 591; *TA*, Sept. 1, 1883; *NYTr*, Aug. 23, 1883. On the blacklist (which was not aimed solely at union activists), see also *EA*, June 1, 1886.

53 *JSP*, Dec. 12, 16, 1883. See also McNeill, *Labor Movement*, 392.

54 *BH*, Aug. 11, 1883; *NYT*, Aug. 17, 1883; *BG*, Aug. 18, 19, 1883; *BET*, Aug. 18, 1883. See also *TA*, Aug. 16, Sept. 1, 1883; *AC*, Aug. 23, 1883; *Operator*, Sept. 1, 1883; *NOP*, Aug. 19, 1883; *NYT*, Aug. 19, 20, 1883; *BH*, Aug. 12, 19, 1883; *NYTr*, Aug. 18, 1883.

55 *EA*, June 1, July 1, 1886.

56 Ibid., June 16, 1886; Terence V. Powderly *The Path I Trod*, ed. H. Carman, H. David, P. N. Guthrie (New York, 1940), 106–108. See also *NYTr*, July 18, 19, 24, 1883; *BG*, July 14, 22, Aug. 22, 1883; *TA*, Sept. 1, 1883; *NYT*, July 28, 29, Aug. 4, 20, 1883; *CPD*, Aug. 22, 1883; *HDT*, Aug. 20, 1883; *BH*, July 12, Aug. 3, 11, 1883; *IW*, Sept. 1, 1883.

57 Senate, *Labor and Capital*, 1:372, 820. See also *JSP*, June 1, 1884.

58 *JUL*, Nov. 1882; *EA*, July 1, 1886; Ware, *Labor Movement*, 129; Layton to TVP, Aug. 2, 1883, Powderly Papers; TVP to John B. Barnes, Aug. 18, 1883, Powderly Papers.

59 Rockwood to TVP, July 10, 1883, Powderly Papers; TVP to Layton, Aug. 6, 1883, Powderly Papers; Layton to TVP, Aug. 18, 1883, Powderly Papers. See also TVP to Layton, Aug. 8, 1883, Powderly Papers; Ware, *Labor Movement*, 129–130.

60 *EA*, July 1, 1886. On McClelland's behavior during the strike and the subsequent controversy, see ibid., June 1, 16, July 1, Aug. 16, 1886; TVP to Robert Layton, Oct. 9, 1883, Powderly Papers. On McClelland's character and post-brotherhood career, see Kealey and Palmer, *Dreaming of What Might Be*, 371. For an indignant appeal to the Knights for funds after the strike, see H. O. Steltz to TVP, Aug. 25, 1883, Powderly Papers.

61 *AC*, Aug. 22, 1883; *JUL*, Sept. 1883; Ware, *Labor Movement*, 130–133. See also Kealey and Palmer, *Dreaming of What Might Be*, 332, 374; Fink, *Workingmen's Democracy*, 224.

62 Robert Layton to TVP, Sept. 21, 1883, Powderly Papers; TVP to J. S. Ryan, Nov. 2, 1883, Powderly Papers; M. W. Russell to TVP, Oct. 8, 1883, Powderly Papers; Robert L. De Akers to TVP, Sept. 3, 1883, Powderly Papers. See also *JSP*, Nov. 25, 1883.

63 *Operator*, Sept. 1, 1883; *NYT*, Aug. 19, 1883; *TA*, Sept. 1, 1883.

64 *JSP*, Mar. 23, Apr. 27, June 1, 1884. See also Apr. 6, Aug. 24, Nov. 16, 1884, Jan. 11, 1885.

65 *Operator*, July 1, 1884.

66 *JSP*, Apr. 26, Sept. 6, 1885; *Operator*, May 15, 1885. There was also a strike at Buffalo over back pay at about the same time; whether related to the other actions, and what its outcome was, are unclear. New York State BLS, *Third Annual Report*, 206–207, 211.

67 New York State BLS, *Third Annual Report*, 243, 245; Taltavall, *Telegraphers of To-Day*, 273–274; *JSP*, Aug. 9, 1885.

68 *JSP*, June 27, July 18, 1886; *EA*, June 16, Aug. 16, Oct. 1, 1886, Feb. 16, 1887. For the continued labor movement links of another old brotherhood activist, Eugene O'Connor, see *JSP*, Apr. 17, 1887.

69 *JSP*, Dec. 14, 21, 1884, Sept. 20, Dec. 27, 1885. See also Jan. 10, 1886.

70 *EA*, Jan. 1, 16, Oct. 15, 1887. See also ibid., Nov. 1, 1887; *Telegraph Age*, Mar. 16, Nov. 1, 1893, Jan. 16, Nov. 16, 1898.

71 *EA*, Nov. 1, 16, 1886, Jan. 1, Sept. 1, 1887; *Telegraph Age*, June 16, 1893; Jeff W. Hayes, *Autographs and Memoirs of the Telegraph* (Adrian, Mich., 1916), 10.

72 Ulriksson, *The Telegraphers*, chaps. 5–7; *Telegraph Age*, June 16, 1893, Feb. 1, Mar. 16, Apr. 1, 1894, June 16, 1897, Feb. 1, July 1, 1898. On the 1907 strike, see also *Telegraph Age*, Apr. 1, June 1, 16, July 1, Aug. 1, 16,

Sept. 1, Oct. 16, Nov. 16, Dec. 16, 1907. On the ORT, see Licht, *Working for the Railroad*, 265.

73   Nonoperators made up about 9 percent of the total brotherhood membership at the time of the Great Strike. BTUSC, Circular, May 20, 1883.

74   Paul Starr, *The Social Transformation of American Medicine* (New York, 1982); Monte A. Calvert, *The Mechanical Engineer in America* (Baltimore, Md., 1967), xvi, 35, 153, 189 and passim; McMahon, *Making of a Profession*, 29, 36–40.

75   *EA*, Aug. 16, 1886, Feb. 16, 1887; *Operator*, Apr. 15, 1881, July 1, 1884.

76   Mitchell, "Lingo of Telegraph Operators," 155; BTUSC, *Proceedings*, 8; idem, Circular, May 20, 1883. On "tramping" and trade union regulation of the labor market, see Oestreicher, "Solidarity and Fragmentation," 120–121; Hobsbawm, *Labouring Men*, 42, 44, 48.

77   Union Electric Telegraph Co., brochure, box 88, WUCS; *Operator*, June 1, 1875, Sept. 15, 1878, Feb. 15, Nov. 15, 1879, Feb. 1, 1880, Apr. 15, 1881; *Telegrapher*, Sept. 26, 1864, Nov. 1, 1865; *TA*, June 16, 1883, Oct. 16, 1885; *EA*, June 16, Oct. 1, Dec. 16, 1886, July 1, 1887; *Telegraph Age*, June 16, 1893, Jan. 1, 1897; Senate, *Labor and Capital*, 1:192; North Carolina BLS, *Eighth Annual Report*, 274; New York State BLS, *Fourth Annual Report*, 55–57; J. W. Schmults to A. J. Doughty, Feb. 3, 1888, WULB. See also *BH*, July 19, 23, 1883; *JT*, Mar. 16, 1881.

78   *Operator*, Feb. 15, 1879; North Carolina BLS, *Eighth Annual Report*, 274; *TA*, May 10, 1883; *EA*, June 1, 1886. See also *EA*, June 16, Sept. 1, Oct. 1, 16, 1886, Feb. 1, 16, Apr. 1, May 2, Aug. 1, Dec. 16, 1887, Feb. 16, 1888; *Operator*, May 15, Aug. 15, 1877, June 15, Aug. 1, 1879.

79   George D. Penrose to J. E. Wootten, Dec. 30, 1876, box 195, Reading Papers; H. H. Heisen to Wootten, May 7, 1880, box 221, Reading Papers; O. W. Stager to Wootten, Jan. 15, 1881, box 233, Reading Papers; Circular (copy) from R. C. Luther, Dec. 1894, box 144, Reading Papers; L. Horton, Jr., to Theodore Voorhees, July 22, 1897, box 353, Reading Papers.

80   *EA*, June 16, 1887. See also ibid., Nov. 1, 1886, May 16, 1887; J. W. Schmults to A. J. Doughty, Feb. 3, 1888, WULB; Norvin Green to H. Graf, June 17, 1892, WULB; *JT*, Apr. 15, May 1, 1868, May 1, Nov. 1, 1869, Apr. 1, Dec. 15, 1870, Oct. 16, 1871; Senate, *Labor and Capital*, 1:886; *Telegrapher*, Mar. 15, 1873; S. Rept. 577, pp. 255–256. For the early twentieth century, see Senate, *Industrial Relations*, 10:9320–9321, 9398–9399, 9408–9409, 9415–9416, 9423.

81   See Chaps. 2–3, above; Licht, *Working for the Railroad*, 269. For the similar concerns of the brotherhood's predecessor and successor, see *Operator*, Apr. 1, 1882; *Telegraph Age*, Mar. 16, 1893.

82   BTUSC, *Proceedings*, 11, 24; *TA*, July 1, 1883; Connecticut BLS, *Second*

Annual Report (Hartford, Conn., 1886), 75; O. W. Stager to J. E. Wootten, May 21, Aug. 4, 1883, box 250, Reading Papers. See also Senate, *Labor and Capital*, 1:125, 126, 194, 227. For later demands to control teaching, see Ulriksson, *The Telegraphers*, 69.

83 Senate, *Labor and Capital*, 1:126, 227; *Telegrapher*, Jan. 28, 1871. On unions and apprenticeship generally, see Lloyd Ulman, *The Rise of the National Trade Union* (Cambridge, Mass., 1966), 312–313.

84 Calvert, *Mechanical Engineer*, 27, 189; *BG*, Aug. 2, 1883; New York State BLS, *Sixth Annual Report* (Albany, 1889), 1040; Iowa BLS, *Twelfth Biennial Report*, 193, 200; idem, *Thirteenth Biennial Report*, 253; North Carolina BLS, *Eighth Annual Report*, 274; *EA*, Feb. 16, 1888. See also *TA*, July 1, 1883; and for an argument against licensing, *EA*, Apr. 1, 1888.

85 BTUSC, *Proceedings*, 17.

86 *EA*, Mar. 1, 1887.

87 Parsons, "Telegraph Monopoly," pt. 5, *Arena*, May 1896, p. 953; Phillips, *Sketches*, iv; *Operator*, Sept. 1, 1882, Feb. 21, 1885; Thayer, *Wired Love*, 10.

88 *EA*, July 1, 1886; North Carolina BLS, *Eighth Annual Report*, 273; *Operator*, Sept. 15, 1874, Nov. 1, 1881, Sept. 1, 1882; Senate, *Labor and Capital*, 1:119, 156, 934; S. Rept. 577, p. 21; Michigan BLS, *Third Annual Report* (Lansing, 1886), 151; *NYT*, Aug. 3, 1883; *NYTr*, July 15, 1883; Ohio BLS, *Twenty-fourth Annual Report* (Columbus, 1900), 324–327, 330–331. See also Iowa BLS, *Eleventh Biennial Report*, 385–388; idem, *Twelfth Report*, 184–185, 199, 234–235; and interview with Carl H. Scheele, Oct. 14, 1986.

89 *EA*, July 1, 1886; *JT*, Feb. 15, 1871; *Telegraph Age*, July 1, 1897; *TA*, July 1, 1883; Stilgoe, *Metropolitan Corridor*, 203–209; interview with Carl H. Scheele, Oct. 14, 1986. See also H. W. Spang to J. E. Wootten, July 16, 1878, box 211, Reading Papers; D. Vetter to Spang, July 20, 1878, box 211, Reading Papers; North Carolina BLS, *Eighth Annual Report*, 274.

90 *RTT*, Aug. 15, 1882.

91 O. W. Stager to J. E. Wootten, July 6, 26, 1883, box 250, Reading Papers; BTUSC, Circular, May 20, 1883; John Campbell to W.[*sic*] E. Wootten, Aug. 4, 1883, box 250, Reading Papers. See also Stager to Wootten, July 23, 1883, box 250, Reading Papers; *BG*, Aug. 9, 15, 1883.

92 *SR*, July 20, 1883; *Nation*, Aug. 9, 1883; *BG*, Aug. 1, 15, 1883; *BH*, July 28, 1883; *NYT*, Aug. 7, 1883. See also *EA*, July 1, 1886; *NYTr*, July 19, 1883; *BH*, Aug. 2, 1883; *NYH*, July 19, 1883; *CPD*, July 25, 1883; *BG*, July 21, 1883.

93 *Operator*, Sept. 15, 1884; *EA*, Feb. 16, 1887, May 1, 1888; *JSP*, May 23, June 27, 1886; New York State BLS, *Sixth Annual Report*, 1040; North

Carolina BLS, *Eighth Annual Report*, 272; Iowa BLS, *Eleventh Biennial Report*, 170–177, 180–181, 192–195, 198–199, 219; *Telegraph Age*, June 16, 1893, June 16, 1897, July 1, 1898.

94   *NYT*, July 20, 1883. See also *NOP*, July 20, 1883.

95   Senate, *Labor and Capital*, 1:199; *EA*, June 16, Nov. 1, 16, 1886; *BG*, July 20, 1883; *CPD*, July 21, 1883; *NYTr*, July 26, 1883; *Telegrapher*, Oct. 16, 1865.

96   *NYT*, July 16, 1883. For the leadership age profile I averaged Thomas Hughes (25), Eugene O'Connor (34), John Taltavall (27), P. J. Tierney (28), John Campbell (35), Harry Orr (30), Mortimer Shaw (30), John Mitchell (33), John McClelland (31), Horace Steltz (29), and Frank Phillips (25). Senate, *Labor and Capital*, 1:168, 191, 225; *BH*, July 23, 1883; *EA*, Nov. 1, 1886; *Operator*, Apr. 1, 1882; Census Manuscript Schedules, 1880, Baltimore City.

97   *Telegraph Age*, Aug. 1, 1898, Aug. 1, Dec. 1, 1907; Taltavall, *Telegraphers of To-Day*, 178–179, 199; *EA*, Nov. 1, 1886, July 1, 1887; Postal Telegraph Company, menu, dinner of May 24, 1894, box 19, WUCS. On Shaw's later tragic decline, see *Telegraph Age*, Aug. 1, 1897, Aug. 1, Sept. 1, 1900.

98   Harrisburg record books, box 65, WUCS; *HDT*, July 20, 23, 26, 1883; *EA*, Mar. 1, 1888.

99   Oestreicher, "Solidarity and Fragmentation," 27, 46. On the specific tensions between white- and blue-collar workers, see Jones, "Working-Class Culture," 507.

100   *BG*, July 24, 1883.

101   *CPD*, July 26, Aug. 16, 1883; *NYT*, July 31, Aug. 9, 1883; *BH*, Aug. 16, 1883.

102   *BG*, July 20, 23, 24, Aug. 6, 1883; *NOP*, July 30, 31, Aug. 2, 1883; *NYT*, July 22, 23, 28, Aug. 6, 12, 1883; *CPD*, July 26, 27, 1883; *BH*, July 26, Aug. 1, 1883; *NYTr*, July 27, 1883.

103   *IW*, Aug. 18, 1883. For labor support, see *NYTr*, July 22, 23, Aug. 1, 13, 1883; *NYT*, Aug. 1, 3, 14, 16, 1883; *BG*, July 19, 23, 25, 28, 29, 30, Aug. 2, 5, 8, 13, 1883; *NOP*, July 25, Aug. 2, 1883; *BH*, Aug. 13, 1883; *CPD*, July 19, 24, 27, Aug. 3, 1883; *AC*, July 24, 1883; J. F. Busche, Jr., to TVP, Aug. 22, 1883, Powderly Papers; *JUL*, Aug. 1883. On the indifference or hostility of the railroad brotherhoods, see *NYT*, July 28, Aug. 6, 9, 1883; *BG*, Aug. 7, 1883; *NOP*, Aug. 8, 1883.

104   Ohio BLS, *Second Annual Report* (Columbus, 1879), 284; *Operator*, Sept. 1, 1883. See also ibid., Oct. 15, 1883; and for later examples of the same kind of superciliousness and anti-unionism (from, ironically, John Taltavall), *Telegraph Age*, Sept. 1, Dec. 1, 1907. For the brotherhood's gentlemanly image during the strike, see *NYTr*, July

22, 1883; *TA*, Aug. 16, 1883; *NYT*, July 25, 1883; Senate, *Labor and Capital*, 1:554.

105 Hayes, *Autographs*, 7; *NYTr*, July 20, 1883; *NYT*, July 20, 24, 1883; *BET*, July 20, 1883. See also *BG*, July 21, 1883; Senate, *Labor and Capital*, 2:55; *IW*, Aug. 4, 1883; *NYTr*, July 18, 19, 21, 1883; *BH*, Aug. 18, 1883.

106 *NYT*, July 21, Aug. 1, 11, 12, 1883; *NYH*, Aug. 9, 1883; *NYTr*, July 23, 1883; *BG*, Aug. 11, 1883.

107 *NYTr*, Aug. 4, 7, 1883. See also *BH*, July 22, 1883. For charges of operators using intimidation or violence, see *BH*, July 26, 27, Aug. 11, 20, 1883; *BG*, July 30, 1883; *NYT*, Aug. 8, 17, 1883; *NYTr*, Aug. 8, 10, 1883; *BET*, Aug. 8, 1883; *NOP*, Aug. 16, 17, 1883. For the cryptic account of an alleged plot to carry out violent sabotage against the Western Union, see Powderly, *Thirty Years*, 275–276, idem; *Path I Trod*, 109–112.

108 *IW*, Aug. 25, Sept. 1, 1883.

109 Ibid., Sept. 1, 15, 1883.

110 *BH*, Aug. 18, 1883; Terence Lynch to TVP, Sept. 2, 1883, Powderly Papers. See also *NYH*, Aug. 21, 1883; *Operator*, Jan. 15, 1884.

111 *NYT*, Aug. 20, 1883.

112 Senate, *Labor and Capital*, 1:603, 1073; *EW*, Dec. 13, 1890; S. Rept. 577, pp. 15–16; Parsons, "Telegraph Monopoly," *Arena*, Jan. 1896, p. 257; Kealey and Palmer, *Dreaming of What Might Be*, 120.

113 *TA*, Sept. 1, 1883.

114 Kealey and Palmer, *Dreaming of What Might Be*, 67–68, 148, 293, 338; Fink, *Workingmen's Democracy*, 154; Melton Alonza McLaurin, *The Knights of Labor in the South* (Westport, Conn., 1978), 45, 46.

115 Grob, *Workers and Utopia*, 189 and passim. Contra Grob, see Oestreicher, "Solidarity and Fragmentation," esp. 320–329; Kealey and Palmer, *Dreaming of What Might Be*; and Fink, *Workingmen's Democracy*.

116 On the relation of firm size to white-collar unionism, see Lockwood, *The Blackcoated Worker*, 33.

117 BTUSC, *Proceedings*, 10–11; *EA*, Feb. 16, 1887; Senate, *Labor and Capital*, 1:236; Thomas H. Winsor to TVP, Dec. 14, 1882, Powderly Papers; John Campbell to J. E. Wootten, Aug. 4, 1883, box 250, Reading Papers, *TA*, June 1, 1883. See also *BH*, July 18, 19, 1883; and on the appeal that the material benefits of pure-and-simple unionism offered, Laslett, "Reflections," 635, 647; and Samuel Gompers, *Seventy Years of Life and Labor* (New York, 1925), 1:83.

118 *Operator*, Jan. 15, 1884; Kealey and Palmer, *Dreaming of What Might Be*, 107, 283–289; Oestreicher, "Solidarity and Fragmentation," 218–219; *BG*, July 24, Aug. 1, 1883.

119 Senate, *Labor and Capital*, 1:236. See also *Operator*, Jan. 15, 1884; *NYH*, Aug. 21, 1883.

120 My conclusions on the Knights strongly reflect the insightful interpretations of Kealey and Palmer, *Dreaming of What Might Be*, 54–55, 96, 396; Fink, *Workingmen's Democracy*, 6, 9, 10; and Oestreicher, "Solidarity and Fragmentation," 213–214, 243–244.

121 On eclecticism, see Oestreicher, "Solidarity and Fragmentation," 173–174, 209, 213–214, 243–244, 320–329; Kealey and Palmer, *Dreaming of What Might Be*, 137, 166, 396. On the dramatic rise in Knights membership as a weakness, see Oestreicher, "Solidarity," 317–318.

122 Fink, *Workingmen's Democracy*, 6, 9, 10; Montgomery, *Beyond Equality*, 444–445; *BH*, Aug. 15, 1883.

123 *Operator*, May 15, 1882; *TA*, July 1, 1883; Alfred H. Love to President, Philadelphia, Reading, and Pottsville Telegraph Co., July 20, 1883, box 250, Reading Papers; Gabler, "Kid-Gloved Laborers," 399–400, 406–407, 410–412; *BH*, Aug. 10, 1883.

124 *NYH*, Aug. 21, 1883; *TA*, Oct. 16, 1885; *EA*, Nov. 1, 1886, Jan. 16, 1887. See also *EA*, June 16, July 1, 1886, Feb. 16, 1887; *Operator*, Apr. 1, 1882, Jan. 15, 1884, Feb. 21, 1885; New York State BLS, *Third Annual Report*, 242; *Telegraph Age*, Mar. 16, 1893.

125 *EA*, Apr. 1, 1887; *TA*, July 16, 1883; *Operator*, Feb. 15, 1881; *HDT*, July 18, 1883; Louisville record book, box 16, WUCS; interview with Carl Scheele, Oct. 14, 1986.

126 *NYT*, July 20, 21, 22, 24, 1883; *CPD*, July 19, 1883; *BG*, July 17, 18, 22, 1883; *BH*, July 20, 24, 1883; *NYTr*, July 19, 21, 1883; *BS*, July 20, 1883. See also *EA*, Nov. 1, 1886, Mar. 1, 1887; *Telegrapher*, Dec. 18, 1875.

127 *JT*, Feb. 1, 1873; Licht, *Working for the Railroad*, 56; William J. Dealy to Employes of the General Operating Department, Feb. 22, 1892, box 48, WUCS; Theodore Voorhees to H. J. Brown, Apr. 22, 1895, box 144, Reading Papers; *Shaffner's Telegraph Companion*, May 1854; *Operator*, Apr. 1, 15, 1876, Jan. 15, 1877, Nov. 1, 1879, Jan. 15, 1882; *Telegrapher*, Dec. 26, 1864, Feb. 27, Nov. 15, 1865, Dec. 10, 31, 1870, Jan. 7, Apr. 15, June 24, 1871; *Telegraph Age*, Mar. 16, Apr. 16, 1893.

128 William Orton to George F. Davis, Mar. 15, 1866, WULB; Ulriksson, *The Telegraphers*, 19; *EA*, Feb. 1, 1887; Reid, *Telegraph in America* (1886), 740; Norvin Green to Edward Chapman, Aug. 1, 1879, Green to John Van Horne, Nov. 17, 1879, WULB; E. R. Adams to Theodore Voorhees, June 10, 1893, box 124, Reading Papers; *EA*, Oct. 1, 1886, Feb. 2, Oct. 15, 1887; Henry F. Sherman to George E. Todd, Oct. 17, 1876, box 23 ("Telegraph"), Warshaw Collection of Business Americana, Archives Center, National Museum of American History; *JT*, Apr. 1, 1868, Apr. 15, 1870, Oct. 15, 1872; Senate, *Labor and Capital*,

1:941; *Operator*, Dec. 1, 1874; *TA*, June 1, 1883. See also *JT*, May 1, 1872; C. M. Lewis to Theodore Voorhees, Aug. 28, 1901, Voorhees to Lewis, Sept. 4, 1901, box 432, Reading Papers; Robert Mecredy to J. E. Wootten, Aug. 20, 1880, box 225, Reading Papers; and for later welfare capitalism, in the Postal Telegraph Co., *Telegraph Age*, Nov. 1, 1907.

129 *Telegrapher*, Oct. 8, 29, Dec. 31, 1870; *Operator*, Dec. 1, 1883. On the loose contemporary distinctions between cooperatives and profit-sharing plans, see Montgomery, *Beyond Equality*, 444.

130 Norvin Green to Amasa Stone, Dec. 13, 1882, Green to Sidney Shepard, Dec. 15, 1882, Green to Zenas M. Crane, Dec. 15, 1882, WULB.

131 Ware, *Labor Movement*, chap. 7; Knights of Labor Executive Board, Order of Assessment, Oct. 8, 1883, Powderly Papers; Kealey and Palmer, *Dreaming of What Might Be*, 67–68, 111; Oestreicher, "Solidarity and Fragmentation," 231; Gompers, *Seventy Years*, 1:96.

132 Senate, *Labor and Capital*, 1:144, 210. See also *NYTr*, Aug. 18, 1883.

133 On republicanism and the labor movement, see, e.g., Montgomery, *Beyond Equality*; Nick Salvatore, *Eugene V. Debs, Citizen and Socialist* (Urbana, Ill., 1982); Oestreicher, "Solidarity and Fragmentation"; Alan Dawley, *Class and Community* (Cambridge, Mass., 1976); Bruce Laurie, *Working People of Philadelphia, 1800–1850* (Philadelphia, 1980); Fink, *Workingmen's Democracy*, 4; Sean Wilentz, *Chants Democratic* (New York, 1984).

134 *BH*, July 29, Aug. 10, 1883; *JSP*, Dec. 16, 1883; *EA*, Oct. 1, 1887; *Telegraph Age*, Mar. 16, 1893. See also *Telegraph Age*, June 16, 1893; Senate, *Labor and Capital*, 1:122–123; *NYTr*, July 21, 1883; *BG*, Aug. 9, 1883; *IW*, Aug. 18, 1883; *Telegrapher*, Feb. 4, 1871; *CPD*, July 30, 1883. For examples of republican rhetoric used against telegraph unionism, see *JT*, Jan. 15, 1870; *Hampshire Gazette and Northampton Courier*, July 24, 1883; *NYT*, July 18, 26, 1883; *BH*, July 14, 15, 1883.

135 Grob, *Workers and Utopia*, 187–188.

136 Oestreicher, "Solidarity and Fragmentation," 2, 192, 241, 452; Kealey and Palmer, *Dreaming of What Might Be*, 278–279, 292; Fink, *Workingmen's Democracy*, 220–221.

137 Grob, *Workers and Utopia*, 44, 47. See also Ware, *Labor Movement*, chap. 14, where he argues that the co-op vision was "archaic" because of the small scale contemplated. The fault in this thesis (forgetting the inherently large size of the telegraphers' plan) is that it assumes that the industrial capitalist models of the Gilded Age were somehow economically (if not morally) right and inevitable—a moot point. On scale and productivity, see Kirkpatrick Sale, *Human Scale* (New York, 1980), 310–318.

138 *Telegrapher*, Mar. 11, 1871.

139 BTUSC, *Proceedings*, 22; *TA*, June 1, 1883. The plan outlined in the editorial was hardly "communistic," since it did not mandate equal shareholding.

140 *TA*, July 16, 1883; *Operator*, Nov. 18, 1882. There is a possibility that the poem envisioned a profit-sharing plan rather than a cooperatively owned firm. On the ambiguity surrounding such distinctions in the era, see Montgomery, *Beyond Equality*, 444.

141 Senate, *Labor and Capital*, 1:148, 178–179.

142 Ibid., 1:214–215.

143 Ibid., 1: 138, 179, 216, 218, 236. On working-class radical theory, see Montgomery, *Beyond Equality*, 249–260; Oestreicher, "Solidarity and Fragmentation," 324–325. For the proclivity of another labor radical, John Swinton, for large-scale (though publicly owned) enterprise, see Senate, *Labor and Capital*, 1:1113.

144 *BG*, July 23, 27, 28, 29, 1883; *NYT*, July 27, 28, 31, 1883.

145 *BG*, July 28, 29, 1883.

146 Ibid., July 28, 1883; R. H. Ferguson to TVP, July 29, 1883, Powderly Papers.

147 *Operator*, Nov. 15, 1883; Gabler, "Kid-Gloved Laborers," 410–412; *NYTr*, July 28, 1883. See also *SR*, July 28, 1883; *NOP*, Sept. 1, 1883. On earlier and later co-op telegraph schemes, see *Telegrapher*, Apr. 15, 1871; *EA*, Feb. 16, 1887. On the fate of Knights co-ops in general, see Ware, *Labor Movement*, chap. 14.

148 Montgomery, *Beyond Equality*, 432. On the Knights' ambivalence and view of the state as a mediator rather than "ultimate antagonist" or "source of salvation," see Fink, *Workingmen's Democracy*, 23, 34.

149 Oestreicher, "Solidarity and Fragmentation," 231; *EA*, Apr. 1, 1888. For antimonopoly sentiment, see also ibid., Sept. 1, 1886. For an earlier view of the state as captive to the interests of capital and thus incapable of passing "impartial laws" (hence the need for a strong operators' union), see *Telegrapher*, Feb. 4, 1871.

150 Gabler, "Kid-Gloved Laborers," 413–424. For a reformist attack on laissez faire and Social Darwinism during the Great Strike, see *BH*, Aug. 10, 1883. For the statist strain within the Knights, see Sidney Fine, *Laissez Faire and the General Welfare State* (Ann Arbor, Mich., 1956), 319; and for a discussion of natural monopolies and statism in the period, Fink, *Workingmen's Democracy*, 31.

151 Gabler, "Kid-Gloved Laborers," 413–418.

152 Senate, *Labor and Capital*, 1:385; *EA*, Nov. 1, 1886. See also ibid., Sept. 16, Nov. 16, 1886, Feb. 16, 1888; *Operator*, Jan. 15, 1881, Feb. 21, 1885; *BH*, Aug. 12, 1883.

153   *EA*, Oct. 1, 16, 1886, May 2, 1887; Grob, *Workers and Utopia*, 86–87, 164–165; Ray Ginger, *The Age of Excess* (New York, 1965), 59–61; *NYT*, Sept. 19, 1887.

154   *EA*, Nov. 1, 1886. On Henry George's ideology, see Fine, *Laissez Faire*, 294; and Chester McArthur Destler, *American Radicalism, 1865–1901* (New London, Conn., 1946), 22–23, 200–201.

155   *EA*, Oct. 15, 1887. See also June 1, 16, July 1, 16, Sept. 1, Oct. 1, 1887.

156   *EA*, May 16, June 1, 1887. See also June 16, July 1, Aug. 1, Sept. 1, 1887.

157   Eric Foner, *Politics and Ideology in the Age of the Civil War* (New York, 1980), 184–189, chap. 8.

158   *IW*, Aug. 4, Sept. 1, 15, 1883.

159   Foner, *Politics and Ideology*, 194, 198–199; *EA*, Oct. 15, 1887.

160   Oestreicher, "Solidarity and Fragmentation," 81; and for a contemporary Knights statement of purpose, *AC*, Aug. 19, 1883.

EPILOGUE

1   Frank Ackerman, *Reaganomics: Rhetoric vs. Reality* (Boston, 1982), 110, 113.

2   *NYT*, Aug. 4, 1981.

3   Ackerman, *Reaganomics*, 111; *NYT*, Aug. 4, 7, 1981.

4   *NYT*, Aug. 7, 25, Oct. 23, 1981; Ackerman, *Reaganomics*, 111–112.

5   On the Association of Professional Flight Attendants, see *NYT*, Aug. 15, 1981; and Cindy Hounsell, "Grounded," *Democratic Left*, Sept.–Oct. 1986. For the educational requirements for air traffic controllers, see *NYT*, Aug. 4, 1981.

BIBLIOGRAPHY

PRIMARY SOURCES

Manuscripts

Anglo-American Telegraph Company, Heart's Content (Newfoundland) Cable Station Letter Books, microfilm of originals at Heart's Content Cable Museum, in Division of Electricity and Modern Physics Archives, National Museum of American History (NMAH), Smithsonian Institution, Washington, D.C.

Baltimore & Ohio Railroad Papers (Ms. no. 2003), Manuscripts Division, Maryland Historical Society, Baltimore, Maryland

Garrett Family Papers (Ms. no. 979), Manuscripts Division, Maryland Historical Society

Obituary Scrapbooks, Dauphin County Historical Society, Harrisburg, Pennsylvania

Terence V. Powderly Papers, microfilms of originals at Catholic University, Washington, D.C.

Reading Railroad Papers (Ms. no. 1520), Hagley Museum and Library, Wilmington, Delaware

U.S. Census Manuscript Population Schedules, Ninth Census (1870), Dauphin County, Pennsylvania

———, Ninth Census, Norfolk County, Massachusetts

———, Tenth Census (1880), Baltimore City, Maryland

———, Tenth Census, Dauphin County, Pennsylvania

———, Tenth Census, New York City

———, Tenth Census, Norfolk County, Massachusetts

———, Twelfth Census (1900), Dauphin County, Pennsylvania

Warshaw Collection of Business Americana, Archives Center, NMAH

Western Union Collection, Archives Center, NMAH

Western Union Telegraph Company, Presidents' Letter Books, Secretary's Office, Western Union Corporation, Upper Saddle River, New Jersey
————, "Records, Directors and Stockholders" (Minute Books), Secretary's Office, Western Union Corporation
————, "Statistics of the Western Union Telegraph Company for the Years ended 30th June 1867–1875," Western Union Papers, Manuscript Division, New York Public Library
Charles F. Wood Correspondence, Division of Electricity and Modern Physics Archives, NMAH

Government Documents

Connecticut Bureau of Labor Statistics (BLS). *Second Annual Report*. Hartford, 1886.
Illinois BLS. *Third Biennial Report*. Springfield, 1884.
Iowa BLS. *Sixth Biennial Report*. Des Moines, 1895.
————. *Eleventh Biennial Report*. Des Moines, 1905.
————. *Twelfth Biennial Report*. Des Moines, 1907.
————. *Thirteenth Biennial Report*. Des Moines, 1908.
Kansas Bureau of Labor and Industrial Statistics (BLIS). *Third Annual Report*. Topeka, 1888.
Maine BLIS. *Second Annual Report*. Augusta, 1889.
Massachusetts BLS. *Third Annual Report*. Boston, 1872.
————. *Sixth Annual Report*. Boston, 1875.
————. *Fifteenth Annual Report*. Boston, 1884.
Michigan BLS. *Second Annual Report*. Lansing, 1885.
————. *Third Annual Report*. Lansing, 1886.
————. *Tenth Annual Report*. Lansing, 1893.
New York State BLS. *Third Annual Report*. Albany, 1886.
————. *Fourth Annual Report*. Albany, 1887.
————. *Sixth Annual Report*. Albany, 1889.
North Carolina BLS. *Eighth Annual Report*. Raleigh, 1894.
Ohio BLS. *Second Annual Report*. Columbus, 1879.
————. *Twenty-fourth Annual Report*. Columbus, 1900.
U.S. Census Bureau, Ninth Census. *Statistics of the Population of the United States*. Vol. 1. Washington, D.C., 1872.
————. Tenth Census. *Statistics of the Population of the United States*. Vol. 1. Washington, D.C., 1883.
————. Eleventh Census. *Report of the Population of the United States*. Pt. 2. Washington, D.C., 1897.
————. Twelfth Census. *Special Reports, Part 2: Occupations*. Washington, D.C., 1904.
U.S. Commissioner of Labor. *Fourth Annual Report*. Washington, D.C., 1888.

_____. *Fifteenth Annual Report*. Washington, D.C., 1900.

U.S. Department of Commerce. *Historical Statistics of the United States*. Washington, D.C., 1975.

U.S. Department of Commerce and Labor. *Statistical Abstract of the United States*. Washington, D.C., 1911.

U.S. House of Representatives. *Postmaster General's Report*. 51st Cong., 2d sess., 1890, House Exec. Doc. 1, pt. 4.

U.S. Senate. 43d Cong., 1st sess., 1874, S. Rept. 242.

_____. 48th Cong., 1st sess., 1884, S. Rept. 577.

_____. *Report of the Committee of the Senate upon the Relations between Labor and Capital*. Washington, D.C., 1885.

_____. *Wholesale Prices, Wages, and Transportation*. 52d Cong., 2d sess., 1893, S. Rept. 1394, pt. 4.

_____. *Report on Conditions of Women and Child Wage Earners in the United States*. 61st Cong., 2d sess., 1911, S. Doc. 645.

_____. *Final Report of Testimony Submitted to Congress by the Commission on Industrial Relations*. 64th Cong., 1st sess., 1916, S. Doc. 415.

Books and Articles

Barnard,Charles. "The Telegraph of To-Day." *Harper's New Monthly Magazine*, (Oct. 1881).

Bates, David Homer. *Lincoln in the Telegraph Office*. New York, 1907.

Bowker, R. R., ed. "Great American Industries. 12—Electricity." *Harper's* (Oct. 1896).

Brackbill, Hervey. "Some Telegraphers' Terms." *American Speech* (Apr. 1929).

Buckingham, Charles L. "The Telegraph of To-Day." *Scribners* (July 1889).

Bunnell, J. H., & Co. *Students' Manual for the Practical Instruction of Learners of Telegraphy*. New York, 1882.

Butler, Elizabeth Beardsley. *Women and the Trades*. New York, 1911.

Carnegie, Andrew. *Autobiography of Andrew Carnegie*. Boston, 1920.

Churchill, Lida A. *My Girls*. Boston, 1882.

Garland, Charles H. "Women as Telegraphists." *Economic Journal* (June 1901).

Gompers, Samuel. *Seventy Years of Life and Labor*. New York, 1925.

Grant, E. B. *The Western Union Telegraph Company: Its Past, Present and Future*. New York, 1883.

Harrisburg, Pennsylvania, City Directory, 1880, 1882, 1890, 1900 eds.

[Harrison, Jonathan Baxter.] "Study of a New England Factory Town." *Atlantic Monthly* (June 1879).

Hayes, Jeff W. *Autographs and Memoirs of the Telegraph*. Adrian, Mich., 1916.

Hoerle, Helen. *The Girl and Her Future*. New York, 1932.

Hoerle, Helen Christene and Saltzberg, Florence B. *The Girl and the Job*. New York, 1919.

Johnston, W. J. *Telegraphic Tales and Telegraphic History.* New York, 1880.

Kelker, Luther Riley. *History of Dauphin County, Pennsylvania.* New York, 1907.

Louisville, New Albany & Chicago Railway. *Rules of the Transportation Department.* Chicago, n.d.

McNeill, George E., ed. *The Labor Movement: The Problem of To-Day.* Boston, 1887.

Manson, George J. *Work for Women.* New York, 1883.

Mitchell, Minnie Swan. "Lingo of Telegraph Operators." *American Speech* (April 1937).

Parsons, Frank. "The Telegraph Monopoly." *Arena* (May 1896).

Penny, Virginia. *The Employments of Women.* Boston, 1863.

Phillips, Walter P. *Sketches Old and New.* New York, 1897.

Powderly, Terence V. *The Path I Trod,* ed. H. Carman, H. David, and P. N. Guthrie. New York, 1940.

————. *Thirty Years of Labor.* Philadelphia, 1890.

Rayne, Martha Louise. *What Can a Woman Do?* Detroit, 1885.

Reid, James D. *The Telegraph in America.* New York, 1879, 1886.

Rhodes, Albert. "Women's Occupations." *Galaxy* (Jan. 1876).

Richardson, Dorothy. *The Long Day.* In *Women at Work,* ed. William L. O'Neill. Chicago, 1979.

Riordan, R. "Recent Advances in Telegraphy." *Popular Science Monthly* (May 1876).

Shaffner, Taliaferro P. *The Telegraph Manual.* New York, 1859.

Sinclair, Upton. *The Jungle.* Reprint. New York, 1960.

Taltavall, John B. *Telegraphers of To-Day.* New York, 1893.

"The Telegraph." *Harper's New Monthly Magazine* (Aug. 1873).

Thayer, Ella Cheever. *Wired Love.* New York, 1879.

Western Union Telegraph Co. *Rules, Regulations, and Instructions.* Cleveland, 1866.

————. *Rules and Instructions.* New York, 1870.

————. *Rules.* N.p., 1884

Willard, Frances E. *Occupations for Women.* New York, 1897.

Journals

Atlanta Constitution
Baltimore Sun
Boston Evening Transcript
Boston Globe
Boston Herald
Charities and the Commons
Cleveland Plain Dealer

Electric Age
Electrical Review
Electrical World
Frank Leslie's Illustrated Newspaper
Godey's Lady's Book
Hampshire Gazette and Northampton Courier
Harper's Weekly
Harrisburg Daily Telegraph
Irish World and American Industrial Liberator
John Swinton's Paper
Journal of the Telegraph
Journal of United Labor
Life
Magnet
Nation
New Orleans Picayune
New York Herald
New York Times
New York Tribune
Operator
Puck
Review of the Telegraph and Telephone
Shaffner's Telegraph Companion
Springfield Republican
St. Louis Post Dispatch
Telegraph Age
Telegrapher
Telegraphers' Advocate

SECONDARY SOURCES

Books and Articles

Ackerman, Frank. *Reaganomics: Rhetoric vs. Reality*. Boston, 1982.
Aron, Cindy S. "'To Barter Their Souls for Gold': Female Clerks in Federal Government Offices, 1862–1890." *Journal of American History* (March 1981).
Baker, Elizabeth Faulkner. *Technology and Women's Work*. New York, 1964.
Blumin, Stuart M. "The Hypothesis of Middle-Class Formation in Nineteenth-Century America: A Critique and Some Proposals." *American Historical Review* (April 1985).
Braverman, Harry. *Labor and Monopoly Capital*. New York, 1974.

Calvert, Monte A. *The Mechanical Engineer in America, 1830–1910.* Baltimore, Md., 1967.

Chandler, Alfred D., Jr. *The Visible Hand.* Cambridge, Mass., 1977.

Cochran, Thomas C. and Miller, William. *The Age of Enterprise.* New York, 1942.

Cohen, Lizabeth A. "Embellishing a Life of Labor: An Interpretation of the Material Culture of American Working-Class Homes, 1885–1915." In *Material Culture Studies in America,* ed. Thomas J. Schlereth. Nashville, Tenn., 1982.

Cott, Nancy F. *The Bonds of Womanhood.* New Haven, Conn., 1977.

Czitrom, Daniel J. *Media and the American Mind.* Chapel Hill, N.C., 1982.

Davies, Margery W. *Woman's Place Is at the Typewriter.* Philadelphia, 1982.

Dawley, Alan. *Class and Community.* Cambridge, Mass., 1976.

Destler, Chester McArthur. *American Radicalism, 1865–1901.* New London, Conn., 1946.

Diner, Hasia R. *Erin's Daughters in America.* Baltimore, Md., 1983.

Douglass, Elisha P. *The Coming of Age of American Business.* Chapel Hill, N.C., 1971.

Dublin, Thomas P. *Women at Work.* New York, 1979.

Dyer, Frank Lewis and Martin, Thomas Commerford. *Edison: His Life and Inventions.* New York, 1929.

Fine, Sidney. *Laissez Faire and the General Welfare State.* Ann Arbor, Mich., 1956.

Fink, Leon. *Workingmen's Democracy.* Urbana, Ill., 1983.

Foner, Eric. *Politics and Ideology in the Age of the Civil War.* New York, 1980.

Frisch, Michael H. and Walkowitz, Daniel J. eds. *Working-Class America.* Urbana, Ill., 1983.

Ginger, Ray. *Age of Excess.* New York, 1965.

Gordon, David M., Edwards, Richard, and Reich, Michael. *Segmented Work, Divided Workers.* Cambridge, England, 1982.

Gray, Robert Q. *The Labour Aristocracy in Victorian Edinburgh.* Oxford, England, 1976.

Green, James R. *The World of the Worker.* New York, 1980.

Grob, Gerald N. *Workers and Utopia.* New York, 1969.

Grodinsky, Julius. *Jay Gould.* Philadelphia, 1957.

Harlow, Alvin F. *Old Wires and New Waves.* New York, 1936.

Hobsbawm, E. J. *Labouring Men.* New York, 1967.

Horlick, Allan Stanley. *Country Boys and Merchant Princes.* Lewisburg, Pa., 1975.

Hounsell, Cindy. "Grounded." *Democratic Left* (Sept.–Oct. 1986).

Jones, Gareth Stedman. "Working-Class Culture and Working-Class Politics in London, 1870–1900." *Journal of Social History* (Summer 1974).

Josephson, Matthew. *The Robber Barons*. New York, 1934.

Katzman, David M. *Seven Days a Week*. New York, 1978.

Kealey, Gregory S. and Palmer, Bryan D. *Dreaming of What Might Be*. Cambridge, England, 1982.

Klein, Maury. *The Life and Legend of Jay Gould*. Baltimore, Md., 1986.

Laslett, John. "Reflections on the Failure of Socialism in the American Federation of Labor." *Mississippi Valley Historical Review* (March 1964).

Laurie, Bruce. *Working People of Philadelphia, 1800–1850*. Philadelphia, 1980.

Lebergott, Stanley. *Manpower in Economic Growth*. New York, 1964.

Levine, Susan. *Labor's True Woman*. Philadelphia, 1984.

Lewis, Gordon K. *Puerto Rico: Freedom and Power in the Caribbean*. New York, 1963.

Licht, Walter. *Working for the Railroad*. Princeton, N.J., 1983.

Livesay, Harold C. *Andrew Carnegie and the Rise of Big Business*. Boston, 1975.

Lockwood, David. *The Blackcoated Worker*. London, 1958.

McLaurin, Melton Alonza. *The Knights of Labor in the South*. Westport, Conn., 1978.

McMahon, A. Michael. *The Making of a Profession: A Century of Electrical Engineering in America*. New York, 1984.

Mills, C. Wright. *White Collar*. New York, 1951.

Montgomery, David. *Beyond Equality*. New York, 1967.

_____. *Workers' Control in America*. Cambridge, England, 1979.

Paine, Albert Bigelow. *Theodore N. Vail: A Biography*. New York, 1929.

Peel, Mark. "On the Margins: Lodgers and Boarders in Boston, 1860–1900." *Journal of American History* (Mar. 1986).

Peiss, Kathy. *Cheap Amusements*. Philadelphia, 1986.

Reynolds, Lloyd G. *Labor Economics and Labor Relations*. 8th ed. Englewood Cliffs, N.J., 1982.

Ryan, Mary P. *Womanhood in America*. New York, 1975.

Salvatore, Nick. *Eugene V. Debs; Citizen and Socialist*. Urbana, Ill., 1982.

Schlesinger, Arthur M. *Learning How to Behave: A Historical Study of American Etiquette Books*. New York, 1947.

Starr, Paul. *The Social Transformation of American Medicine*. New York, 1982.

Stilgoe, John R. *Metropolitan Corridor*. New Haven, Conn., 1983.

Taylor, George R. *The Transportation Revolution*. New York, 1951.

Thompson, Dorothy. *The Chartists*. New York, 1984.

Thompson, E. P. *The Making of the English Working Class*. New York, 1964.

Thompson, Robert Luther. *Wiring a Continent*. Princeton, N.J., 1947.

Tyack, David B. *The One Best System*. Cambridge, Mass., 1974.

Ulman, Lloyd. *The Rise of the National Trade Union*. Cambridge, Mass., 1966.

Ulriksson, Vidkunn. *The Telegraphers: Their Craft and Their Unions*. Washington, D.C., 1953.

Walkowitz, Daniel J. *Worker City, Company Town*. Urbana, Ill., 1981.

Ware, Norman J. *The Labor Movement in the United States, 1860–1895*. New York, 1929.

Wilentz, Sean. *Chants Democratic*. New York, 1984.

Woody, Thomas. *A History of Women's Education in the United States*. New York, 1929.

Unpublished

De Vault, Ileen A. "Work and Honor: The Daughters of Pittsburgh's Skilled Workers."

Gabler, Edwin. "Kid-Gloved Laborers: Gilded Age Telegraphers and the Great Strike of 1883." Ph.D. diss., University of Massachusetts at Amherst, 1986.

Israel, Paul B. "Invention and Corporate Strategies: Western Union and Competition." Paper delivered to the Society for the History of Technology, Oct. 1986.

Oestreicher, Richard Jules. "Solidarity and Fragmentation: Working People and Class Consciousness in Detroit, 1875–1900."

Scheele, Carl H. (B & O Railroad telegrapher, 1944–46). Interview, Oct. 14, 1986.

INDEX